History of the Captivity of Napoleon at Helena Volume II

General Count Montholon

BIBLIOLIFE

HISTORY

OF THE

CAPTIVITY OF NAPOLEON

AT

ST. HELENA.

BY

GENERAL COUNT MONTHOLON,

THE EMPEROR'S COMPANION IN EXILE,

AND TESTAMENTARY EXECUTOR.

VOL. II.

LONDON:

HENRY COLBURN, PUBLISHER,

GREAT MARLBOROUGH STREET.

[Entered at Stationers' Hall.]

1846.

CONTENTS OF VOL. II.

CHAPTER I.

GENERAL CONSIDERATIONS ON FRANCE.

CHAPTER II.

SITUATION OF ITALY IN THE SPRING OF THE YEAR 1796. NEGOTIATION WITH THE REPUBLIC OF GENOA.

CHAPTER III.

TOLENTINO.

CHAPTER IV.

LÉOBEN.

CHAPTER V.

VENICE.

CHAPTER VI.

NAPOLEON DURING 1797.

CHAPTER VII.

PEACE OF CAMPO-FORMIO.

CHAPTER VIII.

NAPOLEON IN PARIS AFTER THE CAMPAIGN OF ITALY.

CHAPTER IX.

CONDUCT OF NAPOLEON AS CONSUL. (DICTATION.)

CHAPTER X.

THE DUKE D'ENGHIEN.

CHAPTER XI.

ON STATE PRISONS. (DICTATION.)

CHAPTER XII.

BRIEF VIEW OF THE CONSULAR PERIOD. (DICTATION.)

CHAPTER XIII.

GENERAL CONSIDERATIONS ON THE POLICY OF FOREIGN GO-
VERNMENTS, AND ESPECIALLY OF THOSE OF ENGLAND
AND AUSTRIA. (DICTATION.)

CHAPTER XIV.

GENERAL POLICY OF SPAIN TOWARDS FRANCE DURING THE REIGN OF FERDINAND

CHAPTER XV.

AFFAIRS OF ROME, AND CONCORDAT OF FONTAINEBLEAU.
(DICTATION.)

CHAPTER XVI.

CORSICA. (DICTATION.)

CHAPTER XVII.

MEMOIRS OF BONAPARTE WHEN YOUNG. CROWNED AT THE ACADEMY OF LYONS.

CHAPTER XVIII.

CHAPTER XIX.

CHAPTER XX.

LORD AMHERST.

HISTORY

OF THE

CAPTIVITY OF NAPOLEON

IN ST: HELENA.

CHAPTER I.

GENERAL CONSIDERATIONS ON FRANCE.

"FRANCE, by her geographical situation, the fertility of her soil, the energy and intelligence of her inhabitants, is the arbitress of European states. She departs from the character assigned her by nature when she becomes a conquering power. She descends from it, when she consents to obey the obligations of any alliance whatsoever. She is among the nations of Europe what the lion is amongst the other animals which surround him. She cannot move without being either a protectress or a destroyer. She lends the assistance of her arm, but never exchanges aid for her own personal interest, or to augment the weight of her influence in the scale of nations. Her own force is always sufficient; for, even when she is momentarily affected by the malady of nations—intestine divisions

—she recovers, by convulsive efforts, the power of punishing her enemies for having dared to provoke her to the combat. In 1793 and 1794, the whole of Europe formed a coalition against her; 100,000 fanatical Vendeans, armed and paid by England, threatened Paris ; 1,300,000 Frenchmen instantly flew to arms, from the love of their country, and not, as has been said, through fear of the guillotine. Europe was conquered—condemned to recognise the French republic, and to submit to the empire of those principles of liberty and equality by which France had just been regenerated. There is nothing great of which the French are not capable; danger electrifies them; it is their Gallic inheritance. The love of glory is with them like a sixth sense; and when, after many years of peace, the wailings of a few mothers shall no longer find an echo, the conscription will become a point of honour, and the nation will be able to defy reverses, invasion, and ages!

" Those who are called to hold the reins of such a kingdom should comprehend the full value and bearing of the favourable position which France enjoys, and never suffer a *nation which was destined to be a sun, to degenerate into a satellite.*

" The whole of my policy was uniformly directed by this opinion, both during the consulate and the empire. I was ambitious to effect the fusion of all the great interests of Europe, as that of parties had been effected in France—to become the arbiter between nations and their kings; but for this, it was first necessary to gain the confidence and the friendship of the latter, which could only be acquired at the expense of my popularity with the former. I knew it, but I felt myself to be all-powerful, and took little note of those murmurs which would have been soon replaced by gratitude, had the great work of my ambition been accomplished. It was with this view, that, after the battle of Austerlitz, I gave liberty to Alexander, who, being hemmed in at Holich, asked it of me, and gave me his imperial word that he would lead back into Russia, by hasty marches, the shattered remnants of the Russian army, and no longer mix himself in the quarrels of Austria ;— that after Wagram I did not partition Austria; I could have done it—nothing would have been easier; for one of the arch-dukes begged me to separate the crowns of Bohemia and Hungary from that of Austria; and he said to me—' Place me upon the throne, I will give you every possible guarantee that you can require, and then only you will have nothing to fear from the Austrian power, whose policy is the depression of France. Metternich is your personal enemy; my brother suffers himself to be led blindfold by him; and, whatever may be said, he will still remain master under the reign of my nephew.'

" I, however, believed the protestations of the Emperor Francis. I suffered the triple crown t remain upon his head, but I was wrong. I committed a fault, also, in marrying the arch-duchess Marie-Louise, because from that day I looked upon the

house of Austria as a part of my family, and if I had
not been ruled by my own impressions of the sacred-
ness of family bonds, I would have waited for the
pacification of Spain before I engaged in the affairs of
the north, and the re-establishment of the kingdom
of Poland. Had I not reckoned on the integrity of
the Austrian alliance, the war in Russia would not
have taken place. It could have been avoided in
principle. It would have been enough for that purpose not to have interfered with the infractions of the
treaty of Tilsit, and to have allowed Russia to sell her
natural productions to England in exchange for English
manufactures.   This was the vital question of the
quarrel.

" Each of my victories was a diplomatic step in my
aim of restoring peace to Europe. After the battle of
Marengo, as well as after those of Austerlitz, Jena,
Wagram, and Dresden, I always offered a general peace;
and when 400,000 Frenchmen and allies of France were
on the banks of the Niemen, and whilst the Emperor
of Austria and the King of Prussia were waiting for
a friendly reception on my passage, I still stretched
out the hand of a brother to the Emperor Alexander,
and renewed to him the solemn declaration, that all
my conquests beyond the natural limits of France,
were neither made nor retained for any other purpose than that of compensation or exchange at a
general peace.

" Had I reigned twenty years longer, I would have
shown the difference between a constitutional emperor

and a king of France. The kings of France have never done anything but for the interests of their dynasty, and with a view of increasing their feudal power by the depression of the high nobility, the extinction of the great fiefs and their reunion with the crown.

" Henry IV. was a valiant captain, but he owed his crown more to his double abjuration than to his victories. His memory is only popular, because by a *bon-mot* he gave evidence of some sympathies for the people. But, in fact, he never did anything for them.

" Louis XIV. was a great king. He did great things, and nobly maintained the honour of the nation, both in his wars and by his diplomatic acts; but the whole spirit of his reign may be compressed into the single phrase—' *L'état c'est moi*' (I am the state). All his actions and thoughts were directed towards the attainment of personal greatness. He acted and created from pride, and not from patriotism.

" The national character sank under the reign of the kings of the third race: everything for the moment and the fancy, and nothing for the future; such was the principle and such were the manners which they conferred on the French nation. I would have changed the face of France and of Europe. Archimedes promised to move the world, if they only furnished him with a fulcrum for his lever; I would have made a fulcrum for myself, wherever I could have placed my energy, my perseverance, and my budgets. With budgets well employed, a world may be regenerated; with

budgets squandered, a world may be ruined. Had the
city of Paris employed, in solid buildings, all the
money which it wasted for ten centuries on structures
of wood and painted cloth, to feast its kings, Paris
would have been a wonder worthy of fabulous times:
wherever my dominion has extended, there remain
durable monuments of its benefits.

"The magnificent docks of Antwerp and Flushing
are capable of containing the most numerous fleets and
sheltering them both from the fury of the tempest and
the attacks of enemies—the hydraulic works of Dunkirk, Havre, and Nice—the gigantic harbour of Cherbourg—the maritime works in Venice—the beautiful
roads from Antwerp to Amsterdam—the plan and
commencement of the canal, intended to connect
Amsterdam with Hamburg and the Baltic — the
road along the banks of the Rhine — the road
from Bourdeaux to Bayonne—the passes of the Sim-
plon, Mont Cenis, Mont Genêvre, and the Corniche,
which open up the Alps in four directions, are works
which exceed in boldness, grandeur, and art, anything
ever attempted by the Romans. The bridges of Jena,
Austerlitz, Sèvres, and Tours—that over the Durance—
those of Bourdeaux, Moissac, Rouen, Turin, and Lisere
—the canal which connects the Rhine and the Rhone
by the Doubs, and unites the German ocean with the
Mediterranean—that which unites the Scheldt and the
Somme, and forms a channel for commerce between
Amsterdam and Paris—that which joins the Rance
and the Vilaine—the canal of Arles, that of Pavia, and

that of the Rhine—the draining of the marshes of Bour-
goin, Cotentin, and Rochefort—the works undertaken
for draining the Pontine marshes, which would have
been completed in 1820—the rebuilding and reparation
of almost all the churches in France, demolished or
injured in the revolution—the construction, in eighty-
three departments, of buildings, as establishments for
the extirpation of mendicity, by offering work and a
refuge to the poor against the infirmities of age, and
the evils of destitution—the embellishments of Paris,
the Louvre, the Exchange, the square on the Quai
d'Orsay, the triumphal arch of the Barrière de l'Etoile,
the granaries, the Madeleine, the canal of Ourg, and
the subterraneous channels for the distribution and
the construction of sewers—the restoration of the
monuments of Rome, the re-establishment of the manufactories of Lyons, and the reconstruction of its
buildings and streets destroyed in 1793—the erection
of many hundred manufactories of cotton, of beet-root
sugar, or of wood, all raised by the aid of millions
supplied from the civil list—50,000,000 employed in
repairing and embellishing the palaces of the crown—
60,000,000, in furniture placed in the royal residences
in France, Holland, Turin, and Rome—60,000,000, in
diamonds as a dotation to the crown of France, all
purchased with my treasures—the Musée Napoleon,
estimated at more than 400,000,000, created by my
victories, and containing nothing but objects legitimately acquired by treaties;—these are the monuments left by my passage; and history will record

that all this was accomplished in the midst of continual wars, without a loan, whilst the public debt
was in the course of extinction every year, with a
normal budget of less than 800,000,000 for more than
40,000,000 of people in the empire, and when the
army amounted to 600,000 men, with the crews of
100 sail of the line.

"France was in want of a great naval harbour
in the channel, as was often felt during the last war;
Louis XVI. had undertaken to form one at Cherbourg,
which was a gigantic undertaking for the means at
his disposal at that period, in which the finances of the
country were in a deplorable condition.   The protection of the roads by a breakwater presented the greatest difficulties; it was suggested to employ cones
constructed on shore, towed to the spot destined for
the breakwater, then filled with stones, and sunk for a
foundation; this was extremely ingenious.   From
rivalry, however, the project failed. The genius which
was to have constructed defences on shore, which were
to serve as auxiliaries to those of the dike, constructed
them in such a manner in the Isle of Pelet, and at
Fort Querqueville, that the breakwater became no
longer the principal part, and that which had been
intended to cover and protect a great navy, whether
collected to terrify the enemy, or driven in for refuge
in the chances of war, offered only an asylum for a
small number of ships, when it ought to have contained
100 at least. The additional accommodation might
have been gained at a small increase of expense, by

carrying the breakwater further out into the roads.
There was another inexcusable circumstance connected with the execution of these works, and one
very characteristic of this period of decay. All the
works connected with the Eastern entrance were
finished before it was even thought necessary to try,
by actual soundings, whether ships of war could enter
at low water without striking, and it was discovered
also that the western passage would be impracticable
for ships drawing more than eighteen feet water, unless
they diminished the length of the breakwater, leaving
the passage 2400 yards wide, which would have rendered the fire from Fort Querqueville very uncertain
in its effect.

" One of my first cares was to complete the works
of Cherbourg. After a long examination of the whole
subject, I gave orders for the elevation of the breakwater, and for the construction of three strong forts,
one at each extremity, and the third in the centre.
In less than a year there sprang up, as if by magic,
a real island, crowned with batteries of the heaviest
calibre. Till this time, the English merely laughed
at our efforts, which they believed would lead to no
result. The cones, they said, would go to pieces in
time, the stones would be scattered by the force of
the sea, and French fickleness would do the rest.
But now it became another affair. The western passage was still too wide, a cross fire could not have
been maintained with effect, and a bold enemy might
have renewed the disasters of Aboukir. I gave orders

for the construction of an enormous elliptical fort within the breakwater. This fort was at its centre, designed for its support, and commanding the central battery. It was two stories high, fitted with casements, and bomb proof, mounted with fifty heavy guns, and twenty mortars of large dimensions. The docks, excavated in the granite rocks, are works worthy of the greatest periods of Rome, and the Romans never executed anything more magnificent. All these works were completed in 1814. I had thus obtained a means of sheltering fifty additional ships of the line, but this was not enough to complete my conception. I proposed to renew the wonders of Egypt at Cherbourg. I had built my pyramid in the sea, and I now wished for my lake Mœris. I was desirous of concentrating at Cherbourg an immense naval force, in order to have it always in my power to threaten England, and to attack her with great force in case of necessity. I took up a position in which the two nations could fight, as it were, at close quarters, and the issue could not be doubtful, for it would have been the struggle, hand to hand, of forty millions of Frenchmen against from fifteen to twenty millions of Englishmen. It would have been terminated by a battle of Actium, and then what would I have done with England?—destroyed her? Certainly not. I would only have required from her that the term of her naval domination should cease, that her intolerable usurpation, her enjoyment of the rights imprescriptible and sacred to all, should have an end.

I would have required the freedom, the liberty of the seas, the independence and honour of the flags of all nations, and I should have had on my side the power, the good rights, and the wishes of the whole continent.

" The convention had no desire for a war with England, and had a good negotiator in London ; Chauvelin, the ambassador, was no longer recognised, but Maret, who then had charge of foreign affairs, was directed to treat. He made very reasonable overtures, which were rejected. Having returned with new powers, he made important concessions, very advantageous both to England and Holland; but Pitt dreaded the degree of power to which France might raise herself, if she were allowed peaceably to establish her revolution, and he never thought that he would imperil the destiny of the whole of Europe by taking up arms against French liberty.

" The convention had sacrificed Louis XVI. The great crime was committed : but England was the only power in Europe which had no pretence of right to punish them for it. It was England, nevertheless, that undertook to perform an act of vengeance which would have been quite natural for the houses of Spain or Austria. It was evident that after having dared to commit such a crime, the convention neither had the inclination nor the power to shrink before any menaces, nor to retrograde in its career. The warlike enthusiasm, but, above all, the revolutionary enthusiasm, which had been exhibited in France after the

battle of Jemappes, ought to have led men to foresee,
that in the moment of the most serious danger, when
the armies of Clairfait and the emigrés were threatening the country, there would be a great national
demonstration — an unanimous rising *en masse*
throughout the whole of France for its defence.
England, however, which assumed the lead in
forming the coalition, knew well that she would only
occupy the second line in the war, and would even
scarcely appear otherwise than in her subsidies.   It
was of great importance to her, that continental
Europe should be embroiled in dangers; the supremacy which she aimed at usurping would thus become more certain, and she would rule over Europe
by the evils which she was instrumental in causing—
she would curb and delay the progress of French
industry, by keeping the French people busy in the
field of battle.   She supported within the republic
those factions which were to tear it to pieces; she refused to negotiate with the convention, and she promised
herself to nourish terror; she wished to be heir of the
death of Louis XVI., and dispute its results with the
republic.   Chauvelin was dismissed on the 24th of
January, 1793; Maret remained till February 3rd,
but he also was ordered to leave the country when
war became imminent; he carried back with him the
conviction, that Pitt was the irreconcilable enemy of
the prosperity of France.   England carried with her,
in her hatred, all Europe, except Denmark, which
always remained faithful to France, and Tuscany,

governed by the wise and liberal Leopold. This was
a sentence of death to Holland, which was so placed as
to receive the first fire of the republic; but William V.
who had destroyed that fine country, to which his
ancestors had been invited with such glorious hos-
pitality, was, in consequence of his eagerness to accede
to the wishes of England, obliged to submit to the
results of his usurpation and his servility. The convention declared war against England, and against
Holland, which had become her satellite.

" It would be a magnificent field for speculation, to
estimate what would have been the destinies of France
and of Europe, had England satisfied herself with
denouncing the murder of Louis XVI., which would
have been for the interest of public morality, and
listened to the counsels of a philanthropic policy by
accepting revolutionized France as an ally. Scaffolds
would not then have been erected over the whole country;
kings would not have shaken on their thrones, but
their states would have all, more or less, passed
through a revolutionary process, and the whole of
Europe, without a convulsion, would have become
constitutional and free, without jealousy and without
ambition. The fancy of the Abbé de St. Pierre
would have been realized. The French republic would
have felt secure in her own resources and surrounding
safety, and would not have entertained the idea, or
felt the wish, of invading other states. She would not
have felt the necessity of victory, and the implacable
legislation which supported that necessity within her-

self would not have shed those torrents of blood which have steeped the soil of France: no other superiority, except that of law, would have sprung up in her bosom, and there would have been no room for the display of private ambition. Her whole glory would have been in her tribunes and on her seats of justice, and all her interests would have constrained the development and perfection of industry. Commerce and agriculture, with the arts, would have become the patrimony of liberty. A single campaign, perhaps, would have taken place in the commencement, which would have fixed the limits of France at the Rhine, the Alps, and the Pyrenees. This would have been her only conquest. France would then have been the greatest miracle in civilization; she would have re-vived the Rome of the Scipios, and the Greece of Miltiades and Leonidas. England would have been merely a manufactory and a counting-house, because France would have become the metropolis of the world. The sentence of death was passed upon France by England, but events seemed to arrest the judgment and to give hopes of its revocation.

"A king does not belong to nature, but only to civilization, and he must march at its head. The ancient crown of the Bourbons was broken, and Louis XVI. brought to the scaffold, because royalty had not kept pace with the progress of civilization. The French people said of Napoleon, ' HE IS OUR KING—the others are THE KINGS OF THE NOBLES.' The confidence of the people constituted his power.   The people were right; all Napoleon's thoughts when on the throne were for France; all his wishes in exile were for her happiness; and if he gained the affection of the French people, it was because he deserved it, by never promising anything which he did not perform.   The first duty of a prince is to fulfil the wishes and meet the expectations of his people, but what the people wish seldom corresponds with what they say; the wishes and wants of the people are found less in their mouths than in the heart of the prince.   Every system may be maintained, that of affability as well as that of severity; both have their chances of success and their dangers.   I often affected severity in order to spare myself the necessity of doing that which policy demanded.   The archives of my ministers, those of my cabinet, have fallen into the hands of my most implacable enemies, and what have they found there to impugn my justice, and the rigid probity of my administration?   Nothing.   Where is the sovereign who, in my position, in the midst of factions, disturbances and unceasing conspiracies, would have inflicted fewer punishments, or had less recourse to the executioner?   And, notwithstanding, what was the calm which pervaded France on my elevation to the head of affairs as First Consul!   All my disinterestedness and all the inflexibility of my character were absolutely necessary to change the modes of administration and to put an end to that frightful spectacle of demoralization organized in the saloons of Barras, which recalled the monstrous disorders of the times of the regency.

" Immorality is, unquestionably, the worst and most destructive disposition which a sovereign can possess, because it becomes the fashion and a means of success to courtiers, among whom all vices find their natural support; it poisons the very sources of all virtue, and infects the whole social body like an epidemic.   It is, in short, the most dreadful of all national scourges. Public morality, on the contrary is the natural complement of law, and has an especial code of its own. There is no doubt, that revolutions regenerate morals, in the same manner as the richest manure produces the most splendid vegetation.

" The occupation of Amsterdam by our troops, was ordered by me, because of the necessity for shutting all the coasts and the ports of Holland against English commerce.   I ordered the French division ofour garrison, which was cantoned at Utrecht, to guard the coasts of the Zuyder Zee.

" The king abdicated.   If he had had more confidence in me, he would have remained King of Holland; the Dutch loved him, and justly, and would have preserved him at the peace ; the esteem and love of his people, would have done for him what the treaty of 1813 did for Murat.

" The dangers of France brought back Louis to me; he came to offer me his services like a good brother and a good Frenchman.

" The expedition against Walcheren and against Antwerp was the means of proving his worth as a king and as a general. His instantaneous and energetic decision saved Antwerp; Holland was almost destitute of troops; all the disposable forces of the Dutch army were on the Elbe. Louis did not hesitate to confide the crown to the patriotism of the Dutch, and he arrived at the head of the royal guards to the assistance of Antwerp; he had escaped every danger, and had paralysed the English expedition, when Bernadotte arrived there. France will acknowledge, sooner or later, when her hour of reverses shall come, the good conduct of all my brothers. All eagerly advanced to offer for her service their persons and their fortunes; my sisters even sacrificed with joy their jewels to pay for the recruiting of the army. Proscription and ruin are the effects of French gratitude at the present day."

———

It appears to me that the proper place for the two following letters, is at the end of this dictation; they explain the causes of the bad understanding between the two brothers as sovereigns :

" When your majesty ascended the throne of Holland, one part of the Dutch nation wished for a union with France ; the esteem which history made me conceive for this brave nation, made me desirous that it should retain its name, and its independence. I myself framed its constitution, which was to form the foundation of the throne of your majesty, and I placed you on it.

" I cherished the hope that your majesty, educated according to my principles, would have perceived that Holland, which had been conquered by my subjects, and which only owed its existence and independence to their generosity,—that Holland, weak, without allies, without an army, could be and ought to be conquered the very day that she should attempt any direct opposition against France,—that your majesty would not separate your policy from mine,—that Holland, in short, was bound by treaties to me. I had hoped that by placing on her throne a prince of my own blood, I had found the *mezzo termine* which would conciliate the interests of the two states, by uniting them in a common interest, and in a common hatred of England; and I was proud of having given to Holland a government suited to it, as I had given one to Switzerland by my act of mediation. But I have not been slow in perceiving that I deceived myself with vain hopes; my expectations have been disappointed; your majesty has, on ascending the throne of Holland, stretched all the springs of your reason, and tormented the delicacy of your conscience, to persuade yourself that you are Dutch.

" I carry in my heart, and I have raised upon the bayonets of my soldiers, the estimation and honour of the French name too high, for Holland or *any one* to insult it with impunity.

" Of what do the Dutch complain? Have they not

been conquered by our armies? Do they not owe their
independence to the generosity of France, which has
consequently opened to their commerce its rivers, and
its ports, which has only made use of its conquest to
protect them, and which has, till this hour, made no
other use of its power, than to consolidate their independence?

"You must understand that I do not separate
myself from my predecessors, that I consider myself
the representative of them all, from Clovis down to the
committee of public safety, and that the evil said out
of pure gaiety of heart against the governments which
preceded me, I consider said with the intention of
offending myself. I know that it has become the
fashion among certain persons to praise me, and to
decry France; but those who do not love France, do
not love me, and I consider those my greatest enemies
who calumniate my people.

"Your majesty has deceived yourself respecting
my character; you have a false idea of my kindness,
and of my feelings towards yourself.

"You have disarmed your squadrons, dismissed
your sailors, disorganized your armies, so that Holland
is at present without an army and without a fleet,
as if magazines, merchandise, and merchants could
consolidate one's power: all this constitutes a rich
community, but there cannot be a king without
means of raising an army, and without a fleet.

"The Dutch merchants have taken advantage of
the period when I was engaged on the Continent, to

renew their relations with England, and thus to defeat the only means of injuring that nation. I have clearly shown my dissatisfaction at this conduct by closing France against them, and I have given you to understand that without any assistance from my armies, and by merely shutting up the Rhine, the Weser, the Scheldt, and the Meuse, as far as Holland is concerned, I should place her in a more critical position than if I declared war against her, and that I should isolate her in such a manner as to annihilate her utterly.

"This intention was known in Holland; your majesty appealed to my generosity, to my sentiments as a brother, in order to change my intentions; I considered that this hint of my wishes would be sufficient, and removed the prohibition from my custom-houses; but your government has soon returned to its former system.

"All the American vessels which presented themselves at any of the Dutch ports, whilst they were not permitted to enter those of France, have been received by your majesty. I was obliged a second time to close my ports against Dutch traders; certainly I could not well have made a more definite declaration of war. In this state of things, we were at liberty to consider ourselves as really at war. In my address to the legislative body, I partly expressed my dissatisfaction, and I will not conceal from you, that it is my intention to annex Holland to France, as the most dreadful blow I can give to England.

"In fact, the mouth of the Rhine and that of the

Meuse ought to belong to us. The principle in France, that the Rhine is our natural limit, is a fundamental principle. Your Majesty writes to me, in your letter of the 17th, that you are certain of being able to hinder all commerce with England; that you can have finances, fleets, and armies; that you will re-establish the privileges of the constitution, by allowing of no principles exclusively belonging to the nobility, by reforming the marshals—a rank which is nothing but a caricature, and which is incompatible with a power of the second rank; finally, that you will command the seizure of the depôts of colonial merchandise, and everything which has arrived in American vessels, and which should not have been permitted to enter the port. My opinion is, that your Majesty is making engagements which you will not be able to fulfil; and that the union of Holland to France is only deferred for a time. I confess that I have no more interest in uniting the right bank of the Rhine with France, than I have in incorporating with it the duchy of Berg or the Hanseatic towns. I have no objection, therefore, to leave Holland in possession of the right bank of the Rhine; and I shall remove the prohibition given to my custom-houses, whenever the existing treaties, which shall be renewed, are fulfilled. These are my demands—

" ' 1. Interdiction of all commerce and of all communication with England.

" ' 2. A fleet of fourteen ships of the line, seven frigates, and seven brigs or corvettes, armed and fully equipped.

" ' 3. An army of 25,000 men.

" ' 4. Suppression of marshals.

" ' 5. Destruction of all the privileges of the nobility, contrary to the constitution, which I have
given and guaranteed.'

" Your Majesty can negotiate on these principles with the Duke of Cadou, by means of your
ministers; but you may be certain that the first
packet, the first vessel of any kind that is introduced into Holland, I shall re-establish the closing of
my ports; that the first insult that is offered to my
flag, I shall seize by force, and have hanged at the
yard-arm the Dutch officer offering the insult to my
Eagle. Your Majesty will find in me a brother, if I
find in you a Frenchman upon the throne of Holland;
but if you forget the sentiments which attach you to
our common country, you will not be surprised if I also
forget those bonds which nature has placed between us.
In a word, the union of Holland with France is that
which is most useful to France, to Holland, and to the
Continent; for it is what would be most injurious to
England. This union may be effected by mutual
arrangement, or by force. I have sufficient cause of
complaint against Holland to declare war against her;
but I will place no difficulties in the way of any
arrangement which will yield to me the boundary of the
Rhine, and by which Holland will bind herself to
fulfil the conditions above stipulated.'

" Your affectionate brother,

(Signed)   " NAPOLEON.

" Trianon, July 21, 1809."

" MON FRÈRE,—I have received your letter of the
16th of May. In the situation in which we are, it is
necessary always to speak openly. You know that I
have heard of some of your tricks, which were not
intended to fall under my eyes. I know your most
secret feelings, and everything you can say in contradiction will be of no avail. You need not speak of
your feelings, and of your childhood; experience has
taught me how much regard I am to pay to such
phrases. Holland is in a disagreeable situation, it is
true. I can well understand that you would like to
be out of it, but I am surprised at your addressing
yourself to me on the subject. I can do nothing in
the matter; it is yourself and yourself alone who can
produce any effect. As soon as you conduct yourself
in such a manner as to persuade the Dutch *that you
act according to my advice*—that all your proceedings, and all your feelings are in accordance with mine,
you will be beloved and esteemed, and you will
acquire the power necessary to re-constitute Holland.
This illusion sustains you somewhat even yet.

" *Your late journey to Paris*—your return, and
that of the Queen, and some other circumstances, have
made your people believe that it is still possible
you may return to my system and to my opinions;
but you alone can confirm this hope, and destroy every
doubt of such a termination. There is not one of
your actions which your clumsy Dutchmen do not
weigh, as they would weigh matters of credit or of
commerce; they know, therefore, with what they have

to do. When, to be a friend of France and of me, is sufficient reason for being in favour at your court, all Holland will perceive this—all Holland will rejoice at it, and will consider this a natural situation; but all this depends upon yourself, and since your return you have done nothing to forward it. Do you wish to know what will be the result of your conduct? Your subjects, finding themselves tossed about from France to England, and from England to France, not knowing what hopes to form, what wishes to express, will throw themselves into the arms of France, and will loudly demand their union with that country, as a refuge against so much uncertainty. Your government aims at being paternal, and is, in fact, only weak.

" Even in Zeeland, where everything is Dutch, the people are content to be united to a great country, in order to be freed from this fluctuation, which they cannot conceive.

" Do not deceive yourself, every one knows that without me there is no credit—that without me you are nothing; if, then, the example that you have had in Paris—if the knowledge of my character, which is, to go straight to my end without allowing myself to be stopped by anything, has not sufficiently enlightened you, what would you have me do? Having possession of the Meuse and of the Rhine, as far as their *embouchure*, I can do without Holland; Holland cannot do without my protection. If, subject to one of my brothers, and only expecting its safety from me, it does not see in you my image; if, when you speak, it is not I who speak, you will destroy your own sovereignty. Do not believe that you can deceive anybody. Do you wish to see the course which good policy recommends to you? Serve France—serve glory; it is the only way to remain King of Holland. Under a king, the Dutch have lost the advantages of a free government; you were, then, for them a harbour of refuge, but you have spoiled this harbour; you have strewn it with reefs, by wishing to be King of Holland before being my brother.

"Do you know why you were a harbour of refuge to the Dutch? It is because you were the pledge of an eternal union between France and Holland, the bond of a community of interest between myself and that country, which had become, by means of you, a part of my empire; a province, moreover, particularly dear to me, because I had given to it a prince who was to me almost as a son. If you had been what you ought to have been, I should take as much interest in Holland as in France; its prosperity would be a matter of as much anxiety to me as that of France.

"If you had understood me, you would be at present king of 6,000,000 of subjects. I should have considered the throne of Holland as a pedestal upon which I should have set up Hamburg, Osnaburg, and a part of the north of Germany: this would have been the kernel of a people which would have assisted in destroying the national feeling of the Germans, which

is the principal object of my policy.   Far from doing
this, however, you have followed a course diametri-
cally opposed to it; I have been compelled to forbid
you France, and to take possession of a part of your
country.

"You do not say a word in your advices, or inform
me of a single circumstance, which is not already
known to me, which does not turn to your disadvan-
tage and injure you ; for, in the mind of the
Dutch, you are a Frenchman, in the midst of them
for four years only; they only see in you a representative of me, and the advantage of being freed from
all subaltern robbers and agitators, who have harassed
them since their conquest. If you wish to make yourself a Dutchman, you would be less to them than a
Prince of Orange, to whose race they owe their standing as a nation, and a long course of prosperity and
glory. It is proved to Holland that your removal
from my policy has caused them to lose advantages
which they would not have lost under Schimmelpen-
nynck or a Prince of Orange.   Be first the brother of
the Emperor, and you may be sure that you will be on
the road to promote the advantage of Holland.   But
to what purpose is all this?   The die has been cast;
you are incorrigible.   Already you are driving out
the few French who remain with you; I can no longer
give you counsel or advice, but must make use of
threats and force.

"What is the use of these prayers and mysterious

fasts, which you have ordered. Louis, you do not wish to reign long. All your actions reveal, better than your confidential letters, the secret feelings of your soul. Listen to a man who knows more of it than you; return from your false course, and believe me,

"Your affectionate brother,

(Signed) "NAPOLEON."

CHAPTER II.

" My first acts, as General, after my entrance into Milan, were the pacification and re-organization of Italy.

" The minority of the aristocracy which governed the republic of Genoa, the majority of the third class, and the whole of the population on the shores of the Ponente, were favourable to French ideas. The city of Genoa was the only one in this state which had stability; it was defended by a double circle of fortifications, a great number of cannon, 6000 regular troops, and a national guard amounting to the same number.

" At the first signal from the senate, 30,000 men, collected from the inferior corporations, such as those of the colliers and porters, the peasants of the valleys of the Polcevera, the Besagno, and the Fontana-Bona, were ready to rise in defence of their prince.

" An army of 40,000 men, the whole *equipage de siége*, and two months' labour, would be required in order to take this capital. In 1794, 1795, and the beginning of 1796, the Austro-Sardinian army covered it on the north, and communicated with it by the Bochetta ; the French army covered it on the west, and communicated with it by the corniche of Savona. Being thus placed between the two belligerent armies, Genoa was in a position to be equally succoured by both,—she held the balance between them ; the one in whose favour she should decide, would gain a great advantage; she was, there-fore, in the existing circumstances, of great weight in the affairs of Italy. The Genoese senate felt all the delicacy, and, at the same time, the strength of this position; it availed itself of them to remain neuter, and constantly resisted the offers and threats of the coalition. The commerce of the town became more extensive, and brought immense riches into the republic; but its port had been forcibly entered by the English squadron; the catastrophe of the frigate " La Modeste " had deeply affected every French heart; the convention had dissimulated, but only awaited a favourable opportunity for exacting a signal repara-tion. Several noble families, who were the most attached to France, had been banished; this was a fresh insult which the government had to redress. After the battle of Loano, in the winter of 1796, the directory thought that the favourable moment for its purpose was now arrived; so much the more so, as the penury which its Italian army was then suffering, made it attach great importance to an extraordinary aid of five or six millions. These negotiations were proceeding at the time when Napoleon was raised to the command of the army; he disapproved of this sordid policy, which could have no success, and the necessary effect of which would be to embitter the minds of the inhabitants of this important capital, and render them unfavourable to the French. ' We must either,' said he, ' scale the ramparts, establish ourselves by a vigorous stroke, and destroy the aristocracy, or respect the independence of the town, and above all, leave it its money.' A few days afterwards, the enemy having been driven beyond the Po, and the King of Sardinia having laid down his arms, the republic of Genoa was at the mercy of France.

" The directory would have wished to establish a democracy in this state, but the French armies were already on their way from Genoa. The presence, and perhaps the sojourn of a body of 15,000 French soldiers under its walls, would have been necessary to secure the success of such a revolution.

" The march of Wurmser, who was then crossing Germany and entering the Tyrol, was already echoed on all sides. After that time, the defeat of Wurmser, the manœuvres in the Tyrol and among the defiles of the Brenta, and the movements made by Alvinzi for the purpose of relieving Wurmser, who was blockaded in Mantua, rendered it necessary that the army should be concentrated on the Adige; the army had besides nothing to fear from the Genoese—their nobles were divided among themselves, and the people were favourable to the French.

" Girola, the imperial minister, profiting by the absence of the French army, and secretly favoured by the feudatory families, had kindled an insurrection in the imperial fiefs, and had formed bands composed of Piedmontese deserters, of vagabonds left without any employment, in consequence of the disbandment of the light Piedmontese troops, and of Austrian prisoners, who had been carelessly guarded by the French, and had escaped on the march. These bands infested the Appenines, and harassed the rear of the French army. Matters went so far, that in the month of June it was found absolutely necessary to put an end to this state of things; a detachment of 1200 men, and the presence of the general-in-chief at Tortona, sufficed to re-establish order. Napoleon gave instructions to the French minister at Genoa, Faypoult, to commence negotiations, for the purpose of increasing the influence of France with the government, as far as this could be done without rendering the presence of an army necessary. He required—1stly, the expulsion of the Austrian minister, Girola; 2ndly, the expulsion of the feudatory families, conformably to one of the statutes of the republic; and finally, the recall of the banished families.

" These negotiations were drawn out to a great

length. While they were going on, five French merchant vessels were carried off from the port of Genoa,
without any attempt being made to protect them,
although they lay close under the Genoese batteries;
the senate, alarmed at the threats of the French
agents, sent to Paris the senator, Vincentes Spinola,
a man very favourable to France, who, after some
negotiation, signed, on the 6th of October, 1796, an
agreement with Charles Lacroix, minister of foreign
affairs. All the complaints of France against Genoa
were sunk in oblivion, the senate paid a contribution of four millions, and recalled the banished
families; France ought, perhaps, to have profited by
these favourable circumstances, to bind the republic
by an offensive and defensive alliance, to add the imperial fiefs and Massadi Carara to its territories, and
to draw from it a contingent of 4000 infantry, 400
cavalry, and 200 artillery. But the utility of this
system of alliance with the oligarchs was repugnant
to the democrats of Paris.

" By this agreement, however, tranquillity was restored, and lasted till the treaty of Montebello, in
1797; and during the whole time that the French
army was in Germany, no cause of complaint arose
from the conduct of the people of Genoa.

" The armistice of Cherasco with the King of Sardinia, had isolated the Austrian army, and had given
the French an opportunity of expelling it from Italy,
investing Mantua, and occupying the line of the Adige.

" The peace concluded at Paris in the month of

May following, placed all the fortresses of Piedmont, except Turin, in the power of France. The King of Sardinia thus found himself at the disposal of the republic. His army was reduced to 20,000 men; his paper money threatened the ruin of the private gentry, and of the state; his subjects were malcontent and divided—even French ideas had partisans, though but few. Politic statesmen would have wished to revolutionize Piedmont, in order to leave nothing which might harass the rear of the army, and to increase the means of France against Austria; but it would have been impossible to overthrow the throne of Sardinia, without intervening directly and with imposing forces; while the scenes which were passing before Mantua sufficiently occupied all the republic's Italian troops; and, besides, a revolution in Piedmont might lead to a civil war; it would, in this case, be necessary to leave in Piedmont, for the purpose of keeping it in order, more French troops than could be supplied by Piedmontese levies; and in case of a retreat, the population, which would have been put into a state of excitement, would run into inevitable excesses; and moreover, might not the Kings of Spain and Prussia be alarmed at seeing the French republic, the hater of kings, overthrow with its own hands a prince with whom it had but shortly before signed a treaty of peace? These considerations determined Napoleon to come to the same result by an opposite road— viz., an offensive and defensive alliance with the King of Sardinia; this plan united all advantages,

and had no drawback.   In the first place, this treaty
would in itself be a proclamation, which would restrain the malcontents; they would no longer be able
to give credit to the protestations of the democrats of
the army, who did not fail to promise them the
support of France; the country would, therefore, remain quiet; 2ndly, a division of fine old troops, of
10,000 Piedmontese, would reinforce the French
army, and would give it fresh chances of success;
3rdly, the example of the court of Turin would have
a happy influence on the Venetians, and would contribute towards determining them to seek, in an
alliance with France, a guarantee for the integrity of
their territories, and the maintenance of their constitution; at the same time, the Piedmontese troops
which were enrolled in the French army would become imbued with its spirit, and would be attached to
the general who should lead them to victory; in any
case, they would be hostages placed in the centre of
the army, and would be guarantees for the disposition
of the Piedmontese, and if it was true that the King
of Sardinia could not maintain his position, surrounded as he was by the democratic republics of
Liguria, Lombardy, and France, his fall would be
the result of the nature of things, and not that of a
political act, of a nature to alienate the other allied
kings from France.

" The alliance of France with Sardinia," said Napoleon, " resembles a giant embracing a pigmy; if he

stifles him, it is against his will, and solely the effect of the extreme difference in their bodily strength."

The directory *would* not understand the wisdom and depth of this policy; it authorised the opening of the negotiations, but shackled their conclusion. Monsieur Poussielgue, secretary of legation at Genoa, had conferences at Turin during several months; he found the court disposed to form an alliance with the republic; but this not very skilful negotiator allowed himself to be drawn into granting concessions which were evidently exaggerated; he promised Lombardy to the King of Sardinia. Now, such a project was not at all to be brought into consideration—to increase this prince's territories, and give him hopes which were never to be realized; he would reap sufficient advantage from a treaty, in the guarantee that his kingdom would be kept entire.

When Mantua opened its gates, and Napoleon marched to Tolentino in order to dictate from thence the terms of peace to the Holy See, and afterwards to proceed to Vienna, he fully saw how important it was to bring the affairs of Piedmont to a conclusion, and authorised General Clarke to negotiate with Monsieur de Saint Marson an offensive and defensive alliance; this treaty was signed at Bologna, on the 1st of March, 1797; the King received from the republic the guarantee of his states; he furnished to the French army a contingent of 8000 infantry, 2000 cavalry, and twenty pieces of cannon.

The court of Turin, entertaining no doubts of the ratification of a treaty set on foot by the general-in-chief, hastened to assemble its contingent, which would have rejoined the army then in Carinthia; but the Directory hesitated to ratify the treaty, and the contingent remained in Piedmont, cantoned near Novarro, during the whole of the campaign of 1797.

The policy to be pursued towards the Infant, the Duke of Parma, was prescribed by our relations with Spain; an armistice was first granted, on the 9th of May, 1797, and some months afterwards, the Infant signed at Paris his treaty of peace with the republic; but the French minister did not understand how to realize the aim which the general-in-chief had proposed to himself.   The success of the French army in Italy had determined the King of Spain to conclude, in the month of August, 1796, an offensive and defensive alliance with the republic; consequently, it would have been easy to persuade the court of Madrid to send a division of 10,000 men to the Po, for the purpose of guarding the Duke of Parma, and, by help of the bait of an addition to the territories of this prince, to have enlisted this division under the French standard.   Its presence would have awed Rome and Naples, and would have contributed, in no small degree, to the success of all the military movements; the alliance with Spain having determined the English to evacuate the Mediterranean, the French and Spanish squadrons were masters of it, and this facilitated the movements of the Spanish troops in Italy.   The sight of a Spanish division in the ranks of a French army would have a fortunate influence in deciding the senate to form an alliance with France, and this alliance would bring to the army a reinforcement of 10,000 Sclavonians.

The armistice of Milan, of the 20th of May, 1796, had suspended the hostilities which had been carried on against the Duke of Modena; the French army was not large, and the space of country which it occupied, immense; it would, therefore, have been very unwise to have taken a detachment of two or three battalions from it for a secondary object. The armistice with Modena placed all the resources of that duchy at the disposal of the army, and did not require the employment of any troops for the maintenance of the public tranquillity. Commander d'Este, furnished with powers from the Duke, commenced at Paris negotiations for a definitive peace; the French ministry acted wisely, and did not hasten to come to any conclusion. The Duke, who was entirely devoted to the Austrians, had retired to Venice, and the regency which governed his states had sent several convoys of provisions into Mantua, at the moment when the blockade was raised at the end of August and the beginning of September; as soon as the general-in-chief was informed of this direct violation of the armistice, he complained of it to the regency, who vainly attempted to justify itself on the ground of the existence of former treaties. In the meantime, however, a detachment of the garrison of Mantua, which had passed the Po at Borgo-forte, was intercepted; it

marched to Reggio on the 20th of October, intending
to proceed to Tuscany; the inhabitants of Reggio
closed the gates of their town; the detachment then
took refuge in the fort of Monte-Cherisio, where the
patriots surrounded it, and forced the soldiers to lay
down their arms: two Reggians were killed in the
struggle; they were the first Italians who sealed the
liberty of their country with their blood. The prisoners were conducted to Milan by a detachment of
the national guard of Reggio, and were received there
in triumph by the congress of Lombardy, the national
guard, and the general-in-chief; and this event was
the subject of several civic fêtes which contributed to
excite the imaginations of the Italians. Reggio proclaimed its liberty; the people of Modena wished to
do the same, but were restrained by the garrison ; in
this state of things, there was but one plan of action
to be pursued. The general-in-chief declared that the
armistice of Milan had been violated by the regency in
re-victualling Mantua; he sent garrisons to the fortresses of the three duchies of Reggio, Modena, and
Mirandola; and, in virtue of his right of conquest,
proclaimed their independence. This revolution
ameliorated the position of the army, as a provisional
government, entirely devoted to the French cause, was
now substituted for the former unfriendly regency;
national guards, composed of warm patriots, were
formed in every duchy. Hostilities with Rome having
been suspended by the armistice of Bologna, June
23rd, 1796, the papal court sent Monsignor Pétrarchi

to Paris. After passing some weeks in conferences, Pétrarchi sent to Rome a prospectus of the treaty proposed by the directory. The assembly of cardinals gave their opinion that it contained things contrary to the faith, and was not admissible; Pétrarchi was recalled. In September, the negotiations were recommenced at Florence; the government commissioners then with the army were invested with the powers of the directory. After one or two conferences, the commissioners presented to Monsignor Galeppi, plenipotentiary of the pope, a treaty of sixty articles, as a *sine quâ non*, declaring that they could make no change in any part of it.

The cardinals decided that this treaty also contained things contrary to the faith; and the negotiations were broken off, on the 25th of September. The court of Rome, no longer doubting that France was bent upon its destruction, gave itself up to despair, and resolved to ally itself exclusively with the court of Vienna. It began by suspending the execution of the armistice of Bologna; it had still to pay sixteen millions, which were now on the way to Bologna, where they were to be paid into the treasury of the army; these convoys of money returned to Rome; their re-entrance was a triumph. Monsignor Albani set out on the 6th of October for Vienna, there to solicit the support of the Austrian government; the Roman princes offered patriotic gifts and levied regiments, and the pope issued proclamations for the purpose of kindling the holy war.

All the efforts of the court of Rome were calculated to be able to raise an army of 10,000 men, of the most miserable troops possible; but it counted on the assistance of the King of Naples, who secretly engaged to support it with an army of 30,000 men; and although the inimical disposition and bad faith of the Neapolitan cabinet were well known at the Vatican, the pope still invoked its aid.

" Any means are welcome to them in their delirium," wrote the minister Cacault; " they would cling to red hot iron."   This state of affairs had a vexatious effect on the whole of Italy.   Napoleon was in sufficiently embarrassing circumstances without this fresh addition; he was already menaced by Alvinzi, whose troops were being collected in the Tyrol and on the Piave; he reproached the French ministry for having left him ignorant of negotiations which he alone could direct.   Had he been entrusted with their direction, as he ought to have been, he would have delayed the overture for two or three weeks, in order to have received the sixteen millions owed by the Holy See, in fulfilment of the armistice of Bologna.   He would not have allowed spiritual and temporal affairs to have been brought forward at the same time in the treaty; for, let the latter, which formed the essential part of it, once be arranged, a few months delay in coming to an understanding concerning the former, would have been indifferent; but the mischief was done, and the French government, which now perceived it, invested him with the authority necessary to remedy it, if this should be possible. The essential thing was, to gain time, to calm the passions which had been roused, to restore confidence, and to restrain within bounds the alarmed spirits of the Vatican. He commissioned M. Cacault, the French agent at Rome, to disavow, confidentially, all the spiritual matter contained in the negotiations of Paris and Florence; and to inform the papal see that Napoleon was now charged with the negotiation, and that it would no longer have to do either with the directory or the commissioners, but with him. These overtures produced a good effect. In order the more to strike the minds of the people, the general went to Ferrara, on the 21st of October, drove to the house of Cardinal Mattei, arch-bishop of that city, and had several conferences with him; he convinced him of his pacific intentions, and sent him to Rome with a direct message of peace to the pope. The hopes to which the army of Alvinzi had given rise in Italy, were, a few days afterwards, extinguished by the battle of Arcola. Napoleon thought this a favourable moment for terminating the affairs of Rome; he went to Bologna with 1500 French troops and 4000 Cispadans and Lombards, and threatened to march against Rome; but this time the papal see laughed at his menaces, it was negotia-ting a treaty through its minister at Vienna, and knew that two fresh and large armies were advancing into Italy; the cardinal and the Austrian minister at Rome said, haughtily—" Should it be necessary, the pope will evacuate Rome; for the further the French

general removes his army from the Adige, the nearer
we shall be to our safety." And, in fact, Napoleon,
being a few days afterwards informed of Alvinzi's
movements, recrossed the Po and marched quickly to
Verona. But the battle of Rivoli, fought in the
month of January, 1797, destroyed for ever the hopes
of the enemies of France. Mantua shortly after opened
its gates—the moment for chastising Rome had arrived;
a small Gallo-Italian army marched to the Appenines.
All the difficulties between France and the papal see
were settled by the treaty of Tolentino, as will be seen
in the next chapter.

The Grand Duke of Tuscany was the first prince in
Europe who acknowledged the French republic. At
the time when the French army invaded Italy, he was
at peace with France, his states, which lay beyond
the Appenines, exercised no influence on the theatre
of the war. It is true, that after the investiture of
Mantua, a French brigade marched upon Livorno,
but this was only for the purpose of expelling English
commerce from it, and facilitating the deliverance of
Corsica; in every other affair, the states of Tuscany
were respected. The garrison of Livorno was never
above 1800 men; it was doubtless a sacrifice to employ three battalions for a secondary object; but the
soldiers employed in this service were those of the 57th
half brigade, who had suffered much, and needed
repose.

Manfredini, the prime minister of the grand duke,
showed skill and activity in removing any obstacles

which might injure his master, and to him the duke owed the preservation of his states. Three or four agreements of slight importance were signed between the French general and the Marquis Manfredini; by the last, signed at Bologna, it was agreed that the French garrison should evacuate Livorno; on this occasion the grand duke, in order to liquidate old accounts, put two millions into the treasury of the army. On the conclusion of the peace of Campo-Formio, this prince preserved his states entire; he had experienced some annoyance, but nothing more ; during the Italian war, no injury was done to him, partly out of respect for existing treaties, and partly on account of the desire entertained by France to soften the animosity with which the house of Lorraine was animated against the republic, and to detach it from England. When the French army had reached the Adige, and central and lower Italy thus found themselves cut off from Germany, Prince Pignatelli came to headquarters, and demanded and obtained for the King of Naples an armistice, which was signed on the 5th of June, 1796. The division of Neapolitan cavalry, consisting of 2400 horsemen, which formed a part of Beaulieu's army, went into cantonment around Brescia, in the centre of the French army. A Neapolitan plenipotentiary was dispatched to Paris, with powers to negotiate and sign a definitive treaty of peace with the republic; this treaty met with difficulties from the ill-timed cavils which were carried on at Paris, and from the effects of the constant and well-known bad faith of the court of the two Sicilies. The directory should have thought itself only too happy in being able to make peace with the King of Naples, since this prince had 60,000 men under arms, and had from 25 to 30,000 men at his disposal to send to the Po. Napoleon incessantly urged the conclusion of this treaty. The French minister of foreign affairs demanded from Naples a contribution of some millions, which that government refused, and with justice, to pay; but in the month of September, when it was acknowledged by all parties that the alliance of Spain with France, and the deliverance of Corsica from the English yoke, had determined the cabinet of St. James's to recall its squadrons from the Mediterranean, thus leaving that sea and the Adriatic in the power of the French squadrons, the court of Naples, alarmed at these events, subscribed to all the demands made by the directory, and the peace was signed on the 8th of October.

But the hatred and bad faith of this cabinet, and its little respect for its signature and its treaties, were such, that it continued, long after the peace had been signed, to harass Italy by the movements of troops on its frontiers, and by menaces of attack; conducting itself, in fact, just as if it had been in a state of war. It would be difficult to express the indignation excited by this want of all shame and respect, which finally brought on the ruin of this cabinet. In the beginning of September, when the French armies of the Rhine, Sambre, and Meuse, were still in Germany, the French government instructed Napoleon to write to the Emperor, threatening that if he would not consent to peace, the French armies would destroy his maritime establishments at Fiume and Trieste. Nothing was to be hoped from so inexpedient a step. Afterwards, when the armies of the Sambre, Meuse, and Rhine had been thrown back into France, and the bridge-entrances of Kehl and Honingen were besieged, Moreau proposed an armistice, which the arch-duke refused, declaring that he intended to get possession of both; but as Marshal Wurmser, with nearly 30,000 Austrians, was blockaded in Mantua, and as Alvinzi's efforts to relieve him had just been defeated at Arcola, the directory conceived the hope of obtaining the acceptance of a general armistice, which would preserve Honingen and Kehl to France, and Mantua to Austria. In consequence of this project, General Clarke received the necessary powers, and went to Vienna to propose this armistice, which was to last till the month of June, 1797; the sieges of Kehl and Honingen were to be raised, and the *statu quo* established, as regarded Mantua; Austrian and French commissaries were to send into the town the provisions necessary for the inhabitants and troops. General Clarke arrived at Milan, on the 1st of December, in order to arrange matters with the general-in-chief, who was commissioned to take the necessary steps in order to obtain for the plenipotentiary all the passports which he needed. Napoleon said to him—" The sieges of Kehl and Honingen are easy to raise; the arch-duke has but 40,000 men before Kehl; let Moreau sally out at break of day from his entrenched camp with 60,000 men, defeat him, take his artillery and provisions, and destroy all his works; and besides, Kehl and Honingen are not equal in value to Mantua; there would be no means of feeding the number of inhabitants—men, women, and children—not even that of the garrison. Marshal Wurmser, by reducing all the inhabitants to half rations, would in six months save enough to live on for another six; if the government propose that this armistice shall serve as an opportunity for commencing negotiations for peace, this is an additional reason for not proposing it as long as Mautua remains in the power of the Austrians; we ought to gain a battle under the walls of Kehl, and await the surrender of Mantua, before offering an armistice and peace." The orders of the government were, however, decisive: General Clarke wrote to the Emperor, and sent him a letter from the directory. In consequence of this proceeding, Baron Vincent, aide-de-camp to the Emperor, and General Clarke, met at Vicenza, on the 3rd of January; they had two conferences there. Baron Vincent declared that the Emperor could not receive at Vienna the plenipotentiaries of a republic which he did not acknowledge; that, moreover, he could not detach himself from his allies; and that, finally, if the French minister had any communications to make, he might address himself to Monsieur Giraldi, the Austrian minister at Turin. Thus, this disastrous idea of an armistice was happily eluded by the enemy.

The French minister had scarcely returned to the Adige, when Alvinzi began manœuvring to relieve Mantua; this gave rise to the battles of Rivoli and La Favorite, as will be seen in the account of the Italian wars.

The cabinet of Luxembourg, however, saw in this answer of Baron Vincent's, it knew not why, an open tendency towards negotiations, and during the month of January, 1797, it addressed to General Clarke instructions for negotiating a peace, which he was authorised to sign—on condition, 1stly, that the Emperor should renounce Belgium, and the province of Luxembourg; 2ndly, that he should acknowledge to the republic the cession of Liege and other small enclosures of principalities which had been made; 3rdly, that he should use his influence in order to give to the stadtholder an indemnity in Germany; 4thly, that the republic, on its part, should restore to Austria all its Italian states; these conditions did not obtain the approbation of Napoleon, who thought that the republic had a right to require the limits of the Rhine, and a state in Italy, which might nourish French influence, and keep the republic of Genoa, the King of Sardinia, and the Pope, in their state of dependence, for Italy could no longer be considered as it was before the war; if the French ever repassed the Alps, without leaving a powerful auxiliary in Italy, the aristocracies of Genoa and Venice, and the King of Sardinia, influenced by the necessity of securing their interior existence against democratic and popular ideas, would attach themselves to Austria by indissoluble bonds. Venice, which, for a century past, had had no influence in the balance of Europe, enlightened now by an experience of the dangers she had just seen, would have energy, money, and armies, to reinforce the Emperor, and repress the ideas of liberty and independence which were nourished on the main land. Pontiffs, kings, and nobles, would unite in defending their privileges, and closing the Alps against modern ideas.

Three months afterwards, Napoleon signed the preliminaries of peace, on the basis of the limits of the Rhine; that is to say, with an acquisition to the republic of the fortress of Mayence, and a population of 1,500,000 persons over and above what the Directory required, and the existence of one or two democratic republics in Italy, which communicated with Switzerland, forming a line across the whole of Italy from north to south, from the Alps to the Po, surrounding the King of Sardinia, and covering, along the line of the Po, the centre and south of Italy.

In case of need, the French armies, pouring in through Genoa, Parma, Modena, and Bologna, might appear suddenly on the Piave, having passed the Mincio, Mantua, and the Adige. Genoa, this republic of 3,000,000 inhabitants, would secure the French influence over the 3,000,000 inhabitants of the kingdom of Sardinia, and the 3,000,000 of the states of the church and Tuscany, and even over the kingdom of Naples.

The course of conduct to be pursued towards the people of Lombardy was a delicate matter; France was willing to conclude a peace as soon as the Emperor should renounce Belgium and Luxembourg. No engagements could, therefore, be contracted ; no guarantee given, which was contrary to these secret arrangements of the cabinet. On the other hand, all the expenses of the army had to be borne by the country, and they not only absorbed the revenues, but gave rise to an overplus of charges, greater or smaller in proportion to the number of troops which were quartered in different places. In France, the system of indirect taxation had been suppressed. The system of contributions was very insufficient; the treasury was not under proper control; everything was conducted in an irregular, corrupt, and unskilful manner; all the wants of the army were left unprovided for; it was necessary to supply them by contributions raised in Italy; considerable sums were sent from thence to aid the armies of the Rhine, the squadrons of Toulon and Brest, and even the administration of Paris.

In the meantime it became essential to counterbalance in Italy the influence of the Austrian party, which was composed of the nobility, and a part of the clergy, on whom the influence of Rome acted with more or less success. Napoleon supported the party which wished for the independence of Italy, yet without compromising himself; and in spite of the critical state of the times, he gained over the opinion of the majority of the nation. He not only had a great

respect for religion, but he neglected nothing which
was likely to conciliate the minds of the clergy.   He
made use, at the right moment, of the talismanic words,
liberty and national independence, which, since the
times of Rome, have never ceased to be dear to the
Italians.   He confided the administration of the provinces, towns, and communes, to the inhabitants, by
choosing from among them such men as were most to
be recommended, and who enjoyed the greatest proportion of popular favour; he appointed, as police, the
national guards, who were levied throughout the whole
of Lombardy, in imitation of those of France, under
the Italian colours—red, white, and green.

Milan had been attached to the Guelph party, and
such was still the general tendency of the inhabitants.
The patriot party was daily increasing in number;
French ideas were daily making fresh progress, and
the state of the public mind, after the entire defeat of
Wurmser, was such, that the general-in-chief authorised the Lombard congress to make a levy of a legion
of 3000 men.   In the course of November, the Polish
generals, Zayonyerk and Dombrouski, hastened from
Poland with a great number of their officers, to offer
their services to Italy; the congress was authorised to
levy a legion of 3000 Poles.   These troops were not
brought forward against the Austrians, but served to
maintain public tranquillity, and to restrain the
pope's army. When difficult circumstances determined
the general-in-chief to proclaim the Cispadan republic,
the Lombard congress was greatly alarmed, but it

was soon made evident that this was the effect of the difference of circumstances. The army's line of operations did not pass through the Cispadan territories; and, in short, it was not difficult to convince the most enlightened members of the assembly, that, even were it true that this proceeding originated in the desire felt by the French government not to enter into engagements which the issue of the war might not enable it to fulfil, this ought not to be any cause of alarm; for that, in fine, it was evident that the fate of the French party in Italy depended on the hazards of the battle-field; and that, moreover, the guarantee which France henceforth gave to the Cispadan republic, was equally favourable to them; since, if circumstances should one day oblige the French to consent to the return of the Austrians into Lombardy, the Cispadan republic would then be a place of refuge for the Lombards, and a central point where the flame of Italian liberty might be preserved and cherished.

Reggio, Modena, Bologna, and Ferrara, embraced the whole extent of the country, from the Adriatic to the states of Parma, by which they were joined to the republic of Genoa, and through this to France.

If the French government thought it should be obliged to restore Lombardy to Austria in order to facilitate peace, it felt so much the more strongly the importance of preserving, on the right shore of the Po, a democratic republic, over which the house of Austria could establish neither right nor claim.

These four states preserved, for several months,

their independence, under the government of their
municipality; a junto of general safety, composed of
the Capratas, &c. &c., was organized for the purpose
of concerting means of defence, and restraining the
malcontents.   A congress, composed of a hundred
deputies, assembled at Modena during the month of
November; the Lombard colours were there declared
to be the colours of Italy; some bases of a government
were decreed—viz., the suppression of feudality and
the equality of the rights of man; these small republics formed a confederation for the common defence,
and united to raise an Italian legion, containing 3000
men.   The congress was composed of persons of all
ranks: cardinals, nobles, merchants, lawyers, and men
of letters.   Insensibly, ideas became more enlarged,
the press more free, and at length, in the beginning of
January, 1797, after some resistance, the spirit of
locality was conquered; these different republics
united themselves into one, under the name of the
Cispadan republic, of which Bologna was declared the
capital, and adopted a representative constitution.
The counter-blow of this event made itself felt at
Rome.

The organization and disposition of these new republicans formed an efficacious barrier against the
spirit which was being propagated by the Holy See,
and against the troops which it was collecting in
Romagna.   The Lombard congress formed a close
alliance with the Cispadan republic, which thenceforth
attracted the eyes of all Italy.   Of all the cities of

Italy, Bologna is the one which has constantly exhibited the greatest degree of energy and of true enlightenment. In February, 1797, after the peace of Tolentino, Romagna having been ceded by the pope, was naturally joined to the Cispadan republic, and increased its population to nearly two millions. Such was the state of Italy at the end of the year 1796, and the spring of 1797, when the French army resolved to cross the Julian Alps, and march against Vienna.

CHAPTER III.

TOLENTINO.

CARDINAL BUSCA had, six months before, succeeded
Cardinal Zelada in the office of secretary of state in
Rome.   He had broken with France, and openly
formed a connexion with Austria, and laboured with
more zeal than success in the attempt to form a respectable army.   He was anxious to restore those
times when the pontifical armies decided the fate of
the Peninsula.   He had contrived to stimulate the
Roman nobles to such a degree, that, with greater
emphasis than sincerity, they offered to provide regiments fully equipped, horses, and armies.   The cardinal had great confidence in the attachment of the
Italians to their religion, and in the naturally warlike
spirit of the people of the Apennines.   Napoleon had
dissembled amid many outrages, and many insults; but
the fall of Mantua placed him in a situation to take
a splendid vengeance.

On the 10th of January, 1797, a courier sent with despatches from Cardinal Busca to Monsignor Albani, *chargé d'affaires* at Vienna, was intercepted near Mezzolo, and the whole policy of the Roman Government was unveiled. The contents of these despatches were as follow: " That the French were desirous of peace, and even solicited it with importunity; but that he would obstruct and prolong its conclusion, because the Pope had determined to trust entirely to the fortune of the house of Austria ; that the conditions of the armistice of Bologna neither had been nor would be executed, notwithstanding the loud complaints of Cacault, the French minister; that fresh troops were in the course of being levied with activity in the states of the church; that his holiness accepted General Colli, whom the court of Vienna proposed, as the commander of the papal armies ; that it was necessary for this general to bring with him a good number of officers, especially of engineers and artillery; that orders had been given at Ancona for their reception ; that he was sorry to see that Colli would be obliged to come to an understanding with Alvinzi, with whose manœuvres he was dissatisfied; and that it would be well for him to go and review the Pope's troops in Romagna, before coming to Rome."

A courier was instantly dispatched to Cacault, the French minister, with orders to leave Rome " for several months." Napoleon wrote to him: " They have loaded you with humiliations, and have had recourse to all possible means to lead you to depart from Rome. Now, resist all their urgent solicitations to induce you to remain; set out immediately on the receipt of this letter."

Cacault wrote to Cardinal Busca, secretary of state, in the following terms: " I have been recalled by my government, and am obliged to set out this evening for Florence, of which I have the honour to give your eminence due notice, and subscribe myself," &c.

Busca kept up the game till the very last, and replied: " Cardinal Busca was far from expecting to receive such news as that which the honourable Monsieur Cacault has just communicated to him. His sudden departure for Florence does not allow Cardinal Busca to do more, than assure him of his profound esteem."

At the same moment, General Victor crossed the Po at Borgo-Forte, at the head of 4000 infantry, and 600 horse, and formed a junction at Bologna with the Italian division of 4000 men under General Lahoz. These 9000 men were quite sufficient to conquer the states of the church.

A few days afterwards, Napoleon went to Bologna, and published a manifesto in the following terms:

" Art. 1. The Holy See has formally refused Articles 8 and 9 of the Armistice concluded at Bologna, on the 20th of June, under the mediation of Spain, and solemnly ratified in Rome, on the 27th of the same month.

" 2. The Roman government has never ceased to arm and excite the people to war, by means of manifestoes; it has caused the territory of Bologna to be violated; its troops have ˙ advanced to within ten miles of that city, and threatened to occupy it.

" 3. His holiness has entered into negotiations with the court of Vienna, hostile to France, as is proved by the letters of Cardinal Busca, and the mission of Bishop Albani to Vienna.

" 4. He has confided the command of his troops to Austrian generals and officers, recommended and sent by the court of Vienna.

" 5. He has refused to give any reply to the official notes addressed to the Roman government by citizen Cacault, minister of the French republic, with a view of opening negotiations for a peace.

" 6. The treaty of armistice has therefore been broken and infringed by the Holy See, in consequence whereof, I hereby declare the armistice concluded between the court of Rome and the French republic on the 20th of June, to be at an end.'

In support of this manifesto, Cardinal Busca's intercepted letters were published, and many other documents might have been added, but these letters revealed the whole.

Cardinal Matteï, after having been three months in a college at Brescia, had obtained permission to return to Rome. Availing himself of the opportunity which he had had of knowing the general, he had written to him several times, and the latter profited

by the circumstance to forward to this Cardinal in
Rome the intercepted letters of Cardinal Busca. The
reading of these communications filled the whole of
the sacred college with confusion, and effectually
closed the mouths of that minister's partisans.

On the 2nd of February, head quarters were
established at Imola, in the palace of Bishop Chera-
monte, afterwards Pope Pius VII. On the 3rd, the
small French army arrived at Castel-Bolognese, in
presence of the Pope's army, which was drawn up in
position on the right bank of the Senio, in order to
dispute the passage of the bridge. This army was
composed of from 6 to 7000 regular troops, or peasants collected by the tocsin, commanded by monks,
and inspired with fanaticism by the preachers and
missionaries. It had eight pieces of cannon. The
day's march had been long, and as the French were
placing their guards, the bearer of a flag of truce
presented himself in a burlesque manner, and declared, on behalf of his eminence, the cardinal-in-
chief, that if the French army continued to advance,
he would fire upon them. This terrible menace
caused a fit of hearty laughter. An answer was returned, that there was no desire to expose the French
army to the cardinal's fire, and that the army
was only taking up its position for the night. Cardinal Busca, however, had succeeded in his expectations. Romagna was on fire, a holy war had been
proclaimed; the toscin had never ceased for three
days, and the lowest classes of the people were in a

state of frenzy and madness. The forty hours' prayers, missions in the public places, indulgences, and even miracles, had all been put in requisition. Here were martyrs, whose wounds had bled; there Madonnas which had shed tears; everything announced a fire ready to consume that beautiful province. Cardinal Busca had said to Cacault, the French minister: "We shall make a Vendée of the Romagna; we shall make one of the high lands of Liguria; we shall make one of all Italy."

The following proclamation was posted at Imola— " The French army is about to enter the Pope's territories. It will be faithful to the maxims which it professes; it will protect religion and the people.

" The French soldier carries in one hand the bayonet as a guarantee of victory; in the other, the olive branch as a symbol of peace, and the pledge of protection. Woe to those, who, seduced by profoundly hypocritical men, shall draw down upon themselves and their houses, the vengeance of an army, which, in six months has made prisoners of 100,000 of the Emperor's best troops, taken 400 pieces of cannon, 110 stand of colours, and destroyed five armies."

At four o'clock in the morning, General Lannes, commanding the advanced guard of the small French army, ascended the Senio for a league and a half, passed the river at a ford at daybreak, and formed in order of battle in the rear of the Pope's forces, cutting off their retreat to Faenza.

General Lahoz, supported by a battery, and covered

by a line of sharpshooters, passed the bridge in close column. In a moment, the whole of the armed multitude were in disorder, the artillery and baggage were taken, and between 4 and 5000 cut down. A few monks, chiefly of the mendicant orders, fell with crucifixes in their hands—almost all the troops of the line were taken prisoners. The cardinal-general made his escape. The battle did not last an hour, and the loss, on the part of the French, was very small. On the same day they arrived at Faenza, where they found the gates shut and the tocsin ringing; the ramparts were mounted by a few pieces of cannon, and the people in their fury provoked their conquerors by every species of insult. On being summoned to open their gates, an insolent reply was returned from the town.

It became, therefore, necessary to break them down and to enter by main force. " The case is the same as that of Pavia!" cried the soldiers—which was a request to be allowed to pillage. " No," replied Napoleon; " at Pavia, the people, after having taken an oath of obedience, revolted, and attempted to murder our soldiers who were their guests. These people are only mad, and must be subdued by clemency." A few convents only were maltreated. This interesting town being saved from its own madness, the French next proceeded to deliver the province. Agents were sent throughout the country to enlighten the minds of the people, and to calm their agitation and frenzy which were extreme; the most effectual means, however, was the restoration of the prisoners of war.

The prisoners taken at the battle of the Senio were collected in the garden of one of the convents in Faenza. The first moments of terror still continued, and the prisoners, in fear of losing their lives, fell on their knees, and begged for mercy with loud cries, on the approach of Napoleon. He addressed them in Italian, and said: " I am the friend of the whole people of Italy, and particularly of those of Rome. I come among you for your good—you are free; return to the bosom of your families, and tell them that the French are friends of religion, of order, and of poor people." Joy succeeded consternation—the unfortunate prisoners gave way to their feelings of gratitude with all that vivacity which belongs to the Italian character.

From the garden, Napoleon went to the refectory, where the officers were assembled, of whom there were several hundreds, and among them some members of the best families of Rome. He conversed with them for a long time, spoke of the liberty of Italy—of the abuses of the pontifical government—of those who acted in opposition to the spirit of the gospel, and of the folly of attempting to resist a victorious and well disciplined army, which had seen so much service. He gave them permission to return to their respective homes, and, as the price of his clemency, he requested them to make known the sentiments with which he was animated towards the whole of Italy, and especially towards the people of Rome.   These prisoners became so many missionaries, who spread themselves over all the states of the church, and never ceased to pour out eulogies upon the good treatment which they had experienced.   They carried with them proclamations, which by these means reached the most remote villages in the Apennines. The plan was successful, the public mind underwent a complete change, and when the army arrived successively at Forli, Casino, Rimini, Pegaro, and Sinigaglia, the people showed themselves most favourably disposed.   They had passed from one extreme to another, and now received, with every demonstration of joy, those Frenchmen whom a few days before they had been taught to consider, and did consider, as the enemies of their religion, pro- perty, and laws.   The monks themselves, with the exception of the mendicant orders, calculating on the interests which they had really at stake, seriously applied themselves to the task of informing the masses respecting the real state of the question. There were among them many men of real merit, who were groaning under the follies of the government.

Colli, who was at the head of the Pope's army, had commanded the Piedmontese forces at Mondovi and Cherasco; he knew whom he had to deal with; and on this occasion he chose an excellent position on the heights in advance of Ancona, and there formed a camp with the 3,000 men who remained with him.

But under various pretexts, he and his Austrian officers retired to Loretto as soon as the French army appeared. The position occupied by the Romans was excellent. General Victor dispatched an officer with a flag of truce, to summon them to submit, and whilst the conferences were taking place with this view, the French and Italian troops extended their line to the right and left, surrounded them, took them prisoners without firing a shot, and entered the citadel without resistance.

The same course was pursued respecting the prisoners, as had been adopted in the case of those taken at the battle of the Senio; they were sent home, well supplied with proclamations, and formed a body of new missionaries, who preceded the march of the army. Ancona is the only port in the Adriatic between Venice and Brindisi, which is at the extremity of the most easterly point of Italy; but it was then in such a neglected condition, that even frigates could not enter the harbour. It was on this occasion that Napoleon perceived what was necessary to be done to fortify the place and improve the port. Great works were executed at Ancona, during the existence of the kingdom of Italy; and now, ships of any size, even three-deckers, can enter the harbour with safety. The Jews, who are very numerous in Ancona, as well as the Mahometans of Albania and Greece, were there subjected to ancient and humiliating restrictions, only fit for a barbarous age. One of the first acts of the

Emperor was to strike off their bonds and set them free. In spite, however, of the presence of the army, the people ran in crowds to throw themselves at the feet of a Madonna which shed tears. Some sensible citizens gave intelligence of this proceeding, and Mœnge was sent thither. He reported that in reality the Madonna did weep. The chapter was ordered to bring her to head quarters, and it was discovered that the whole was an optical illusion, very skilfully managed by the assistance of a glass. The next day the Madonna was replaced in the church, but without the glass ; she wept no more. A chaplain, who had been guilty of this piece of knavery, was arrested. It was regarded both as an offence against the army, and a means of bringing religion into contempt.

On the 10th, the army encamped at the church of our lady of Loretto. This is a bishop's see, and the seat of a magnificent convent; the church and the buildings are splendid. There are immense and beautifully furnished apartments for the treasures of the Madonna, and the lodgings of the clergy, the chapter, and the pilgrims. The church contains the *casa-santa*, or dwelling of the Virgin at Nazareth, the very place in which she was visited by the angel Gabriel. This dwelling consists of a small house, of ten or twelve yards square, in which there ·is a Madonna placed under a canopy. The legend says, that angels carried it from Nazareth to Dalmatia, when the infidels overran Syria, and from thence across the Adriatic to the summits of

Loretto. The shrine of the Virgin is visited by pilgrims from all parts of Christendom. Presents, consisting of diamonds and all sorts of precious stones and metals, sent from various countries, formed her treasury, which amounted to many millions. The court of Rome no sooner knew of the approach of the French army, than they ordered all the treasures of Loretto to be packed up and placed beyond the reach of danger; above a million, however, was still found in gold and silver. The Madonna itself was sent to Paris and deposited in the national library, where it was to be seen for many years. It was a statue very rudely carved, which was a proof of its antiquity. The first consul restored this relic to the Pope on the conclusion of the concordat, and it has been replaced in the *Casa-Santa.*

Several thousand French priests, who had left their country, were now sojourning in Italy; and, in proportion as the French army advanced into the Peninsula, the tide was rolled back upon Rome. As soon, however, as the army entered the papal states, they found themselves deprived of further means of retreat or refuge. Some of the more timid had crossed the Adige in good time, and returned into Germany, for Naples had refused them an asylum. The heads of the different convents, on whose resources they were a heavy burden, seized upon the pretext of the arrival of the army, and affected to fear that the presence of the French priests would draw down the vengeance of the conqueror upon their convents, and they drove away these unfortunate men. Napoleon made a decree, and issued a proclamation, in which he relieved the apprehensions of the French priests, and commanded the convents, bishops, and chapters, to receive them, and to furnish them with everything necessary for their support and comfort. He prescribed to them the duty of looking upon those priests as friends and countrymen, and ordered them to receive and treat them as such. The whole army became animated by the same feelings, and this led to a great number of very affecting scenes; many of the soldiers recognised their old pastors, and these unfortunate old men, living in exile many hundred leagues from their own country, received, for the first time, marks of respect and affection from their countrymen, who, until then, had treated them as enemies and criminals. The news of this measure was spread abroad throughout the whole of Christendom, and especially in France. Some critics were unfavourable to this policy, but their views were stifled by the feeling of general approbation, and especially by that of the directory.

In the meantime, consternation reigned in the Vatican. One piece of bad news rapidly succeeded another. The government first learned that the papal army, on which they had placed such confidence, had been completely destroyed, without having opposed the slightest resistance. The couriers, who afterwards arrived, bringing intelligence of the arrival of the French in the various cities, made them acquainted with the complete change of opinion which had taken

place in the public mind, and informed them that sentiments of friendship and a desire for liberty had taken
the place of hatred and fanaticism. Busca soon became convinced that a *Vendée* was not a thing to
be created at pleasure; that if extraordinary circumstances do create it, nothing but grave faults can
give it consistency and duration. It was soon known
that the French army had taken possession of Ancona,
Loretto, and Macerata, and that the advanced guard
was already on the summits of the Apennines.
" The French do not march," said the prelates; " they
run."

In the meantime, the officers and soldiers who had
been taken prisoners and sent home from Faenza and
Ancona, diffused the feelings of confidence, by which they
themselves were animated, throughout all the quarters
of Rome. The partisans of liberty raised their heads,
and showed themselves openly in the city itself. The
members of the sacred college, no longer seeing any
ground of hope, began to think of their own safety.
All the necessary preparations were made for their
departure to Naples. The carriages of the court were
ready, when the general of the *Camaldules* arrived at
the Vatican, and prostrated himself at the feet of the
holy father. On passing through Casena, Napoleon
had recognised him, and, knowing the confidence which
Pius VI. had in this monk, he commissioned him to
go and assure his holiness that his life was not in
danger, that the French general would respect his
person and office—that he might remain in Rome—

that he would only have to change his cabinet and to
send plenipotentiaries, with full powers, to Tolentino,
to conclude and sign a definitive peace with the
republic. The general of the Camaldules acquitted
himself of his mission with success; the Pope took
confidence, dismissed the ridiculous Busca, and called
Doria to the head of affairs, who was well known for
the judicious moderation of his opinions. He further
countermanded his departure from Rome, and named
plenipotentiaries to conclude and sign a definitive
peace.

The instructions of the directory were opposed to
all negotiations with Rome. The members were of
opinion that the time was come to put an end to the
temporal reign of the Pope, and to have no more
trouble on that score; that it would be impossible to
find any occasion on which the court of Rome should
be more obviously in the wrong; and that it was
nothing less than folly to think of a sincere peace with
a set of theologians, who were so strenuously opposed
to those principles on which the new republics were
founded. Undoubtedly, the temporal power of the
Pope appeared incompatible with the prosperity of
Italy. Experience had proved, that neither moderation nor good faith was to be expected from that court;
but Napoleon was of opinion, that he could neither
revolutionize Rome, nor unite its territory to the
transpadane republic, without marching upon Naples
and overthrowing its throne. In Naples, the liberal
party was numerous enough to give considerable dis-

quiet to the court, but too weak to be a support or
to offer effectual assistance to the French army. The
court of Naples felt that a revolution in Rome would be
the forerunner of its fall. In order, however, to undertake an expedition against Naples, an army of at least
25,000 men was necessary, and the employment of so
great a force in that direction was not compatible with
the great design of dictating the terms of a peace
under the walls of Vienna.

The advanced guard of the French army had
crossed the Apennines. It was within three days'
march of Rome; and, on the 13th of February, the head-
quarters were in Tolentino. Cardinal Mattei, Monsignor
Galeppi, the Duke of Braschi, and the Marquis Massini,
the Pope's ministers plenipotentiary, arrived there
on the 14th ; Monsignor Galeppi conducted the
conference. This prelate was endowed with great
fertility of mind, and deeply versed in homilatic
learning; but the court of Rome was in the wrong, and
ought to be punished. This could only be done by
the cession of the conquered provinces, or by contributions to an equal amount in value.

The three legations, the Duchy of Urbino, the
March of Ancona, and the districts of Macerata and
Perugia, were conquered. The bases being thus
settled, the conclusion of the treaty required only five
days' discussion. Galeppi, who had said a great deal
respecting the total ruin of the papal finances, found
resources wherewith to make compensation for the
conquered provinces, or at least to diminish the

number of those which the Pope should cede. The treaty was signed in the convent occupied as the head-quarters of the French army.

This treaty was concluded on the conditions, and in the form following:

"General Bonaparte, commander-in-chief of the army of Italy, and Citizen Cacault, agent of the French republic in Italy, plenipotentiaries furnished with full powers by the executive Directory, and his Eminence Cardinal Mattei, Monsignor Galeppi, the Duke of Braschi, and the Marquis Massini, plenipotentiaries of his Holiness, have agreed, and do agree, to the following articles:

"Art. 1. There shall be peace, friendship, and a good understanding between the French republic and Pope Pius VI.

"2. The Pope revokes all adhesion, consent, and accession, whether open or secret, given by him to the coalition in arms against the French republic; every treaty of alliance, offensive or defensive, with all powers or states whatsoever. During the continuance of the present war, as well as in all subsequent wars, he engages not to furnish, to any power in arms against the French republic, any succours of any kind or denomination whatsoever, whether in men, ships, munitions of war, provisions, or money.

"3. Within five days after the ratification of the present treaty, his Holiness binds himself to dismiss all levies recently raised, and to preserve only such regiments as existed previous to the armistice signed at Bologna.

" 4. No ships of war, nor privateers, belonging to the powers at war with the French republic, shall be allowed to enter the harbours or roadsteads of the states of the church, and much less to remain in such harbours or roads.

" 5. The French republic, as before the war, shall continue to enjoy all those rights and privileges which France possessed in Rome—shall be treated, in all respects, as the most favoured nations, and especially with respect to its ambassador or minister, consuls, or vice-consuls.

" 6. The Pope fully and clearly renounces all his rights or pretensions over or to the cities and territories of Avignon, the county of Venassin, and its dependencies; and transfers, cedes, and abandons the said rights to the French republic.

" 7. The Pope equally renounces for ever, cedes, and transfers to the French republic, all his rights to the territories comprised under the names of the Legations of Bologna, Ferrara, and Romagna ; no injury shall be inflicted on the Catholic religion in the fore-mentioned legations.

" 8. The town, citadel, and villages, forming the territory of the city of Ancona, shall remain in the hands of the French republic till the conclusion of a continental peace.

" 9. The Pope binds himself and his successors, not to transfer, to any persons whatsoever, any claims or titles to the lordships attached to the territories ceded by this treaty to the French republic.

" 10. His Holiness engages to cause to be paid and delivered at Foligno, to the paymaster of the French army, on the 15th of Ventose inst. (March 5th, 1797), the sum of 15,000,000 of livres—ten millions in currency, and five millions in diamonds and other valuable effects—in addition to 16,000,000 which remain due, according to Article 9 of the armistice signed at Bologna, and ratified by his Holiness on the 27th of June.

" 11. In order fully to discharge the remainder of the obligations contracted by the armistice signed at Bologna, his Holiness agrees to furnish 800 cavalry horses with their accoutrements, 800 draught horses, oxen, buffaloes, and other objects, which are the production of the states of the church.

" 12. Independent of the sum mentioned in the foregoing articles, the Pope will pay to the French republic, in cash, diamonds, and other precious articles, the sums of 15,000,000 of livres tournais * of France, of which 10,000,000 shall be paid in the course of the month of April ensuing.

" 13. Article 8 of the treaty of armistice signed at Bologna, and referring to manuscripts and works of art, shall be executed in full, and as quickly as possible.

" 14. The French army will evacuate Umbria,

* The "livre tournais de France," is equal in value to the French franc, 10d. English.

Perugia, and Camerino, as soon as Article 10 of the present treaty shall be executed and fulfilled.

" 15. The French army shall evacuate the province of Macerata, with the exception of Ancona, Fermo, and their respective territories, as soon as the first five millions of the sum mentioned in Article 12 of the present treaty, shall have been paid and delivered.

" 16. The French army shall evacuate the territory of the city of Fano, and the duchy of Urbino, as soon as the second five millions of the sum mentioned in Article 12 of the present treaty shall have been paid and delivered, and Articles 3, 10, 11, and 12, fully executed.

" The last five millions, constituting a part of the sum stipulated by Article 12, shall be paid at latest in the course of the ensuing month of April.

" 17. The French republic cedes to the Pope all its rights over the different religious foundations in the cities of Rome and Loretto; and the Pope cedes to the French republic all the allodial possessions belonging to the Holy See in the three provinces of Bologna, Ferrara, and Romagna, and especially the district of Mezzola and its dependencies; in case of sale, however, the Pope reserves one-third of the amount of the produce of such sale, to be returned to his permanent funds.

" 18. His Holiness, by his minister in Paris, shall cause the assassination committed on the person of Basseville, secretary of legation, to be publicly disavowed.

"In the course of the year, the sum of 300,000 livres shall be paid by his Holiness, to be divided amongst those who have suffered from this crime.

"19. His Holiness shall set at liberty all persons who may be detained in custody on account of their political opinions.

"20. The commander-in-chief will set at liberty, and enable to return to their own homes, all prisoners of war taken from his Holiness, as soon as the ratification of this treaty shall have been received.

"21. Pending the negotiations for a commercial treaty between the French republic and the Pope, the commerce of the republic shall be placed on the same footing as that of the most favoured nations.

"22. Conformably to Article 6 of the treaty concluded at the Hague, on the 27th Floréal, year 3, the terms of the peace now concluded between the French republic and his Holiness, are declared to be common to the Batavian republic.

"23. The French post shall be re-established in Rome, on the same footing on which it previously stood.

"24. The school of arts, instituted in Rome for all Frenchmen, shall be re-established, and continue to be directed as before the war; the palace belonging to the republic, in which that school was placed, shall be restored without injury.

"25. All the articles, clauses, and conditions of the present treaty are to be of perpetual obligation upon his Holiness Pope Pius VI., and all his successors.

" 26. The present treaty shall be ratified with the least possible delay.

" Done and signed at the head quarters at Tolentino, by the under-mentioned plenipotentiaries, on the 1st Ventose, year 5 of the French republic, one and indivisible (Feb. 19th, 1797).

(Signed)

" BONAPARTE, CACAULT,

" CARDINAL MATTEI, L. GALEPPI,

" L. DUCA BRASCHI-ONESTI, AND

" CAMILLO MARCHESE MASSINI."

Napoleon insisted, for a long time, that the court of Rome should engage to suppress the inquisition. It was represented to him, that the inquisition was no longer what it had been; that, at present, it was rather a tribunal of police than of religious opinion, and that *autos-da-fé* no longer existed. He appreciated these reasons at their just value, and desisted from pressing this article, out of complaisance to the Pope, who was deeply affected, and opened up his views in his private correspondence. He satisfied himself with the cession of the Legations of Bologna, Ferrara, and Romagna, and the occupation of Ancona with a garrison: this was the consequence of the same principle which led him to respect the temporal existence of the Pope. If, as the patriots of the transpadane republic wished, he had increased the territory of this new republic by the addition of the duchy of Urbino, and the provinces of Ferrara and Macerata, and had extended its boundaries to Otranto and the Apennines, it would then have come in contact with the kingdom of Naples. War with this court, would, in that case, have become the infallible consequence, and this war would have taken place, whether France and the court of Naples desired it or not.

The importance which this court attached to the stipulations of this treaty was so great, that its minister, Prince Pignatelli, followed the French head quarters, which was a striking proof of their alarm. This prince was not deficient either in intelligence or activity; but he stopped at no means to keep himself well informed. Many times, but especially at Loretto, and during the negotiations at Tolentino, he was surprised listening at the doors, and exposed himself to the indignity of being driven away by the porters. The peace stopped the advance of the French troops.

After the signature of the treaty, the commander-in-chief entrusted General Victor with the superintendence of its execution, sent his aide-de-camp, Colonel Yanot, to Rome, as the bearer of a respectful letter to the Pope, and set out for Mantua.

This letter, and the Pope's reply, which were published, formed a great contrast with the language then commonly in use, and this peculiarity was remarked.

Mantua had now been for a month in the hands of the republic; the hospitals were still full of Austrians. Napoleon went to the ducal palace and sojourned there for several days. A very great number of beautiful pictures had been found in this city, which

he caused to be sent to the museum in Paris. Titian's
magnificent frescoes of the war of the Titans, the
admiration of all *connoisseurs*, were in the palace of
the *T*. The commission of artists submitted various
plans for their removal and transference to Paris, but
there would have been a great risk of losing and
destroying these *chefs-d'œuvre*. Napoleon caused an
engineering arsenal to be established, and ordered
General Chasseloup, commanding the engineers, to
direct his attention to the improvement of the fortifications; the weak side at that time was that of
La Pradella and Pietolli. From this moment forward, all his efforts were directed to the establishment
and consolidation of his new creations. Having given
orders respecting Mantua, he proceeded to Milan, the
centre of the administration and of Italian politics.
Public opinion in the meantime had made great
progress.

CHAPTER IV

LÉOBEN.

THE news of the battles of Tagliamento and of
Tarwis, of the combat of Gorizia, and of the entry of
the French into Clagenfurt and Laybach, caused a
general consternation in Vienna. The capital was
threatened, and destitute of any means of effectual
defence: the richest furniture was stowed away, and
all the most important papers lodged in security.
The Danube was crowded with boats engaged in con-
veying the valuables of the Viennese to Hungary,
whither the young archdukes and archduchesses were
also sent. Among the latter was the Archduchess
Marie Louise, then about five years and a half old,
who afterwards became empress of the French.

Discontent was general—" In less than a fortnight," said the Viennese, " the French will be under
our walls, the ministry do not think of making peace,

and we have no means of resisting this terrible army of Italy!"

The armies of the Rhine and the Moselle, of the Sambre and the Meuse, were to commence the campaign, and pass the Rhine on the same day on which the army of Italy should pass the Piave, and thus advance rapidly into Germany. Napoleon, in giving an account of the battle of Tagliamento, announced that he was about to cross the Julian Alps in a few days, and push forward into the very heart of Germany; that between the 1st and the 10th of April, he would be at Clagenfurt, the capital of Carinthia—that is to say, sixty leagues from Vienna; that it was, therefore, important to put the armies of the Rhine in motion, and inform them of their line of march. The government replied to him on the 23rd of March, complimented him on the victory of Tagliamento, made excuses for the armies of the Rhine not having already opened the campaign, and assured him, that they should be put in motion without delay. Four days afterwards, however, on the 26th of March, the government wrote to him, that Moreau's army could not commence the campaign, because it had no boats to enable it to cross the Rhine, and that the army of Italy could not, therefore, calculate upon the co-operation of the armies of Germany, but must rely upon itself alone. This despatch, which arrived at Clagenfurt on the 31st of March, gave rise to many conjectures. Was the Directory afraid that these three armies, which constituted the whole force of the

republic, if once united under the same general, would
prove too powerful? Was it the checks which these
armies had suffered in the preceding year, which rendered them timid? Or must this strange pusillanimity
be attributed to want of resolution and courage on the
part of the generals? It was impossible that the
government should wish to destroy or sacrifice the
army of Italy, as it had wished to do in June 1796,
by ordering one half of the troops to march against
Naples. Napoleon, not being able to calculate on the
co-operation of these two armies, could not flatter
himself with being able to enter Vienna, because he
had not cavalry enough to descend into the valley of
the Danube, although he might reach the summit of
the Simmering without destruction. He thought it
his best course, in the position in which he was placed,
to conclude a peace; which was an object of universal
desire in France.

On the 31st of March, twelve hours after having
received the despatch of the Directory, he wrote to
the Archduke Charles, as follows:—" Sir, brave soldiers
make war and desire peace! Has not the present war
now lasted six years? Have we not killed enough
people and inflicted evils enough upon unfortunate
humanity? She utters complaints on all sides.
Europe, which had taken up arms against the French
republic, has laid them down. Your nation alone
remains, and yet blood is about to flow more copiously
than ever. This sixth campaign is announced by
sinister presages. Whatever may be the issue, we

shall destroy, on both sides, thousands of men, and at last be obliged to come to an understanding, because everything has its limits, even the most hateful passions.

" The executive directory of the French republic has already signified to his majesty, the emperor, its desire to put an end to a war so ruinous to the people of both nations. The intervention of the court of London opposed the fulfilment of the wish. Is there no hope of coming to an understanding? Must we, for the interests and passions of a nation removed from the evils of war, continue to slaughter one another? You, sir, who, by your birth, stand so near the throne—you, who are the commander-in-chief, and exalted far above those low passions, by which governments and ministers are often animated, are you determined to deserve the title of a benefactor of humanity and to become the true deliverer of Germany?

" Do not suppose, sir, that I intend by this, to say that it is not possible to deliver the country by force of arms ; but on the supposition that the chances of war should turn in your favour, Germany will not be the less ravaged. For myself, sir, if the overture which I now make to you saves the life of a single man, I shall be prouder of the civic crown which I shall thus have deserved, than of that melancholy glory which is the result of military success."

On the second of April, Prince Charles replied as follows : " Assuredly, General, whilst making war,

and obeying the call of honour and duty, I desire
peace as much as you, for the well-being of the people,
and the interests of humanity. As, however, in the
position in which I am placed, it does not fall within
my sphere either to discuss or terminate the quarrels
of belligerent nations, and as I am not entrusted
with any powers by his majesty to treat, you will see
that I cannot enter into any negotiations on that
subject, and that I must wait for orders upon a point
of such deep importance, and which is not completely
within my power.

   "Whatever may be the future chances of war or
hopes of peace, I beg you to be assured, General, of
my esteem and distinguished consideration."

   In order to support this overture for negotiations,
it was necessary to advance, and approach Vienna.

   The advanced guard at this time occupied St. Veit,
and the head-quarters were in Clagenfurt. At break
of day, on the 1st of April, Masséna advanced on
Friesach; in front of the castle, he found the enemy's
rear guard in charge of considerable magazines, which
the archduke had caused to be there collected. He
pushed rapidly forward, entered Friesach pell-mell
with the enemy's troops, seized upon the whole of the
magazines, and continued the pursuit as far as Neumarkt. On approaching this town, he fell in with
the archduke, with four divisions just arrived from
the Rhine, those of the Prince of Orange, and two
other generals, together with the reserve of grenadiers,
and prepared to dispute the passage of the gorges of

Neumarkt. The commander-in-chief immediately ordered Masséna to collect the whole of his division on the left of the high road; he placed Guieur's division on the heights on the right, and kept the division of Serrurier in reserve. At three o'clock in the afternoon, the 2nd regiment of light infantry belongto Masséna's division, charged the enemy's first line, and covered itself with glory. This regiment was just come from the Rhine, and the soldiers, in allusion to the troops of the German princes, which were not reckoned good, called it the *contingent*. The soldiers of the 2nd, piqued by this ridicule, challenged the old soldiers of Italy to advance as far and as fast as themselves; they performed prodigies of valour. Prince Charles was present in person, but to no purpose; he was driven from all his positions, and lost 3000 men.

The French troops entered Neumarkt at night mixed with the Austrians, took 1200 prisoners, six pieces of cannon, and five stand of colours. It was still four leagues to Scheifling, the point at which the third transverse road abuts. The Austrian general, not being able to delay the conqueror's march, had recourse to a stratagem, in order to gain twenty-four hours, and to give time to General Kerpen to form at Scheifling. He made a proposition for a suspension of arms, in order to enable him, as he said, to take into full consideration the letter written to him on the 31st of March. Berthier replied, that it was possible both to negotiate and fight, but that

no armistice could be agreed to, till the French were
at Vienna, unless to treat for a definitive peace.

At day-break, the French advanced guard commenced their march upon the Muer; strong reconnoi-
tring parties were sent forward as far as Murau, to
meet the corps of General Kerpen. Napoleon himself marched thither, but that general had retired.
General Sporck only, who commanded his rear-guard,
was slightly wounded. The French head-quarters
remained, on the 4th and 5th, at Scheifling, a castle
situated on the banks of the Muer.

The road from Scheifling to Knittelfeld follows the
bank of the Muer, and passes through some frightful
gorges. At every step positions present themselves,
at which the French army might have been stopped.
It was of the highest importance to the archduke to
gain a few days, in order that they might come to
their senses in Vienna, and to enable the troops
who were hastening from the Rhine to arrive and
cover the great capital. The same reasons prescribed
to the French army not to lose a moment in accele-
rating its march. On the 3rd, the advanced guard
fought a very warm engagement in the gorges of
Unzmarkt, overthrew the enemy in spite of their
superiority in numbers, drove them from all their
positions at the point of the bayonet, and entered
Knittelfeld. The loss of the Austrians was considerable—1500 prisoners and four pieces of cannon.
Colonel Carrère, a distinguished officer in command

of the artillery of the advanced guard, was killed,
deeply regretted.   He was an excellent officer in the
field, and one of the frigates at Venice was named
after him, as a mark of honour.   She was one of those
on board of which Napoleon returned from Egypt,
and landed at Frejus.   On the 6th of April, the head
quarters were at Judenburg, the chief town of one of
the circles of Carinthia.

After the affair of Unzmarkt, the army met with
no more resistance, and the advanced guard arrived
at Léoben, on the 7th.   Here, Lieut.-Gen. Bellegarde,
chief of Prince Charles's staff, and General Meerfeld,
presented themselves with a flag of truce, and after a
conference with the commander-in-chief, placed in his
hands the following note: " General, his Majesty the
Emperor and King has nothing more at heart than
to secure the repose of Europe, and to terminate a
war which afflicts both nations.   In consequence of
the overture made in your letter to his Royal Highness Prince Charles, the Emperor has sent us to you,
in order to come to an understanding on this most
important subject.   After the conversation which
we have just had with you, and persuaded of the
goodwill, as well as of the intention of the two
powers to put an end to this disastrous war as speedily
as possible, his imperial highness asks' for a suspension of arms for ten days, in order to be able to arrive
at the desired result without further loss of time, that
all those delays and obstacles arising from a state of

active hostilities may be removed, and everything may contribute to re-establish peace between the two nations."

The French General replied on the same day: " In the military positions of the two armies, a suspension of arms is decidedly contrary to the interests of the French; but should such a suspension lead to a peace so much desired, and so useful to the people, I consent without regret to the proposal. The French republic has often manifested to his majesty its desire of putting an end to this cruel struggle; it continues to hold the same sentiments, and, after the conference which I have had the honour to hold with you, I do not doubt that, in a few days, peace between the French republic and his majesty will be re-established."

The suspension of arms was agreed to, and a paper to that effect signed at seven o'clock in the evening. It was to continue for five days. The whole country, as far as the Simmering, was now in possession of the French army. Gratz, one of the largest cities in the Austrian monarchy, had surrendered with its citadel. Whilst at dinner, General Berthier asked the Austrian commissary generals, where they thought Bernadotte's division was? " At Laybach," they replied. " And Joubert's?" "Between Brixen and Mühlbach." "No," answered he, " both are *en échelon;* the most distant is a day's march from this place." This answer surprised them very much. On the 9th, head-quarters being at Léoben, the advanced guard pushed forward to Brück, sending detachments as far as the Simmering. Adjutant-General Léclerc was dispatched to Paris, to convey the intelligence to the government of an agreement to a suspension of hostilities. This general was a distinguished officer, intrepid on the field of battle, and well versed in business.

From Clagenfurt, the commander-in-chief had, on the 30th of March, sent his aide-de-camp, Lavalette, at the head of a party of cavalry, as far as Lienz, to meet General Joubert. This general had not, however, arrived from the Tyrol, and the towns-people, seeing that the party consisted only of a handful of men, rose upon them; and the detachment owed its safety to the coolness and intrepidity of the aide-de-camp who commanded it. One dragoon only, lost his life. A few days afterwards, General Zagoncheck, with some squadrons of dragoons, took possession of Lienz, and opened a communication with the army of the Tyrol. The town was disarmed, and the inhabitants punished. On the 8th of April, Joubert arrived at Spital, near Villach, formed the left of the army, and immediately placed the prisoners in the rear.

General Bernadotte, after having organized Carniola, received orders to cross the Save and the Muer, and to concentrate himself upon Léoben; he left General Friaud, with a column of 1500 men, to protect the evacuation of Fiume, and to keep Carniola in check. It was easy to foresee, that with such a small force, General Friaud might be repulsed; his orders, in that case, were to defend the Isonzo, and, finally, to throw himself into Palma Nova, to complete the garrison there. What had been foreseen, happened; a force of 6000 Croats attacked him on the 10th of April; though only one against four, his troops repulsed the enemy with considerable loss; but the General felt the necessity of evacuating Fiume; and the truce of Judenburg found him, on the 19th of April, at Materia, covering Trieste. These events, exaggerated like those of the Tyrol, were repeated in Venice, and were the principal cause of the commotion and taking up arms, which caused the ruin of that state. During the five days that the truce lasted, from the 7th to the 12th of April, the division of Masséna established itself at Brück, at the foot of the Simmering, having an advanced guard half-way up the hill, the head-quarters were at Léoben, at the bishop's palace; the division of Serrurier occupied the important city of Gratz, and was causing the castle to be repaired. These five days of repose were necessary and very useful.

The armistice terminated on the 13th; but at nine o'clock in the morning, the Comte de Meerfeld arrived with full power to negotiate the preliminaries for peace, conjointly with the Marquis de Gallo, the Neapolitan ambassador at Vienna, who was in high favour with the Empress, whose influence in affairs of state was very decided. An agreement was signed, prolonging the armistice till the 20th of April, and conferences were begun relative to the preliminaries of peace. On the 16th of April, after a long discussion, they had determined upon three plans which were dispatched by them to Vienna, and to which the French plenipotentiary had given his consent. On the 17th, the answer of the cabinet of Vienna having been brought by the Baron Vincent, aide-de-camp of the Emperor, the preliminary articles, public and private, were agreed upon; the secretaries of legation had rendered neutral a small country-house, about a league from Léoben, where the preliminaries were signed on the morning of the 18th. General Clarke, as we have seen, was provided with full power by the government, but he was then at Turin. Some time was necessary for his arrival; and as he was not at head-quarters on the 18th, Napoleon went a step further on this, as on several other occasions, and signed the preliminaries himself.

Clarke arrived at head-quarters a few days afterwards. The Austrian plenipotentiaries had thought to do something agreeable to the French, by putting in the first article, that the Emperor recognised the French republic. " Strike that out," said Napoleon; " the republic is like the sun, which shines of itself: it is only the blind who do not see it." In fact, this recognition was obnoxious, because, in case the French people should some day erect for itself a monarchy, the Emperor might say, that he had recognised the republic. It was stipulated by the preliminaries that the definitive peace should be treated of at a congress to assemble at Berne, and that the peace of the empire should be the object of another congress which should be held in a German city. The limits of the Rhine were guaranteed to France; the Oglio was to be the limit of the house of Austria in Italy, and of the Cisalpine republic, which was composed of Lombardy, Modena, the Bergomasque, and the Cremasque. The city of Venice was to receive legations from Ferrara and from Bologna; and was to receive the Romagna, as a compensation for the loss of its states on the Continent. By this treaty, the Emperor was to retain Mantua, but the French republic was to obtain Venice. The French armies were allowed to communicate from Milan to Venice, along the right bank of the Po, to pass out at the Piave, and to render null the lines of the Mincio, of the Adige, and of Mantua. No opposition was offered to the two republics forming one, if they both desired it. Venice had existed for nine centuries, without possessing any territory in Italy, and had only been a maritime state; this was the period of its greatest power; besides, it is true that the arrangements were made out of hatred for the Venetians. It was just at the time when the despatches of the 3rd and 5th of April had arrived from General Kilmaine. The French army were full of indignation at the description of the murders committed on their stragglers. An insurrectionary cockade had been set up at Venice, and the English minister wore it in triumph, whilst the lion of St. Mark floated in his gondola. This minister possessed very great influence.

On the 27th of April, the Marquis de Gallo pre-

sented to the general-in-chief, at Gratz, the preliminaries, ratified by the Emperor. If the exchange did
not take place immediately, the reason was that it was
necessary to wait for the ratification of the executive
directory; but as there could be no doubt that they
would then ratify the preliminaries, the army evacuated Styria, and part of Carniola and of Carinthia.
Several overtures having been made by the plenipotentiaries of the Emperor, the aide-de-camp, Lemar-
rois, conveyed the answers to Vienna; he was received
with distinction; it was the first time since the
revolution that the tri-color cockade had been seen in
that capital. It was at one of these conferences at
Gratz, that one of the plenipotentiaries, authorised by
an autograph letter of the Emperor, offered Napoleon
to obtain for him, at the peace, a sovereignty of
250,000 souls in Germany, for himself and his
family, in order to secure him against republican
ingratitude. The general smiled, and commissioned
the plenipotentiary to thank the Emperor, in his
name, for this proof of friendship towards him, and to
say, that he wished for no greatness, no riches, which
were not given to him by the French people; and he
is said to have added—" And with this support,
believe me, sir, my ambition will be satisfied."

The adjutant-general, Dessoles, was dispatched to
Paris with the news of the opening of the negotiations.
General Masséna conveyed to the directory the preliminary treaty; he received a formal audience, on the
9th of May. All the generals, at all distinguished

during the campaign in Italy, had been dispatched to Paris with trophies of the success of the French arms; Masséna alone, who held the first place, by the share he had had in the campaign, had not yet been sent to Paris; it was only just, therefore, to associate his name with this great national festival, since it was the result of the intrepidity and valour of the French arms.

The position of the army of Italy was prosperous; the account of the 19th of April gave 38,500 infantry, 4,500 cavalry, and 120 cannons; on the whole, 43,000 men, united in the same field of battle, and ready to take up their position in a single march on the Simmering. It had experienced but very slight losses since the opening of the campaign. The fortresses of Palma-Nova, Clagenfurt, and Gratz, were victualled and garrisoned, and depôts of all kinds were formed in these places. The morals of the French army were at the highest point; at the battle of Neumarkt, only a third of the division of Masséna was engaged, and it was sufficient to overthrow the élite of the Austrian army, though very favourably posted. The army of the archduke, on the contrary, was demoralized; he had scarcely any of the old Italian army remaining. The six divisions which had arrived from the Rhine, had been successively and considerably broken ; they had been much diminished. Napoleon might then have pushed forward to Vienna, but this would have produced no decisive result; he could not have maintained his position, because the armies of the Rhine had not only not entered on the campaign, but had announced that they could not enter on it. The opinions of the directory were divided; there was a split even among the directors themselves; the government was powerless: there was no public spirit in France, and the finances were in a deplorable state. The army of the Rhine was without pay, and in the greatest poverty. One of the greatest obstacles to his passage of the Rhine, was the fact, that the treasury could not furnish Moreau with the 30 or 40,000 crowns necessary for the construction of the machinery of a bridge. The regiments formed in La Vendée for the recruiting of the Italian army, each about 4000 strong, by means of joining together several corps, arrived at Milan, from 900 to 1000 strong; three-quarters had deserted on the road. The governor had no means of bringing back the deserters, or of recruiting the army.

From the very first conferences, the Austrian plenipotentiaries had granted the cession of Belgium and of the lines of the Rhine; but they required a compensation for this; and when this was offered to them in Germany—in Bavaria, for example—they added immediately that it would be necessary, in that case, to guarantee to the republic of Venice its present constitution, and to consolidate the aristocracy of the golden book; not wishing to allow, under any pretext whatever, that the Italian republic should extend from the Alps and the Apennines, as far as the Isonzo and the Julian Alps. But this would have been to con-

solidate the most active and the most constant enemy
of the republic—an enemy which, perceiving from the
events which had just happened, the dangers to which
it would be exposed, would have henceforth no other
policy than to connect itself to, and to make common
cause with Austria, which, in fact, would have
willingly entered into an offensive and defensive
alliance with the Venetian oligarchy, against the
democratic Italian republic. This, then, would have
been to increase the power of Austria, both by Bavaria
and by the Venetian territory. In the instructions
given by the directory to General Clarke, they had
authorised him to sign much less advantageous conditions. Peace was the will of the people, the government, and the legislative body. Napoleon signed the
preliminaries of it.

Hoche had just been promoted to the command of
the army of the Sambre and Meuse; he was a young
man, full of talent, valour, and ambition. He had
under his orders a splendid army, which he acknowledged contained 80,000 men under arms; he felt
within himself the strength to command it well; he
stamped with impatience at every fresh account of
the victories in Italy. He entreated the directory, by
every courier, to permit him to enter Germany. His
troops shared his ardour; even the inhabitants, informed by their correspondents of the rapid march of
Napoleon towards Vienna, and of the retrograde
movements of the Austrian armies on the Rhine,
decised why the French armies of the Sambre, Meuse,

and Rhine remained inactive, and lost such precious time?

On the 18th of April, Hoche crossed the Rhine by the bridge of Neuwied, while Championnet, who had quitted Düsseldorf, arrived at Turkerath and Altenzirchen.   Kray commanded the Austrian army. Hoche attacked him at Heddersdorf—took several thousand of his soldiers prisoners—seized some of his cannon and standards and threw them into the Maine. He had just arrived before Frankfort, on the 22nd of April, when the staff of General Kray forwarded to him a despatch from General Berthier, announcing the signature of the treaty of Léoben.   He immediately concluded an armistice, and removed his head-quarters to Friedberg, occupying the Nidda and Wetzlar. Moreau was at Paris; he solicited the machinery necessary for the construction of a bridge, for the purpose of crossing the Rhine at Strasburg; but as soon as Desaix, the commander, *pro tempore*, of the armies of the Rhine, learned that Hoche was engaged in battle with the enemy, he threw a bridge, on the 20th of April, at six o'clock in the morning, across the river, at a village several leagues below Strasburg.

On the 21st, at two o'clock in the morning, the army crossed the Rhine. Moreau, who had arrived in great haste from Paris, was at the head of the army at the moment when Sytaray, who had collected 20,000 men and twenty pieces of cannon, attacked it. The combat was warm: the Austrians were completely defeated; they left some prisoners, and twenty pieces of cannon in the hands of the conqueror. All the baggage and equipages of the Austrian chancery were taken; amongst them, the carriage of Klinglin, which contained the correspondence between Pichegru and the Prince of Condé; Moreau kept this discovery secret for four months, without giving any account of it to the government.

After this victory, the army again ascended the Rhine, and took possession of Kehl. Its advanced guard was already beyond Offenburg, in the valley of the Kiutzig. Thither, on the 22nd, a courier of the Italian army brought the news of the signature of the preliminaries at Léoben. Moreau suspended hostilities, and concluded an armistice with Sytaray.

Hostilities did not commence on the Rhine until eight hours after the treaty of Léoben was signed, and Napoleon received intelligence of them a week after the signature of the treaty. Why had they not recommenced five days sooner, or, at least, why had the directory written that the co-operation of the armies of the Rhine must not be reckoned on? But the affairs of the war were directed without vigour and without talent; the administration was corrupted, and led to no satisfactory result. By one of the arrangements of the constitution of the year 3, the treasury was independent of the government, a most false and disastrous idea, and the most absurd which could have been conceived by the metaphysics of our modern legislators! This alone was sufficient to compromise the existence of the republic.

CHAPTER V.

VENICE.

VENICE, founded in the 5th century, by some inhabitants of the districts of Friuli and Padua, who fled to the lagunes in order to shelter themselves from the incursions of the barbarians, originally occupied the sites of Heraclea and Chiozza. The patriarch of Aquilea afterwards established himself, with his clergy, at Grado, on the occasion of the Arian schism. Grado became the capital. Padua at first gave laws and consuls to the Venetians. In 697, they first appointed a doge; Pepin, King of France, built a small fleet at Ravenna, and compelled the Venetians to retreat to Realto and the Sixty Islands which surround it, where they found themselves protected by the lagunes, from Pepin's resentment; this is the present site of Venice. In 830, the body of St. Mark the Evangelist was brought thither from Egypt, and he became the patron

VOL. II.   H

saint of the republic. From the year 960, the Venetians were masters of Istria and of the Adriatic; their
possession of Dalmatia was still disputed by the kings
of Hungary. In 1250, they, in conjunction with the
French, took Constantinople. They had possession of
the Morea, and of Candia, up to the middle of the 17th
century. Italy, a prey to revolutions, has frequently
changed its masters, but Venice, always free and independent, has never acknowledged a foreign power; she
has always found means to throw off the tyrannical
yoke of the Peninsula.

Venice is the best situated commercial port in
Italy. Merchandise from Constantinople and the
Levant arrives there by the shortest route, across the
Adriatic, and from thence is diffused over northern
Italy, as far as Turin, by the Po, and over Germany,
by being carried up the Adige as far as Bolzano, from
whence roads lead to Ulm, Augsburg, Munich, and
Nuremberg.

Venice is the sea-port of the Upper Danube, the Po,
and the Adige: nature destined it to be the storehouse
of the Levant, Italy, and southern Germany. Before
the discovery of the Cape of Good Hope, Venice carried
on the commerce with India by Alexandria and the
Red Sea, and even struggled to intercept the navigation of the Portuguese. It equipped a considerable
fleet in the Red Sea, and established an arsenal,
watering-places, and magazines, near Suez; the remains of these buildings are still to be seen at the
fountains of Moses.

But the Portuguese defeated these fleets, con-structed at so great an expense; and the state of anarchy in which Egypt then was, finally closed this route of Indian commerce.

The Lagunes are formed by the waters of the Piave, the Brenta, and the Livenza; they fall into the sea by three great passages, La Chioggia, Il Malamoco, and Il Lido.

After the abolition of the democracy in 1200, the sovereign power was in the hands of an aristocracy consisting of some hundreds of families, inscribed in the Golden Book, which furnished to the great council as many as 1200 voters. The population of the states of the republic amounted to three millions, and was extended over the rich districts and fertile plains which surrounded Venice. The following were the Venetian territories: the districts of Bergamo, Brescia, Cremona, Vicenza, Padua, Polesina, Treviso, Bassano, Cadorino, Belluno, and Friuli, on the peninsula of Italy; Istria, Dalmatia, and the Gulf of Cattaro, on the shores of the Adriatic; and, lastly, the Ionian islands. Its territories were bounded on the north by the upper range of the Julian Alps, from the Adda to the Isonzo. This chain of mountains is everywhere impassable for carriages; it forms the frontier on the side of Germany, and can only be crossed by three roads, those into the Tyrol, Carinthia, and Carniola. In 1796, this republic had greatly fallen to decay; it was but the shadow of its former self. Three genera-tions had succeeded each other without having been engaged in any war. The sight of a gun made these unworthy descendants of the Dandolos, Zenos, and Morosinis tremble.

During the war of the succession, and those of 1733 and 1740, they had endured, with cowardly resignation, the insults and outrages of the Austrian, French, and Spanish armies.

The Venetian navy consisted of a dozen of sixty-four-gun vessels, as many frigates, and a great number of small ships, which sufficed to awe the barbarians, command the Adriatic, and defend the Lagunes. The army consisted of 14,000 men, was composed of Italian regiments levied in the provinces, and of Sclavonians from Dalmatia; they were brave, and very much devoted to the republic, and the Sclavonians had the advantage of being strangers to the language and manners of the Peninsula.

Those families alone whose names were inscribed in the Golden Book, had a share in the administration; they exclusively composed the senate, the councils, the Council of Forty, and other assemblies: this displeased the nobility of the main land, among whom were included a great many rich, illustrious, and powerful families, who, deprived of all power, and subject to the reigning class of nobles, passed their lives without receiving distinction or honours, and nourished a deeply-rooted jealousy of the sovereign nobility. These families were partly descended from the ancient *condottieri*, *podestà*, or other personages who had played a distinguished part in the republics of their towns, and whose ancestors, after having long opposed the enterprises of Venice, had at last fallen victims; thus, to the dislike with which the nature of the government inspired them, were added many carefully perpetuated historical subjects for resentment.

The people of the provinces were in general discontented; most of them made common cause with their nobles. The Venetian nobles, however, who had estates and establishments in almost every province, had also their partisans. The priests were without credit and without respect in this republic, which had very early freed itself as much as possible from the temporal power of the Pope.

In the year 1792, the allied powers urged Venice to take part in the war; it does not appear that any serious discussions on this subject took place in the senate; the votes were unanimous in favour of neutrality; the republic was so distant from the theatre of war, that it looked upon itself as a stranger to the affairs of France.

When the Count de Lille took refuge at Verona, the senate only granted him permission to remain there by consent of the committee of public safety, who were better pleased that he should be at Verona, than at any other place.

When the French troops marched, in 1794, towards Oneille, Italy was thought to be menaced with an invasion, and several powers assembled at the congress of Milan; Venice refused to send ambassadors to it, not that she approved of the French principles, but be-

cause she feared to give herself up to the mercy of
Austria, and was not willing to give up that cowardly
and enervated policy which she had for several genera-
tions pursued.

But when Napoleon arrived at Milan, when Beaulieu fled terrified beyond the Mincio, and occupied
Peschiera, where he placed his right wing, in the
hope of defending this line, the uncertainty and alarm
of the senate were very great. The great gulf which had
till then defended Venice from the struggle between the
aristocracy and the democracy was now crossed; the
war of opinion and actual war arose in the bosom of
the state; stormy discussions agitated the councils, in
which three different opinions were maintained.

The young oligarchs demanded an armed neutrality; they wished strong garrisons to be placed
in Peschiera, Brescia, Legnago, and Verona; that
these places should be declared in a state of siege;
that the army should be increased to 60,000 men;
that the lagunes should be put into a posture of defence,
and covered with armed chaloupes; that a squadron
should be equipped for the purpose of defending
the Adriatic; and that, in this formidable attitude,
the republic should declare war against the first
who should entrench on its territory. The partisans
of this opinion went even further; they said: "If it
come to the worst, there is less shame in perishing
with arms in our hands. By defending our territory,
we shall prevent French ideas from being propagated
in the large towns of the provinces; we shall obtain

the more regard from the two inimical parties, as being in a condition to exact it. If, on the contrary, we peaceably open our gates, the territories of the republic will become the seat of the war between these two powers, and from that moment, sovereignty will fall from the hands of the prince. His first duty is to protect his subjects: if their fields and lands become the prey of war, the unhappy people will lose all respect and esteem for the government which has abandoned them. The causes of discontent which already exist will be increased to a violent pitch; the republic will expire without exciting a single regret."

The partisans of the old policy declared that they ought not to take any decisive line of conduct; that they ought to beat about in order to gain time, and see how matters would go. They confessed that all these dangers did indeed exist; that they had reason to fear at once the ambition of Austria, and the principles of France; but that these evils were happily transient; that with management and patience, the inconveniences which they feared might be avoided; that the French were of a conciliatory disposition, easily persuaded by caresses; that if they proceeded aright, they could gain over the minds of the chiefs, and obtain their good opinion; that in the present state of the public mind, an armed neutrality would lead to war, which was above all things to be avoided; that Providence had placed the capital in a position which sheltered it from any insult; and that they must oppose to every difficulty, patience, moderation and time.

Battaglia said: " The republic is truly in danger. On one side the French principles are subversive of our constitution; on the other, Austria makes attempts against our independence. Of these two inevitable evils, let us choose the least; the greatest, in my opinion, is Austrian slavery. Let us increase the list of the Golden Book—let us inscribe in it the names of such of the provincial nobility as deserve that honour; by this means we shall conciliate our people, there will no longer be any opposition among ourselves. Let us garrison our strong places, levy our army, equip our fleet, hasten to meet the French general, and to offer him an offensive and defensive alliance. We shall, perhaps, be obliged to make some slight changes in our constitution, but we shall save our independence and our liberty. An armed neutrality has been proposed; two years ago, this plan would have been the best you could have pursued; it would have been just, because equal towards both the belligerent parties; it would have been possible, because there was then time to prepare for it. But now it is otherwise; you cannot forbid the French to do what you have permitted or tolerated from the Austrians; this would be to declare war against the French army, when it is victorious, when in a week it will be at Verona, and that without your even being secure of Austria; but to declare war two months hence against so active and enterprising an enemy—this, of all plans would be the worst—it would be precipitating ourselves into danger, instead of avoiding it.

" The second course of conduct which has been proposed to you—namely, that of patience and time, is as bad as the first; political circumstances are no longer what they were, times are greatly changed, the crisis in which we now stand bears no resemblance to any of those in which the prudence of our ancestors triumphed. French principles are in every mind, and are reproduced under every variety of form ; they are a rushing torrent, whose course it would be in vain to attempt to arrest by patience, moderation, and cunning. The measure which I propose to you can alone save you ; it is simple, noble and generous. We can offer to the French a contingent of 10,000 men, and retain what we require for the defence of our fortresses. They will soon have taken Mantua, and carried the war into Germany. After the first steps have been taken, all will be easy, because all the parties who divide the state will act together in the same spirit—our independence will be saved—we shall save the great foundations of our constitution. Austria has no influence over our people, and lastly, she has no fleet, whilst, at any moment, the fleet of Toulon may be signaled from the Lido."

This opinion excited the passions, and struck every intelligent mind, but it gained few suffrages. Aristocratic prejudices got the upper hand of the interest of the country. This resolution would have been too noble for degenerate men, incapable of elevated ideas.

The proveditor, Mocenigo, received Napoleon at Brescia with great magnificence; he expressed the good feelings of the senate towards France. Splendid festivals established intimacies between the officers of the French army and the principal families of the place. Each noble endeavoured to become the particular friend of a French general. At Verona, the proveditor, Foscarelli, imitated this example, but the pride of his character was unfavourable to dissimulation; he but ill disguised his secret sentiments; he was one of the number of senators who were the most hostile to the new ideas; he had not dared to protest against the entrance of the French into Peschiera, because they succeeded the troops of Beaulieu; but when they demanded from him the keys of the arsenal, for the purpose of strengthening the ramparts, and set about manning the galleys, he complained of this violation of the neutrality of the republic. On Napoleon's arrival at Peschiera, Foscarelli endeavoured to dissuade him from marching to Verona, and even threatened to order the gates to be closed, and the artillery to be brought into play. "It is too late," answered the general; "my troops have entered it—I am obliged to establish my defence on the Adige during the siege of Mantua; 1500 Sclavonians would not enable you to oppose the passage of the Austrian army; neutrality consists in having the same weight, and the same measure for every one; if you are not my enemies, you ought to grant to or tolerate from me, the same as you do from my enemies."

These various disputes being reported to the senate, it was decided to recall Foscarelli, and to replace him by Battaglia, on whom was bestowed the dignity of proveditor of all the provinces beyond the Adige, Verona included; Battaglia was an acute, well-informed man, of mild manners, and sincerely attached to his country, very favourably inclined to the France of former times, and preferring even republican France to Austria.

By degrees the theatre of war extended over the whole of the Venetian possessions, but it was always the Austrians who entered upon any new territory. Beaulieu occupied Peschiera and Verona; Wurmser entered Bassano, and crossed Vicenza and Padua; Alvinzi and Duke Charles occupied Friuli, Palma-Nova, and all the country as far as the eastern boundaries of the republic.

Great agitation was manifested in the provinces—discontent was propagated with rapidity; to the old hatred of the oligarchy was now joined the attraction of the new opinions. Italy was generally regarded as lost to the Austrians, and this would bring with it the fall of the aristocracy.

Napoleon constantly endeavoured to moderate the agitation which was yet more excited by the general spirit of the army. When he returned to Tolentino, entirely occupied with his project of marching to Vienna, he saw himself constrained to pay attention

to this state of things, which embarrassed him. The
irritation had gone on increasing. Brescia and Bergamo were in a state of insurrection. The Fenarolis,
Martinengos, Lecchis and Alessandris were at the head
of the insurgents; they belonged to the first and
richest families. The municipalities of these two
towns exercised great authority; they had the control of the finances, disposed of the revenues, and had
the power of appointing to offices. If the lion of St.
Mark was still to be seen in them, it was rather in
deference to the general-in-chief, than as an act of
submission to the sovereignty.

Continual and violent declamations against the
Venetian nobles—sometimes verbal, sometimes poured
forth through the channel of the press, were heard on
all sides. The injustice of their government was demonstrated with bitterness, and by all possible means:
"What right has Venice," said they, "to rule in our
cities? Are we less brave, less enlightened, less rich,
less noble?" The pride of the senators was deeply
offended at seeing subjects who had for centuries been
submissive to their government, forget the immense
distance which separated them from their masters, and
compare themselves with them. Everything gave
warning of a violent shock. Battaglia, in his despatches
to the senate, concealed as much as possible the outrages of the Brescians, and softened down to the latter
the indignation and passion of the senate. Always
seeking to conciliate, he ceased not, in his frequent in-

tercourse with the general-in-chief, to interest him in the republic.

It would have been dangerous thus to leave, in the rear of the army, three millions of people given up to disorder and anarchy. Napoleon did not conceal from himself that he had no more influence over the friends of France, than over the senate itself. He could suppress their rebellious movements, but he could not prevent them from speaking and writing, from irritating the prince by a mass of details of administration which were strange to him. To have disarmed the patriots of Brescia and Bergamo, declared for the senate, proscribed the innovators, and filled the dungeons of Venice with them, would have been to alienate from him for ever the popular party, without gaining the affection of the aristocracy; and if this cowardly policy could have found place in his projects, its final and infallible result would have been, as in the case of Louis XII., the rising of the whole population against the French party. To persuade the senate to attach itself to France, and to modify its constitution in order to satisfy the wishes of the people of the provinces, was the best and most suitable plan. This was Napoleon's constant aim; after each fresh victory which he gained, he renewed this proposal, but always in vain. A third project suggested itself—namely, to march upon Venice, occupy that capital, effect by force the political changes which circum-stances rendered indispensable, and entrust the govern-

ment to the partisans of France; but Venice could
not be approached as long as Prince Charles kept his
position on the Piave; it would, therefore, be necessary
to commence by defeating the Austrian army, and expelling it from Italy, and should this end be obtained,
would it then be well to lose the fruit of the victory,
and delay the passage of the Alps, for the purpose
of bringing back the war to Venice? which proceeding would give the archduke time to think of himself,
reinforce his troops, and create fresh obstacles.
It was under the walls of Vienna that Napoleon
looked forward to the signing of a peace, which should
crown so many victories. Venice was, besides, very
strong; she was defended by her lagunes, by armed
vessels, and by 10,000 Sclavonians; she was mistɪ
of the Adriatic, and could by this channel recei
fresh troops; and finally, she had within her tl
moral strength of all the ruling families, who woul
feel strongly called upon to struggle for their politicɛ
existence.   Who   could   calculate   how   long   th
French army would be stopped by this enterprise
And should the struggle be at all prolonged, what effec
might not an active resistance have on the rest o
Italy?

   This new war could not fail to meet great opposition at Paris; the minister was very active; the
legislative body was in opposition to the directory
the directory itself was divided. Should it be con
sulted on the subject of the war with Venice, it would
not reply, or would evade the question; should Napo-

leon, as he had hitherto done, act without authority, he would be reproached, except in case of immediate success, with having violated every principle; in his character of general-in-chief, he only had the right to repulse force by force.   To undertake a fresh war against an armed power, without orders from his government, would be to render himself guilty of usurping the rights of sovereignty, and he was already but too deeply engaged in a struggle with republican jealousy.

The episode of Venice might become the principal affair; Napoleon, therefore, decided to take, with regard to the Venetians, simply military precautions; he was secure of Brescia, Bergamo, and the whole right shore of the Adige.   He placed troops in the castles of Verona, St. Felix, and St. Piero, and in the Old Palace; this made him master of the stone bridges. The troops which had been employed in the expedition against the Pope, were now on their return to the Adige; they would form a reserve large enough to awe the senate.   Arrangements were made that all the convalescent and wounded who should leave the hospitals, were to be organized into marching battalions, and added to the reserve; but this, in fact, weakened by so much the acting army.

Napoleon resolved, however, to make one ⸜fresh effort.   He desired an interview with Pesaro, who at that time directed the affairs of the republic.   Pesaro described to him the critical state of the country, the bad disposition of the people, the just complaints of the senate; he said, that these difficult circumstances required the senate to take strong measures, and to raise extraordinary armaments, which, however, ought not to give any umbrage to the French; that the senate was obliged to issue arrests at Venice, and in the provinces; that it would be unjust to consider as rigorous measures against the partisans of France, that which was only a just punishment inflicted on turbulent subjects who were endeavouring to overthrow the laws of their country.

Napoleon granted the critical situation of Venice, but, without losing time in discussing its causes, came immediately to the point: "You desire," said he, "to arrest the proceedings of those whom you call your enemies, but whom I call my friends. You entrust the administration to men distinguished by their hatred to France—you raise fresh troops. What remains for you to do, in order to produce a declaration of war? And yet your ruin would in that case be entire and immediate; it would be in vain for you to rely on the assistance of the archduke; within a week I should drive his armies from Italy. There is one way remaining by which you may deliver your republic from its present difficult situation; I offer you an alliance with France; I offer to secure to Venice her provinces, and even her authority in Brescia; but I demand in return that she shall declare war against Austria, and furnish to my army a contingent of 10,000 infantry, 2000 cavalry, and twenty-four

cannon. I think it would be well done, to enrol in the
Golden Book the principal families of the provinces;
I do not, however, make this a *sine quâ non.* Return
to Venice; let the senate deliberate on these proposals,
and come back to sign a treaty which alone can save
your country." Pesaro agreed to the wisdom of this
project, and set out for Venice, promising to return
within a fortnight.

On the 11th of March, the French army was put
in motion for the purpose of crossing the Piave. Immediately on the arrival of this intelligence at Venice,
orders were issued that fourteen of the principal inhabitants of Bergamo should be arrested and brought
before the Council of Ten. The chiefs of the patriotic
party, informed in time by a Venetian commissary
who was devoted to their cause, intercepted the courier,
arrested the proveditor himself, raised the standard of
revolt, and proclaimed the freedom of Bergamo. The
deputies which they sent to the head-quarters of the
French general, found him on the battle-field of Tagliamento. This event thwarted Napoleon's projects, but it
was irremediable. The Bergamese had already entered
into a confederacy with Milan, the capital of Lombardy, and with Bologna, the capital of the transpadane
republic. The same revolution took place a few days
afterwards at Brescia; the two thousand Sclavonians
garrisoned there, were disarmed; the proveditor Battaglia was respected, but sent back to Verona. The
Venetian General, Fioravante, marched against the

insurgents, occupied Salo, and threatened Brescia;
Lahoz, a Milanese, went to meet him, defeated his
troops, and expelled him from Salo.

Pesaro returned, as he had promised, to the head-
quarters, then at Goritzia. The archduke had been
defeated at Tagliamento; Palma-Nova had opened its
gates; the French standard floated over Tarvis beyond
the Isonzo, and on the summit of the Julian Alps.
" Have I kept my word?" said Napoleon to him:
" The Venetian territories are covered with my troops;
the Austrians flee before me. In a few days I shall
be in Germany. What is the decision of your republic? I have offered her the alliance of France; does
she accept it?"

" Venice," answered Pesaro, " rejoices at your
triumphs; she knows that she can only exist by the
aid of France; but, faithful to her ancient policy, she
is determined to remain neuter. Under Louis XII.
and Francis I. her forces were of some weight in the
field of battle; but now, even were the entire population in arms, of what benefit would our assistance
be to you?"

Napoleon made a last effort; he failed; and said to
Pesaro, on parting, " Since your republic is then determined to remain neuter, so let it be—I consent; but
let it cease raising armaments. I leave sufficient
troops in Italy to support my authority there.

" I am now on my way to Vienna. What I would
have pardoned to Venice when I was in Italy, will
become an unpardonable crime when I am in Germany.

Should my soldiers be assassinated, my convoys ha-
rassèd, or my communications interrupted on the
Venetian territories, your republic will cease to exist;
it will have pronounced its own sentence."

General Kerpen had imitated the movement of
General Joubert, which had been put into operation
on the 20th of March; he had abandoned the Tyrol,
and had passed, by Salzburg and Rottenmann, into
the valley of the Muer, where he hoped to rejoin the
archduke; but having heard, at Scheifling, of the
rapidity of the French army's march, he re-crossed the
mountains, and did not effect his junction till some
time after, in the plain of Vienna. General Laudon,
left by him to guard the Tyrol, with only 2000 regular
troops, succeeded in re-organizing 10,000 Tyrolean
militia, who, discouraged by so many defeats, had
dispersed. This reinforcement gave him greatly the
advantage in numbers over the small guard which had
been ordered by Joubert to cover the road to Trent.

General Serviez had about 1200 men; he evacuated
the two shores of the Tarvis at the approach of the
enemy, and retreated to Monte Caldo. Laudon occupied Trent. Being now master of the whole of the
Tyrol, he inundated Italy with proclamations; he
spread to Venice, to Rome, to Turin, and to Naples,
the news of the defeat of the French. "The Tyrol
had been the tomb of Joubert's troops; Napoleon
had been defeated at Tagliamento; the imperial troops
had gained brilliant victories on the Rhine." He
came down from Trent into Italy with 60,000 men

for the purpose of entirely cutting off the retreat of
the wrecks of the army, which the archduke was pursuing; and, finally, summoned Venice and all Italy to
arms, and to revolt against France.

At this news, the Venetian oligarchy no longer kept
measures. The French minister attempted in vain to
show the senate on what an abyss it stood; he denied
the pretended disasters of Joubert in the Tyrol, as
well as those, quite as false, of the Sambre, Meuse
and Rhine; he proved that hostilities had not yet
been commenced; he went so far as to communicate
the plan of the campaign, from which it resulted that
the abandonment of the Tyrol by Joubert was an
arranged movement; that he was at that moment
marching through Carinthia towards the Pasterthal;
and that, far from having lost his end, he had attained
it. Pesaro gave no credit to these communications;
he too earnestly desired the disasters of the French.
The court of Vienna, on its part, omitted nothing
which might serve to rouse the passions of the enemies
of France. It was an essential part of its plans to
organize insurrections in the rear of the army.

The *corps-de-reserve*, which had been left at Palma-
Nova, the garrison of Osapo, and the prudence of the
proveditor Mocenigo, kept Friuli tranquil; perhaps,
too, the inhabitants of this province, who were nearer
the theatre of action, were better informed respecting
the state of affairs.

The rising *en masse* of the Veronese had long since
been arranged; more than thirty thousand peasants

had received arms, and only awaited the signal for massacre; 3000 troops, composed partly of Venetians, and partly of Sclavonians, had been sent to Verona to form a garrison there. Emile, the proveditor, who was devoted to the senate, conferred with Laudon; he informed him of the weakness of the French garrison, and, as soon as he thought himself secure of the assistance of the Austrian troops, gave the signal for revolt.

On the 17th of April, the second day of the Easter festival, after vespers, the tocsin sounded; the insurrection burst forth; a general massacre of the French commenced; the people, in their fury, even went so far as to murder 400 sick people in the hospitals. General Balland shut himself up in the castle with the garrison. The Veronese authorities, alarmed by the artillery of the forts, which the General directed against the town, decided to demand a parley; but the fury of the populace opposed this measure; a reinforcement of 2000 Sclavonians, sent from Vicenza by the proveditor Foscarini, and the approach of the troops of the Austrian General Neiperg, added still more to the madness of the people, who avenged the mischief done in the town by the bombardment, by massacring the garrison of La Chuisa, who had been obliged to capitulate before the rising of the mountaineers.

General Kilmaine, commander-in-chief of Lombardy, made arrangements for assisting General Balland, on the first intelligence which he received of the insurrection at Verona. On the 21st, the first ranks of his army appeared under Verona. The Generals Chabraud and Chevalier fought several skirmishes, and succeeded in investing the town on the 22nd. On the 23rd the signing of the preliminaries of peace with Austria became known to the insurgents, and almost at the same moment they heard of the arrival of the division commanded by Victor, which was hastening from Treviso. The alarm spread; their dejection was now equal to their former fury; they demanded a capitulation; they accepted on their knees the conditions which Balland exacted; they gave hostages, and order was again established.

The French owed them a heavy debt of vengeance; the blood of their comrades, ignominiously murdered, still flowed in the streets; no such vengeance was, however, taken; three inhabitants only were given up to justice; the people were all disarmed, and the peasants sent back to their villages.

The oligarchy of Venice, not less blind, allowed the crew of a French corvette, which, pursued by an Austrian frigate, had taken refuge under the batteries of the Lido, to be massacred before their eyes. The French minister protested against this violation of the right of nations, and demanded that justice should be exercised against the assassins. The senate laughed at his representations and his threats, and issued a decree, by which it granted rewards to such of its satellites as had taken part in the massacre of Captain Laugier and his crew.

As soon as Napoleon was informed of the disorders and murders which were being committed in the rear of the army, he sent the aide-de-camp Junot to Venice, charging him to deliver to the senate the following letter, dated from Judenburg, the 9th of April:

" Throughout all the provinces the subjects of the illustrious republic are in arms: their rallying cry is—*Death to the French!* The number of French soldiers who have already fallen victims to their rage amounts to some hundreds. It is in vain for you to affect to disavow the tumults which you yourselves have raised. Do you think, that because I am at a distance, in the heart of Germany, I shall not have power to enforce respect towards the soldiers of the first nation in the world? Do you think that the French legions will leave unpunished the assassins stained with the blood of their comrades? There is not a man amongst them who, when charged with this vengeance, will not feel his courage and his means tripled. Do you fancy yourselves still in the age of Charles VIII.? Since then, opinions are changed indeed in Italy!"

Junot had orders to read this letter to the senate, and to express all the indignation of the general-in-chief; but terror had already seized on Venice. The illusion was dissipated; they now knew that the armies on the Rhine had not commenced hostilities; that Joubert was at Villach with his body of troops;

that Victor was close to Verona; that the French were already directing their march to the lagunes; finally, that Napoleon, victorious in every combat, had carried terror to Vienna itself; that he had just granted a truce to the archduke, and that the emperor had sent ambassadors to him to demand peace.

The French minister, L'Allemand, presented Junot to the senate; he fulfilled his mission with all the frankness and roughness of a soldier; the senate was humbled, and endeavoured to make excuses. The friends of liberty raised their heads, and foresaw the moment of their triumph. A deputation was sent to the general-in-chief, then at Gratz, and was commissioned to offer him any reparation which he might desire; the members of this deputation had private instructions to corrupt, by bribes, all such persons as might have influence with the general; but all was in vain.

The senate at the same time dispatched courier after courier to Paris, and put considerable sums at the disposal of the Venetian minister, in the hope of gaining over the leaders of the directory, and causing such orders to be dispatched to the general-in-chief as should save the aristocracy. This intrigue succeeded in Paris: the distribution of ten thousand bills of exchange gained for the Venetian minister the orders which he solicited; but these orders were not clothed with all the legal forms. Despatches intercepted at Milan, gave Napoleon the clue by which to unravel this intrigue; the list of the bills distributed in Paris was in his hands; he annulled them all by his own authority.

On the 3rd of May, he issued, from Palma-Nova, his declaration of war against the Venetian republic, founding this declaration on the principle of repulsing force by force. This manifesto was couched in the following terms:

" While the French army is engaged in the defiles of Styria, and has left far behind it Italy and its principal warlike establishments, where but a few battalions remain, the following is the conduct of the Venetian government.

" It profits by the Holy Week to arm 40,000 peasants—adds to these, ten regiments of Sclavonians, divides them into bodies, and posts them at various points, for the purpose of intercepting the communications of the French army.

" Extraordinary commissaries, guns, ammunition of all kinds and cannon, are sent from Venice itself in order to complete the organization of the different corps. All persons in the provinces who are favourably disposed towards us, are arrested; all those who are known to nourish a furious hatred against the French, and more especially the fourteen conspirators, whom the proveditor Priuli arrested three months ago, as being convicted of plotting a massacre of the French, are loaded with rewards, and enjoy the whole confidence of the government.

" In all market-places, coffee-houses, and other places of public resort, the French are insulted, called

Jacobins, regicides, atheists; they are finally expelled and forbidden to re-enter the town.

" The inhabitants of Padua, Vicenza, and Verona, are ordered to take up arms, and to second the various bodies of troops—to commence, in short, these new Sicilian vespers. ' It is our business,' say the Venetian officers, ' to verify the proverb, that *Italy is the tomb of the French.*' The priests in the pulpit, preach the crusade; and priests, in the Venetian states say nothing but what the government pleases. Pamphlets, perfidious proclamations, anonymous letters, are printed in various towns, and begin to excite the people; and in a state where the liberty of the press is not allowed, in a government as much feared as it is secretly abhorred, the printers print nothing, the authors compose nothing but what suits the senate.

" At first everything seems to favour the treacherous project of the government; French blood flows on every side; convoys, couriers, everything appertaining to the army is intercepted on all the roads.

" At Padua, a commander of a battalion and two other Frenchmen are assassinated; at Castiglione di Mori, unarmed soldiers are murdered; and on the high roads between Mantua and Legnago, Cassano and Verona, more than two hundred French are killed.

" Two battalions, intending to join the army, meet a Venetian division at Chiari, which endeavours to oppose their passage; an obstinate combat ensues, and our brave soldiers cut a passage over the dead bodies of their enemies.

" At Valeggia, there is another combat; at Maleg-
nana, they are obliged to fight once more ; the
French are everywhere few in number, but they are
accustomed not to reckon the number of their
enemies.

" On the second day of Easter, at the sound of the
tocsin, all the French are assassinated in Verona;
neither the sick in the hospitals, nor those just
recovering, and taking the air in the streets, are
respected; they are thrown into the Adige, after
being pierced with a thousand stiletto wounds; more
then 400 soldiers are also massacred.   During a
whole week the Venetian army besieges the three
castles of Verona; the cannons which the Venetians
place as a battery are taken from them at the bayonet
point; the town is set on fire; and the *corps-d'observation* which arrives in the middle of these doings,
completely routs these cowards, and takes 3000
prisoners—among them several generals.

" The French consul's house in Zante is burnt down.
In Dalmatia, a Venetian war ship takes an Austrian
convoy under its protection, and fires several times
upon the sloop *Le Brun.* The *Liberator of Italy,* a
vessel belonging to the French republic, and only
carrying three or four small pieces of cannon, is sunk
in the port of Venice, by order of the senate.

" The young and interesting Lieutenant Laugier,
commander of this vessel, as soon as he sees himself
fired upon from the fort and from the admiral's galley,
being only at the distance of a pistol shot from each,

orders his crew to go down into the hold. He himself mounts the deck alone, amidst a shower of grapeshot, and endeavours, by speaking, to disarm the fury of the assassins; but in vain—he falls! His crew throw themselves into the water, and endeavour to-escape by swimming; they are pursued by six chaloupes, manned by troops in the pay of Venice, who strike down with hatchets the sailors who are endeavouring to find safety in the open sea. A boatswain, wounded, bleeding and exhausted, has the good fortune to gain the shore and to cling to a piece of wood close to the castle; but the commandant himself cuts off his hand with a hatchet.

" Considering the above grievances, authorised by cap. xii., art. 328, of the constitution of the republic, and impelled by the urgency of circumstances, the general-in-chief requires the French minister, now in Venice, to quit the said city.

" He orders the various agents of the French republic in Lombardy, and in the Venetian provinces, to leave the said provinces within twenty-four hours.

" He further orders the various generals to treat as enemies the troops of the republic of Venice; to throw down, in all the towns of the provinces, the Lion of St. Mark; each general will receive to-morrow particular instructions for his ulterior military operations."

On reading this manifesto, the arms fell from the hands of the oligarchs, they no longer thought of defending themselves; the great council of the aristocracy assembled, and gave up the sovereignty to the people; a municipality was the depository of it. Thus did these families, so proud and so long held in regard, and to whom an alliance had been offered in such good faith, fall without offering any resistance. In vain did they, in their anguish, solicit the aid of the court of Vienna; in vain did they entreat it to include them in the truce and in the negotiations for peace. That court was deaf to their prayers; it had its own views.

On the 16th of May, Baragnay d'Hilliers entered Venice; he had been called upon by the inhabitants, who were menaced by the Sclavonians. He took possession of the forts and batteries, and planted the tri-color in the square of St. Mark. The aristocracy was entirely and for ever overthrown; the democratic constitution of 1200 was proclaimed. Dandolo, a man of a quick, warm character, enthusiastic in the cause of liberty, a person of integrity, and a distinguished lawyer, placed himself at the head of the affairs of the city.

The Lion of St. Mark and the Corinthian horses were taken to Paris. The Venetian fleet consisted of twelve ships of sixty-four guns, and as many frigates and sloops. They were manned and sent to Toulon.

Corfu was one of the most important strong places of the republic ; General Gentili, who had taken Corsica, approached it with four battalions and a few companies of artillery, on board a squadron formed of Venetian vessels. He took possession of this place,

the true key of the Adriatic, as also of the other
Ionian Islands, Zante, Cerigo, Cephalonia, St. Maura,
(the ancient Ithaca), &c. &c.

Pesaro was overwhelmed with reproaches, and took
refuge at Vienna; Battaglia sincerely regretted the
fall of his country; he had long disapproved of the
proceedings of the senate, and had but too well foreseen this catastrophe; he died some time afterwards,
sincerely regretted by the good and honourable.   Had
his advice been followed, Venice would have been
saved.   The Doge Manini, at the moment when he
was swearing allegiance to Austria, fell dead into the
arms of Morosini, who had become commissary of the
Emperor.

On the receipt of the declaration of war against
Venice, all the provinces were in arms against the
capital.   Each separate town proclaimed its independence, and constituted a government for itself. Bergamo, Brescia, Padua, Vicenza, Bassano, Odina,
formed themselves into separate republics.   It was
this system which had been the origin of the cispadane
and transpadane republics. They adopted the principles
of the French revolution, abolished convents, but
respected the religion and property of the secular
priests; they constituted national domains, and suppressed feudal privileges.   Chosen men from the
nobility and proprietors of land formed themselves
into companies of hussars and riflemen, under the title
of a guard of honour.   The inferior classes formed
battalions of a national guard.   The colours of these

new republics were those of Italy. Notwithstanding
Napoleon's extreme vigilance in endeavouring to prevent outrages and destruction, more took place at this
period than at any other during the course of the war.
The country was divided into two very violent
factions; all the passions of the people were roused
to a high pitch; at the time of the surrender of
Verona, the *mont-de-piété*, of that town, which possessed from seven to eight millions of francs, was despoiled. Bouquer, the war-commissioner, and Lan-
drieux, a colonel of hussars, were accused of this
robbery, the character of which was rendered still
more shocking by the other crimes, necessary to its
concealment, which preceded and followed it. All
that was found in the houses of the accused persons
was restored to the town, but the loss was nevertheless considerable.

General Bernadotte carried to Paris the standards
which had been taken from the Venetian troops, and
also the remains of those taken at Rivoli and in
Germany from Prince Charles. He presented these
trophies to the directory a few days before the 18th of
Fructidor.

The frequent presentations of standards were, at
this period, very useful to the government; these
manifestations of the disposition of the army confounded the malcontents and made them tremble.

CHAPTER VI.

NAPOLEON, DURING 1797.

MONTEBELLO is a castle situated some leagues from Milan, upon a hill which commands the whole plain of Lombardy. The French head-quarters were there during the months of May and June. The assemblage of the principal ladies of Milan, who came there daily to pay their respects to Josephine; the presence of the ministers of Austria, of the Pope, of the King of the Two Sicilies, and of the republics of Genoa and Venice; those of the Duke of Parma, of the Swiss cantons, and of several princes of Germany; the numerous authorities of the cisalpine republic, and the deputies of cities; the great number of couriers from Paris, from Rome, from Naples, Vienna, Florence, Turin, Venice, Genoa, who came and went at all hours, —in a word, the whole manner of life in this castle, caused the Italians to speak of it as the court of

Montebello; and, in fact, it was a brilliant court. The negotiations of peace with the Emperor—the politics of Germany, the fate of the King of Sardinia, of Switzerland, of Venice and Genoa, were settled there. The court of Montebello made several excursions to Lake Maggiore, to the Borromean Isles, to the Lake of Como; and passed several days in the different country-houses round these lakes. Every town—every village, wished to distinguish itself in showing esteem and respect for the liberator of Italy. The corps diplomatique could not but be surprised at all they saw.

General Serrurier conveyed to the directory the last colours taken from the archduke Charles: " This officer " (we quote from Napoleon's letter) " has displayed in the two last campaigns, as much talent as civism; his division gained the victory of Mondovi, and contributed materially to that of Castiglione, and to the taking of Mantua. It also distinguished itself at the passage of the Tagliamento, at the passage of the Isonzo, and particularly at the taking of Gradisca. General Serrurier is severe to himself; he is so, sometimes, towards others; a firm friend to discipline, order, and the virtues most necessary to the maintenance of society; he disdains all intrigue. These qualities have made him several enemies among men always ready to accuse of incivism those who require them to submit to the laws.

" I consider him very fit to command the troops

of the cisalpine republic. I beg you, therefore, to
send him to his post as soon as possible."

Serrurier was well received at Paris; the frankness
and openness of his character gave general satisfaction.
During his residence in France, he visited his native
department of L'Aisne; he had always been moderate respecting the principles of the revolution, but
when he returned from France, he was very warm in
favour of the republic, so indignant was he at the bad
feeling he had had occasion to remark.

Just as the French army was entering Venice,
Count d'Entraigues escaped from that town. He
was stopped at the Brenta by the troops of Bernadotte's division, and sent to head-quarters at Milan.
The Count d'Entraigues was from Nivernois. As
one of the deputies from the nobility to the constituent assembly, he was an ardent patriot in '88 and
'89; but shortly after the beginning of the general
assembly, being a nephew of M. de St. Priest, he
changed sides, emigrated, and was one of the principal
agents of royalty in other countries, and unceasing in
his intrigues. He had been at Venice for two years,
nominally attached to the English embassy, but in
fact, as minister of the counter-revolution, and putting
himself at the head of all the plots for injuring or
rising against the French army. He was suspected
of having had a share in the massacre at Verona.
Generals Berthier and Clarke searched his papers,
made a list of all the contents of his secretaire, and
sent this list to Paris. The French government sent

an answer, ordering d'Entraigues to be brought before a military tribunal, and judged according to the laws of the republic; but, in the meantime, he had interested Napoleon, who had seen him several times. Not ignorant of the dangers of his position, he took pains to please him who alone had power over his fate; he spoke to him without reserve, discovered to him several intrigues then in progress, and compromised his party much more than he was called on to do. This plan succeeded; he was allowed to reside in the town on his parole, and shortly afterwards made his escape into Switzerland. So little attention had been paid to him, that it was only some six or seven days after his departure from Milan, that it was discovered he had broken his parole. Not long afterwards, a sort of pamphlet by him was spread all over Germany and Italy, calumniating his benefactor. He described the horrible dungeon in which he had been immured, the torments which he had suffered, the boldness which he had displayed, and the risks he had run to obtain his liberty. Every one at Milan, where he had been seen in every company, on the public promenade and elsewhere, was indignant at this conduct; several members of the corps diplomatique shared the general indignation, and even published declarations on the subject.

The republic of Genoa, during the three wars respecting the succession of Parma, of Spain, and of Austria, had taken an active part in the quarrel; its little armies had marched to the field with those of

the crowns of France and Spain. In 1747, the people
had driven out of Genoa the Austrian garrison
commanded by the Marquis of Botta, and since
that time the town had sustained a long and obstinate siege from the army of Maria Theresa. In the
eighteenth century, Genoa had carried on a bloody
war against Corsica. National antipathy gave rise to
interminable skirmishes between the Piedmontese
and the Genoese. This continual recurrence of military events had contributed to keep alive among the
citizens of this republic, weak as it was in respect to
population and extent, an energy which gave it quite
a different standing from that of Venice. Thus the
Genoese aristocracy had successfully resisted the
storm; it had preserved itself free and independent;
it had allowed itself to be dictated to neither by the
coalition, nor by France, nor by the popular party; it
had preserved, in all its purity, the constitution which
Andreas Doria had given it in the sixteenth century.

But the proclamation of the independence of the
cispadane and transpadane republics, the abdication of
the aristocracy of Venice, the establishment of a popular
form of government in the whole of the Venetian
states, and the enthusiasm inspired by the victories
of the French, gave such an increase of weight to the
popular party, that some change in the constitution
became unavoidable. France did not believe itself
justified in placing any confidence in the aristocracy;
but it was considered advisable that the revolution
should take place without any open interference on

its part, and merely by means of the advance and the force of public opinion. Faypoult, the French minister at Genoa, was an enlightened man, moderate in his politics, and rather weak in character; this was an advantage in the then state of things, since he rather restrained than increased the enthusiasm of the revolutionary party.

Those who had observed the course of events, had calculated that matters would come to a crisis about the end of August; they did not believe that the aristocracy could prolong its resistance beyond that term. The revolutionary spirits of the club Morandi, impatient at the slow progress of events, and perhaps too, urged on by secret agents from Paris, drew up a petition in which they demanded the abdication of the aristocracy, and the proclamation of independence.

A deputation presented it to the Doge, who did not show himself averse to give satisfaction to the petitioners; he even named a junta of nine persons, amongst whom, four were to be plebeians, to propose to him the necessary changes in the constitution.

The three state-inquisitors or supreme censors, chiefs of the oligarchy and enemies of France, saw this state of things with grief. Convinced that the aristocracy had but a very little longer time to exist, if they allowed things to go on as they were, and did not take some means of preventing them, they sought for assistance in fanaticism to gain over to their side the inferior corporations. If they could be enabled to gain the coal-porters and the colliers, they would thus acquire assistance sufficient to keep all classes of the citizens in awe. They made use of the confessional, the pulpit, sermons in the squares and streets, miracles, the exposition of the holy sacrament, even the prayers during forty hours, in order to obtain from God, that he would remove from the republic the storm which threatened it; but instead of avoiding the storm, they attracted it by this imprudent conduct. On the other hand, the Morandi Club agitated; they declaimed, printed, excited the people in a thousand ways against the nobles and the priests, and made many proselytes. . They soon considered the moment favourable, and took up arms on the 22nd of May; at 10 o'clock in the morning, they seized the principal gates, particularly those of St. Thomas, of the arsenal, and of the port. The inquisitors, terrified at this, gave the signal agreed on to the coal-porters and colliers, who, conducted by their syndics, rushed with cries of " Viva Maria," to the magazine of arms, and declared in favour of the aristocracy. Thus, in a few hours, 10,000 men were organized and provided with arms, ready to defend the prince. The minister of France, terrified at their vociferations against the Jacobites and the French, proceeded to the palace and endeavoured to conciliate the hostile parties. At the sight of these preparations on the part of the oligarchy, and of this great number of defenders, the patriots felt their weakness; they had reckoned that the mass of the citizens would rise in their favour, and that this would give them the advantage over their adversaries;

but the citizens, terrified at the fury of the coal-porters, remained shut up in their houses. The patriots, thus deceived in their hopes, could not see any means of safety except in adopting the French cockade, which had very nearly produced fatal effects to several French families resident in Genoa.

Every one ran to arms: the patriots were defeated on all sides, and driven from their positions. During the night between the 23rd and the 24th they retained possession of St. Thomas's gate; they lost it, however, early on the 24th. The triumphant party compelled everybody to wear the Genoese cockade; they permitted the pillage of the houses inhabited by French families; and several Frenchmen were even committed to prison.

The minister Faypoult would certainly have been insulted but for a guard of honour that the doge sent to his hotel, consisting of 200 men. Ménard, the commissary of the navy, a prudent man, who had taken no part in the disturbances, was dragged by the hair to the fort of La Lanterne; the house of the consul Lachaise was pillaged; everything French was obliged to be prepared for insults, and even sometimes for wounds.

The citizens were indignant, but dared not make any resistance for fear of the conquerors. From the 23rd to the 29th, the minister Faypoult presented several notes on the subject, without receiving any satisfaction. Just at this time, Admiral Brueys, with two men of war, and two frigates, presented himself at

the port, on his return from Corsica.   The doge
opposed his entrance, under the pretext that his presence would irritate the populace, and that they would
then commit all sorts of excesses against the French.
Faypoult was weak enough to submit to this measure;
he sent orders to Brueys, therefore, to sail for
Toulon.

When the moderate party in the senate observed
upon the imprudence of this conduct, the oligarchs
answered, that as the French were engaged in negotiations with Austria, they would not dare to march a
body of men against Genoa; that the opinions which
prevailed at Paris were not democratic ones; that it
was known that even Napoleon disapproved of the
principles of the club Morandi; and that he would
think twice before exposing himself to the possibility
of blame from his government, and to the hostility of
Clichy's party, which was the most powerful in the
legislature.

All these fallacious hopes were soon dispelled.   As
soon as Napoleon was informed that French blood had
been shed, he dispatched his aide-de-camp, Lavalette,
to Genoa; he required from the doge that all the
French who had been arrested should be immediately
placed at the disposal of the French minister; that the
coal-porters and colliers should be disarmed, and the
inquisitors arrested; declaring, at the same time, that
the heads of the patricians should pay for any French
lives, as well as that the property of the republic
should make reparation for any damage done to theirs.
He desired the minister Faypoult to quit Genoa, and

to retire to Tortona, with all the French residents who chose to follow him, in case these demands should not be complied with in twenty-four hours. Lavalette arrived at Genoa on the 29th of May, at four o'clock in the afternoon; at six, he was presented to the senate, who, after having heard his demands, and seen the letter to the doge, promised to give him an answer the same evening. In fact, the French were immediately set at liberty, and conducted to the hotel of the ambassador in the midst of an immense concourse of people, who testified their sympathy for them. The middle classes and the populace, encouraged by this proceeding of Napoleon's, which convinced them of his protection, roused themselves, and demanded with loud cries, that the cut-throats of the oligarchy should be disarmed. The same evening, 4000 muskets were replaced in the arsenal. The discussion in the senate was warm; the aristocratic party were in the minority. A division of French troops had been sent to Tortona. Genoa, if besieged by sea and land, would have been promptly reduced to humiliation; it is even probable, that the mere sight of the French troops would have been sufficient to give to the citizens, and to the mass of the " tiers état" power sufficient to shake off the yoke of the aristocracy.

In the meantime, the answer of the aristocracy was not satisfactory, being only a sort of compromise. Faypoult determined to leave Genoa. Lavalette was to remain there to protect such French residents as should not leave with the minister. Upon the French minister's demanding his passports, the doge assembled the senate, which alone had the power of granting them. The senate was therefore obliged a second time to take into consideration the position in which the republic was about to be placed. After some discussion, the resolution of giving way to the demands of the general-in-chief was adopted: it was decreed, 1stly, that a deputation consisting of MM. Cambiaso, (doge), Serra, and Carbonari, should be immediately dispatched to Montebello; 2ndly, that the inquisitors should be placed in a state of arrest; 3rdly, that the coal-porters and colliers, who had only acted according to the orders of the prince, and who in reality had no interest whatever in the affair, should become quiet as soon as submission was really determined on.

On the 6th of June, the deputies of the senate signed a convention at Montebello, which put an end to the constitution of Doria, and established at Genoa the democratical form of government. This convention was conceived in the following terms:

" The French republic and the republic of Genoa, wishing to confirm and consolidate the union and harmony of feeling which have always existed between them, and believing that the happiness of the Genoese people requires that the sovereign power should be restored to them: the two states have agreed upon the following articles.

" Art 1. The government of the republic of Genoa recognises the principle, that the sovereign power resides in the united body of all the citizens of the Genoese territory.

" 2. The legislative power shall be confided to two representative councils, composed, the one of 300, the other of 150 members. The executive power shall be delegated to a senate of twelve, presided over by a doge. Both doge and senators shall be chosen by the two councils.

" 3. Each commune shall have its municipality, and each district its administration.

" 4. The mode of election of all the authorities, the divisions into districts, the portion of authority to be confided to each corporation, the organization of the judicial authorities, and of the military force, shall be determined by a legislative commission, which shall be required to frame a constitution, and all the organic laws of the government: taking care at the same time to do nothing contrary to the Catholic religion; to guarantee the consolidated debt; to preserve the free port of the city of Genoa, and the bank of St. George; and to take measures for providing, as far as is possible, for the support of the poor nobles at present in existence. This commission shall complete its task in one month, reckoning from the day of its appointment.

" 5. The people being thus re-established in their rights, every species of privilege or of particular organization, tending to destroy the unity of the state, is, *ipso facto*, annulled.

" 6. The provisional government shall be confided to a commission, consisting of twenty-two members, with the present doge at their head; and this commission shall date from the 14th of the present month of June, being the 26th of Prairial of the year 5 of the French republic.

" 7. Those citizens who shall be called upon to compose the provisional government of the republic of Genoa, shall not be permitted to refuse this office, without being considered as indifferent to the welfare of their country, and condemned to pay a fine of 2000 crowns.

" 8. When the provisional government shall be formed, it shall determine the necessary rules respecting the form of its deliberations. It shall name, in the course of the first week of its appointment, the legislative commission, empowered to frame a constitution.

" 9. The provisional government shall provide for the proper indemnification of all the French residents who shall have suffered loss during the days of the 3rd and 4th of Prairial, (May 22 and 23.)

" 10. The French republic, anxious to give a proof of the interest which it takes in the happiness of the people of Genoa, and desirous of seeing them united and free from factions, grants an amnesty to all the Genoese of whom she might have reason to complain, whether on account of the events of the 3rd and 4th of Prairial, or on account of the several events which have taken place in the various imperial feofs.

" The provisional government shall also endeavour, most anxiously, to put an end to all factions, to unite all the citizens, and to cause them to see the necessity of rallying around the public liberty, granting further, for this purpose, a general amnesty.

" 11. The French republic will grant to the republic of Genoa its protection, and even the assistance of its arms, in order to facilitate, if necessary, the execution of the above-named articles, and to maintain the integrity of the territory of the Genoese republic."

The people triumphed with that vivacity which is the characteristic of a spirit of party and of all southern nations; they even committed some excesses; they burned the Golden Book, and broke the statue of Doria. This outrage, offered to the memory of so great a man, offended Napoleon; he demanded of the provisional government that the statue should be restored.

In the meantime, the exclusives had got the upper hand; the constitution, therefore, was also of the same spirit; the priests were rendered disaffected, and the nobles exasperated; they were both excluded from all offices of state. This constitution was to be submitted to the assembly of the people on the 14th of September; it was printed and posted up in all the communes. Several of the country communes declared that they would not accept it; the priests and nobles endeavoured everywhere to rouse the peasants. At last, the insurrection broke out in the valleys of the Polcevera and of the Besagno; the insurgents took possession of the three bastions of L'Eperon, La Tenaille, and La Lanterne, which latter commands the port. General Duphot, who had been sent to Genoa, to organize the troops of the republic, which amounted to 6000 men, was called upon by the provisional government to fight in their defence. He drove out the insurgents, and recovered the two forts. On the 7th, tranquillity was again established in the valleys; the peasants were disarmed.

Napoleon was displeased at these accounts. He was then entirely occupied with the negotiations with Austria, and had not been able to pay any very particular attention to the affairs of Genoa; but he advised them not to displease the nobles, and to satisfy the priests. He retarded the publication of the constitution; he made all the changes which the priests and the nobles required; and thus, purged of the spirit of demagogy, with which it had been tinged, it was put into execution, with the consent of all ranks. He loved Genoa; he wished to have gone there himself, in order to unite all parties, but circumstances succeeding each other with unexampled rapidity, prevented this design.

After the treaty of Campo-Formio, on the point of quitting Italy, on the 11th of November, 1797, he wrote the following letter to the Genoese government:

" I will respond, citizens, to the confidence you have reposed in me. You feel obliged to diminish the expenses of your administration, in order not to over-tax your people. It is not enough to act in no respect contrary to religion; you must endeavour moreover to give no subject of inquietude to even fearful consciences, and no tool to evil-intentioned persons.

" *To exclude all the nobles from any public
office would be an act of injustice in the highest
degree; you would be doing then what they did
before.* The free port is an apple of discord which has
been thrown in the midst of you . . . The town of
Genoa must hold the freedom of its port from the will
of the legislative body. *Why is the Ligurian
people so changed? Its first impulses of fraternity
have been succeeded by fear and terror. The
priests had first rallied round the tree of liberty;
they first told you that the morality of the gospel is
democratic; but men, paid by your enemies, and
the immediate assistants of tyranny in all revolutions, have taken advantage of the faults, perhaps
even the crimes of some priests, to write against
religion; and the priests have retired. . . You have
proscribed en masse, and the number of your enemies
has increased . . . When in any state, but particularly
in a small state, one becomes accustomed to condemn
without hearing, to applaud a discourse because it
is impassioned, when exaggeration and madness
are called virtue, moderation and equity designated
as crimes, that state is near its ruin.* Believe
me that wherever my duty and the service of my
country may call me, I shall consider *that* one of
the most happy moments of my life, in which I hear
that the people of Genoa are united among themselves
and live happily."

A motion of Sieyes, having for its object the banish-
ment of all the nobles from France, with an equivalent

compensation in manufactured goods for their losses, was just at this time under discussion in the Council of Five Hundred, in Paris; so that this advice given by Napoleon to the republic of Genoa, appears to have been, in fact, intended for the French republic. A' any rate, the latter profited by it; for this extreme and terrible measure, which spread alarm and disorder everywhere, was abandoned, and never more introduced.

No French battalion had passed Tortona. The revolution of Genoa was effected solely by the influence of the " tiers état;" and had it not been for the proceedings of the inquisitors and the club Morandi, it would have been effected without any disorders, without trouble, and without any even indirect interference of France.

The King of Sardinia was placed in a false position; the following treaty, negotiated at Bologna by Napoleon, and signed at Turin by Clarke, existed, yet did not exist.

" The executive Directory of the French republic, and his majesty the King of Sardinia, wishing by all the means in their power, and by a more intimate connexion of their respective interests, to contribute to bring about as quickly as possible, that peace which they both desire, and which must assure the repose and the tranquillity of Italy, have determined upon concluding a treaty of alliance offensive and defensive; and have charged with full powers to that effect—to wit, the Directory of the French republic, General

Clarke; and his majesty the King of Sardinia, the Chevalier D. Clément Damian de Priocca, Knight Grand Cross of the orders of St. Maurice and St. Lazarus, principal Secretary of State of his majesty in the Home Department; who, after having exchanged their respective full powers, have agreed upon the following articles:

. " Art. 1. There shall exist an offensive alliance between the French republic and his majesty the King of Sardinia, until a general peace.

" After that time, the alliance shall be simply a defensive one, and shall be established upon a basis conformable to the reciprocal interests of the two powers.

" 2. As the present alliance has no other object than that of hastening the conclusion of peace, and of assuring the tranquillity of Italy, it shall only be binding during the present war against the Emperor of Germany, being the only one of the continental powers who continues to oppose such salutary intentions. His majesty the King of Sardinia will remain neuter in respect to England and the other powers still at war with the French republic.

" 3. The French republic, and his majesty the King of Sardinia, guarantee to one another, as far as lies in their power, all their present possessions in Europe, during all the time that the present alliance shall continue in force. The two powers will unite their forces against the common enemy from without, and will lend no assistance, direct or indirect, to an enemy within.

"4. The contingent of troops which his Sardiniau majesty shall furnish in consequence of the present alliance, shall be 8000 infantry, 2000 cavalry, and 40 pieces of cannon. In case the two powers shal think it necessary to increase this contingent, this increase shall be agreed upon by commissioners, with ful. powers on the part of the executive directory, and of his majesty the King of Sardinia.

" 5. The contingent of troops and of artillery shall be ready and assembled at Novara—to wit, 500 cavalry, 4000 infantry, and 12 pieces of cannon, on the 30th Germinal of the present year, (April 19, O. S.) the remainder fourteen days later.

" This contingent shall be kept at the expense of his majesty the King of Sardinia, and shall receive orders from the general-in-chief of the French army in Italy.

" A particular convention drawn up in concert with the general, shall determine the mode in which the contingent shall serve.

" 6. The troops composing it, shall share, in proportion to the number actually under arms, in the contributions imposed on the conquered countries reckoning from the day on which the contingent shall have joined the armies of the republic.

" 7. The French republic promises to grant to his majesty the King of Sardinia, at the general' or continental peace, all the advantages that circumstances permit it to procure for him.

" 8. Neither of the contracting powers shall conclude a separate peace with the common enemy, and no truce shall be concluded by the French republic with the armies at present in Italy, without including in it his Sardinian majesty.

" 9. All contributions imposed in the states of his majesty the King of Sardinia, which have not been acquitted or compensated for, shall cease immediately after the exchange of the ratifications of the present treaty.

. " 10. The various equipments which shall have been furnished in the states of his Sardinian majesty to the French troops, as also to the prisoners of war, sent back into France, as well as those which have been the consequence of separate conventions on this subject, in so far as they have not been acquitted or compensated for by the French republic in consequence of the said conventions, shall be repaid in kind to the troops forming the contingent of his Sardinian majesty; and in case the equipments to be restored shall exceed the wants of the contingent, the remainder shall be discharged in cash.

" 11. The two contracting powers shall immediately name commissioners to negotiate in their names a commercial treaty conformable to Art. 7, of the treaty of peace concluded at Paris between the French republic, and his majesty the King of Sardinia; in the meantime, the posts and all commercial relations shall be re-established without delay, as they were previous to the war.

" 12. The ratifications of the present treaty shall be exchanged at Paris with the least possible delay.

" Done and signed at Turin, the 16th Germinal, year 5, of the French republic, one and indivisible, (April 5, 1797, O.S.)

(Signed,)   " M. CLARKE.
CLÉMENT DAMIAN."

The directory did not avow its intentions openly, but it was evident that it did not intend to ratify the treaty. On the other hand, Napoleon persisted in considering this ratification indispensable. He attached importance, as was right, to a division of veteran Piedmontese soldiers, whose value he well knew. Considering himself as personally engaged to the court of Sardinia, he employed all his efforts to secure the interior tranquillity of the states of the king. Meantime, the Piedmontese malcontents became every day more numerous; they ran to arms and were defeated. This position was extremely delicate; it excited in the highest degree the dissatisfaction of the Jacobins in France and Italy; and when the royalist party had triumphed at Turin, the arrests and vexations which they allowed themselves to commit were a continual source of complaint at head-quarters.

At the end of September, the directory, when signing the ultimatum for the negotiations of Campo-Formio, gave Napoleon to understand that they persisted in refusing to ratify the treaty with Sardinia. The minister of foreign affairs, when communicating to him the resolution of the directory, advised him to cause the Sardinian soldiers to be corrupted by some of the Italian recruiters, which would enable him, he said, to obtain the assistance of the 10,000 Piedmontese troops, without any obligation to the court of Turin. But the officer's list of the troops was not to be corrupted; besides which, an operation of this kind could not be completed without losing too much time, for it was necessary to commence the campaign immediately.

This conduct on the part of the directory was one of the causes which decided Napoleon to sign the peace of Campo-Formio, without paying any attention to the ultimatum of the 29th of September, which, in his opinion, could not have been inserted in the protocol, without causing a rupture. In the meantime, the directory finally comprehended the importance of reinforcing the Italian army by the 10,000 men of the Piedmontese contingent; they decided upon ratifying the treaty of Turin, and sent it, on the 21st of October, to the legislative body; but it was too late; the peace of Campo-Formio had been concluded with Austria on the 17th.

Thus, after the campaigns of Napoleon in Italy, the King of Sardinia preserved his throne, weakened, it is true, by the loss of Savoy and Nice, having lost some of his fortresses, a few of which had been demolished, and some garrisoned by the French, but having acquired the immense advantage of becoming the ally of the French republic, which guaranteed to him the in-

tegrity of his states. This prince, however, did not
deceive himself as to his position; he knew that he
owed the preservation of his throne to Napoleon, and
was well aware how insincere was the apparent alliance
of the directory; he had been very near his downfall,
surrounded as he had been by the French, the Ligurian, and the Cisalpine democracies; he had still to
contend against the opinions of his people. The Piedmontese called loudly for a revolution, and the court
began to consider Sardinia as a haven of refuge.

The court of Rome had at first faithfully executed
the stipulations of the treaty of Tolentino; but in a
short time it allowed itself to be influenced by Cardinal Busca and by Albani. It began again to levy
troops, and had the imprudence openly to brave France,
by sending for General Provera to command them. It
even refused to recognise the Cisalpine republic. The
victorious position of the republic, and the threats of
its ambassador, promptly terminated these vain demonstrations of independence. Provera only remained a
few days at Rome, and then set out for Austria. The
Cisalpine republic, glad of the opportunity of taking
possession of some of the provinces belonging to the
papal dominions, declared war against the Vatican.
At the sight of the storm which threatened to burst
over them, these weak and imprudent old men humbled
themselves, and gave to the Cisalpine directory all the
satisfaction they demanded.

If in this conduct we find no trace of that ancient
policy which rendered the Vatican so illustrious during

the last centuries, we must remember that its government was worn out, and that the temporal power of the popes was entirely gone; it ended as the sovereignty of the ecclesiastical electors of the empire also ended.

The court of Naples was directed by the Queen, a woman of remarkable talents, but with ideas as much' disordered as were the passions which agitated her heart. The treaty of Paris of the 10th of October, 1796, had made no change in the dispositions of this cabinet, which did not cease making preparations, and giving trouble during the whole of the year 1797; and yet no treaty could be more favourable. It was conceived in the following terms:

" The French republic and his majesty the King of the Two Sicilies, equally animated with the desire of causing the advantages of peace to succeed the necessary evils of war, have named the following persons, to wit, for the executive directory, Citizen Charles Delacroix, minister of foreign affairs, and for his majesty the King of the Two Sicilies, Prince Belmonte Pignatelli, gentleman of the chamber, and minister plenipotentiary at the court of his Catholic Majesty, to treat in their name of the clauses and conditions proper to re-establish a good intelligence and friendship between these two powers; which persons, after having exchanged their full powers, have agreed upon the following articles:

" Art. 1. There shall be peace, friendship, and a good understanding between the French republic and his majesty the King of the Two Sicilies. In conse-

quence, all hostilities shall definitely cease, reckoning
from the day on which the ratifications of the present
treaty shall be exchanged.

"In the meantime, and until that period, the conditions agreed upon at the armistice of the 17th
Prairial, year 4, (June 4, 1796,) shall continue fully
and entirely in force.

"2. Every prior agreement, engagement or convention, on the part of either of the two contracting
parties, which may be contrary to the present treaty,
is hereby annulled, and is to be regarded as non-
existent; consequently, during the present war,
neither of the contracting powers shall furnish to any
enemy of the other, any assistance in troops, vessels,
arms or munitions of war, provisions, or money, under
any title or denomination whatsoever.

"3. His majesty the King of the Two Sicilies will
observe the strictest neutrality in respect to all the
belligerent powers; he will, therefore, engage to refuse
admittance into his ports to all vessels armed for war
belonging to the said powers, exceeding four in number,
according to the rules of the above-mentioned neutrality. All furnishing of ammunition, or of merchandise known under the name of contraband, shall
be refused to them.

"4. Every security and protection against their
enemies, shall be afforded to all merchant vessels of
the French republic, in whatever number, in all ports
and roadsteads of his majesty the King of the Two
Sicilies, and to all vessels of war belonging to the

republic, not exceeding the number specified in the preceding article.

" 5. The French republic and his majesty the King of the Two Sicilies engage to free from sequestration all effects, revenues, or goods, seized, confiscated or retained from citizens or subjects of either power, in consequence of the present war; and to admit them respectively to the exercise of any rights or privileges to which they may have legal claim.

" 6. All prisoners made on either side, including sailors and mariners, shall be restored within a month, reckoning from the date of the exchange of the ratification of the present treaty, after paying any debts contracted during their captivity; the sick and wounded shall remain in the hospitals until their recovery, when they shall be immediately sent back.

" 7. In order to give a proof of his friendship for the French republic, and of his desire to keep up a good understanding between the two powers, his majesty the King of the Two Sicilies consents to cause to be set at liberty every French citizen who may have been arrested within his dominions, on account of his political opinions in reference to the French revolution; all goods and chattels, which may have been sequestrated or confiscated for the same reason, shall be restored to their owners.

" 8. For the same reason which dictated the preceding article, his majesty the King of the Two Sicilies engages to cause all suitable search for, and to deliver up, if possible, to the rigour of the law, those persons who stole the papers belonging to the last minister of the republic at Naples in 1793.

" 9. The ambassadors or ministers of the contracting powers shall enjoy, in the respective states, the same prerogatives as they enjoyed before the war, with the exception of those which depended on the alliance of the ruling houses.

" 10. Every French citizen and every member of the household of an ambassador or minister, consul, or other agent, accredited and recognised by the French republic, shall enjoy, in the states of his majesty the King of the Two Sicilies, the same liberty of worship as is enjoyed by the individuals of those not Catholic nations most favoured in this respect.

" 11. A commercial treaty shall be negotiated and concluded as soon as possible, between the two powers, founded upon the basis of mutual utility, and such as to secure to the French nation advantages equal to those which the nations most favoured in this respect enjoy in the kingdom of the Two Sicilies. Until the conclusion of this treaty, the commercial and consular relations shall be reciprocally established, such as they were before the war.

" 12. Conformably to Art. 6, of the treaty concluded at the Hague the 27th of Floréal, year 3 of the republic (May 16, 1795), the same peace, friendship and good intelligence, agreed upon in the present treaty between the French republic and his majesty the King of the Two Sicilies, shall be considered to exist between his majesty and the Batavian republic.

" 13. The present treaty shall be ratified, and the ratifications exchanged within forty days from the day of signature.

" Done at Paris, the 19th of Vendemiaire, year 5 of the French republic, one and indivisible, corresponding to October, 10, 1796, O. S.

(Signed) " CHARLES DELACROIX,
" PRINCE DE BELMONTE PIGNATELLI."

Whilst Napoleon was on his march to threaten Rome, the Prince of Belmonte Pignatelli, the Neapolitan minister, who followed the head-quarters, showed him, in confidence, a letter from the Queen, in which she announced to him that she was about to march 30,000 men to cover Rome. " I thank you for this confidence," said the General, " and I will return it with another;" he rang for his secretary, sent for the Neapolitan portfolio, and took from it a despatch, which he had written to the directory in the month of November, 1796, before the taking of Mantua, and read: " The embarrassment which the approach of Alvinzi gives me, would not prevent me from sending 6000 Lombards and Poles to punish the court of Rome; but as it is to be foreseen that the King of Naples might march 30,000 men to the defence of the Holy See, I shall not march upon Rome till Mantua is taken, and the reinforcement you are sending me are arrived: in order that if the court of Naples should violate the treaty of Paris, I may be able to dispose of 25,000 men, with which I can take possession of their capital, and oblige them to retire to Sicily." An extraordinary courier, dispatched in the night by Prince Pignatelli, was, no doubt, commissioned to inform the queen how his insinuation had been received.

Since the treaty of Paris, the Neapolitan legations were generally more hostile and more arrogant towards the French, than during the time of war; and the Neapolitan ambassadors even asserted openly that the peace would not be of long duration. This absurd conduct did not prevent the cabinet of Naples from entertaining ambitious views; during the conferences of Montebello, of Udine, and of Passeriano, the envoy of the Queen of Naples endeavoured to obtain the islands of Corfu, Zante, Cephalonia, Santa-Maura, the Marches of Macerata, of Ferrara, of Ancona, and the duchy of Urbino; he even went so far as to express a desire of enriching himself, at the expense of the Pope and the republic of Venice; and these acquisitions the queen expected to obtain from the protection of France: and it was especially by the mediation of Napoleon, that she expected to obtain her wishes. The throne of Naples survived the peace of Campo-Formio; it would have maintained itself tranquil and happy in the midst of the storms which agitated Europe and Italy, if it had been directed by a sounder policy.

It had been found necessary to yield to the wishes of the Lombards, and to form them into a democratic state, under the name of the Transpadane republic.

This republic included all the left bank of the Po, from the Mincio to the Ticino. The Cispadane republic extended along the right bank of the Po, from the duchy of Parma, exclusive, to the Adriatic.

The constitution of the Cispadane republic had been decided upon in a congress of the representatives of the nation, and then submitted to the acceptance of the people; voted by an immense majority, it had been put in execution at the end of April. The nobles and the priests had been able to get themselves elected to all the offices; the citizens accused them of not being well-intentioned to the new order of things: the discontent was general. Napoleon perceived the necessity of giving a definite organization to these two states.

Immediately after the refusal of the court of Vienna to ratify the convention signed at Montebello, with the Marquis of Gallo, and which contained the basis of a definite peace, Napoleon created the Cispadane and Transpadane republics; which united under the same government 4,000,000 of inhabitants, and composed a force capable of influencing ulterior events. Notwithstanding, the authorities of the Cispadane obstinately refused a union so contrary to all their prejudices. The administrations of Reggio, Modena, Bologna, and Ferrara, submitted with difficulty to the necessity of combining under the same government. The spirit of locality everywhere opposed a resistance to the union of the two nations on the opposite banks of the Po; and the probability is, that this plan of union

would have been wrecked upon the obstinacy of the
people, if they had not been made to believe that this
was only a preliminary to the union of all the inhabitants of the peninsula under one government.   The
desire which all the Italians entertain of forming a
single great nation, overcame the petty jealousies of
the local administrations.   Two particular circumstances assisted this general cause.   Romagna, which
the Pope had ceded by the treaty of Tolentino, had
proclaimed itself independent under the title of the
Emilian republic; it had not chosen to unite with
the Cispadane, on account of its antipathy to Bologna,
but eagerly embraced the idea of joining the Cisalpine; and by numerous petitions it solicited the formation of this republic.   At the same time, Venice
and the states of the Continent, uneasy at the
mystery of the preliminaries, voted in the popular
assembly for the formation of the Italian republic.
These two circumstances smoothed down all the difficulties.   The spirit of locality gave way before public
spirit, private interest before general welfare ; the
union was decreed by common consent.

The new republic took the name of the Cisalpine
republic; Milan was its capital.   This was a fresh subject of dissatisfaction at Paris, where it was wished
that it should have been called the Transalpine republic; but the wishes of the Italians tending towards
Rome, and to the union of the whole peninsula in one
state, the denomination of Cisalpine was one which
flattered their wishes, and which they decided on

adopting, as they did not dare to call themselves the Italian republic.

By the treaty of Campo-Formio, the Cisalpine republic was increased by that part of the Venetian states situated on the right bank of the Adige, which, in addition to the Valteline, made for it a population of 3,600,000 souls. These provinces, the richest and most beautiful in Europe, composed six departments. They extended from the mountains of Switzerland to the Tuscan Apennines, and from the Ticino to the Adriatic.

Napoleon had wished to give the Cisalpine republic a constitution differing in some respects from that of France. He had requested some statesman, such as Sieyes, to be sent to him at Milan; but this idea did not please the directory; they required that the Cisalpine republic should receive the constitution which France had adopted in 1795. The first Cisalpine directory was composed of Serbelloni, Alessandri, Paradisi, Moscati, and Contarini, chiefs of the French party in Italy. Serbelloni was one of the greatest landed proprietors of Lombardy. The inauguration took place in the palace of Milan, on the 30th of June. The independence of the Cisalpine republic had been proclaimed on the 29th, in the following terms:

" The Cisalpine republic has been for a number of years under the government of the house of Austria. The French republic has succeeded them by right of conquest; but it renounces all power over the Cisalpine republic from this day, and proclaims it free and independent. Acknowledged as such by France and by the Emperor of Austria, it will soon be so by all the powers of Europe. The executive Directory of the French republic, not content with having employed its influence, and the victories of the French arms, to assure the existence of the Cisalpine republic, extends its care still further; and convinced that if liberty is the first of blessings, so a revolution which succeeds to it must be the greatest curse; it gives to the Cisalpine people its own constitution, which is the result of the knowledge of the most civilized nation of the world. The Cisalpine people will, therefore, pass from a military to a constitutional government. In order that this change may be effected without trouble or bad feeling, the executive directory has judged fit to name, for this time only, the members of the government and the legislative council; so that the people will only have to name the successors to the vacant places after the lapse of a year, according to the constitution. For a great number of years, no republic has existed in Italy. The sacred fire of liberty has been smothered, and the most beautiful part of Europe has groaned under the yoke of foreign lords. It will be the duty of the Cisalpine republic to convince the world by its wisdom, its prudence, and the good organization of its troops, that modern Italy has not degenerated, and that it is still worthy of liberty.

" Bonaparte, general-in-chief, in the name of the French republic, and in consequence of the preceding proclamation, hereby names the following as members of the directory of the Cisalpine republic—viz., the citizens Serbelloni, Alessandri, Moscati, Paradisi. The fifth shall be named in as short a time as possible. These four members shall be installed to-morrow, at Milan."

A general federation of the national guards and of the authorities of the new republic took place in the Lazaretto of Milan. On the 14th of July, 30,000 national guards and deputies of the departments took the oath of fraternity. They swore also to employ all their efforts for the recognition of liberty and of their country. The Cisalpine Directory named its ministers, the administrative authorities, constituted its military commands, and governed the republic like an independent state. The keys of Milan and of all the strong places were given up by the French officers to the Cisalpine officers. The army quitted the states of the republic, and encamped in the territory of Venice. From this period dates the first formation of the army of Italy, which was afterwards numerous and acquired so much glory.

From this moment the manners of the Italians quite changed; some years afterwards, they were no longer the same nation. The cassock, which had been the general dress for young people, was replaced by the uniform; instead of passing their lives at the feet of women, the young Italians frequented the riding-schools, the fencing-rooms, and the gymnastic exercises; the children even ceased to play at religious services ; they had regiments of tin soldiers, and imitated, in their play, the events of the war.

In plays or in the pieces performed in the streets, there was always an Italian who was represented as very cowardly, and a sort of bully captain, sometimes a Frenchman, but more often a German, very foolish, very brave, but very brutal, who generally ended by administering some gentle correction with a stick to the Italian, amidst great applause from the spectators. Now the people would no longer suffer such allusion; authors were obliged, in order to satisfy the public, to represent the Italians on the stage as brave, putting strangers to flight, in order to uphold their honour and their rights. The national feeling was roused and its spirit formed. Italy had songs at once patriotic and warlike; even the women repulsed with disdain those men, who, in order to please them, affected effeminate manners.

The Valteline is composed of three valleys. The Valteline, properly so called, the Bormio, and the Chiavenna; its population is about 160,000 souls; the inhabitants profess the Roman-catholic religion, and speak Italian. Geographically speaking, it belongs to Italy; it lies along the shore of the Adda, to its embouchure into the Lake of Como, and is separated from Germany by the high Alps. It is eighteen leagues long and six wide; Chiavenna, its capital, is situated two leagues from the Lake of Como, and four-teen leagues from Coire, from which Bormio is seven-teen leagues. It formed part, anciently, of the Milanese

territory, and was given by them to the church at
Coire, in 1404. In 1512, the Grisons were invested
with the sovereignty of the Valteline by Sforza.
by means of the capitularies, for whom the dukes
of Milan were expected to guarantee. The Valteline
was thus subject to the three Grisons, the inhabitants
of which mostly speak German, confess the Protestant
religion, and are separated from it by the high chain
of the Alps.

There is no situation more dreadful than that of
one nation subject to another. It was thus that the
lower Valais was subject to the higher Valais, and
that the Pays de Vaud was subject to Berne. The
unfortunate inhabitants of the Valteline had long
complained of the vexations which they experienced,
and of the humiliating yoke to which they were
obliged to submit. The Grisons, poor and ignorant,
came among them, who were the richer and more
civilized, to enrich themselves. The poorest peasant
of the Grison league considered the same distance to
exist between himself and the richest inhabitant of the
Valteline, as between a sovereign and his subject.
Surely, if any situation can justify a revolution, and
seem to make a change necessary, it is that in which
the Valteline then was.

In the course of May, 1797, the inhabitants of the
three valleys revolted, ran to arms, drove out the
representative of sovereignty, and mounted the Italian
tricolor flag; they then proceeded to name a temporary
governor, and addressed a manifesto to all the powers,

setting forth their wrongs, and expressing their resolution to reconquer those rights of which no people can be justly deprived. They sent as deputies to Montebello, Jindiconni, Planta, and Paribelli, men of worth and character, to demand the execution of the capitulations, which the Grisons had violated in every particular.

Napoleon had a dislike to interfere in any questions which might have reference to Switzerland, and which, in this point of view, were of general importance. However, having caused the documents relating to the affair, to be shown to him, which were preserved in the archives of Milan, he perceived that the Milanese government was called upon to give a guarantee; and as the Grison league also solicited his protection, to cause their subjects to re-enter into their allegiance; he accepted the office of mediator, and ordered the two parties to present themselves before his tribunal, in the course of the following month of July, to defend their respective rights. During this delay, the Grison league implored the assistance of the Helvetic body.

Barthélemy, the French minister at Berne, solicited warmly in their favour. At length, after many proceedings on both sides, Napoleon, before giving a final decision, advised the two parties to have recourse to an amicable arrangement, and proposed to them, as a means of conciliation, that the Valteline should make a fourth in the Grison league, equal in everything to the three others. This advice deeply wounded the pride of the Grison peasants. *They could not understand how a peasant who drank the waters of the Adda, could be the equal of one who drank the waters of the Rhine.* They were indignant at such an unreasonable proposal as that of *equalling catholic peasants, speaking Italian, rich and enlightened,* with *protestant peasants, speaking German, poor and ignorant.* The ringleaders did not share these prejudices, but they were led astray by their interests. The Valteline was for them a very important source of revenue and of riches, which they could not resolve upon giving up. They intrigued at Paris, at Vienna, at Berne. Everywhere they received promises; they were advised to gain time; they were blamed for having invited and accepted any mediation. They declined making any arrangement, and did not even send any deputies at the time appointed for discussing, before their mediator, the question regarding the treaties, in opposition to the deputies of the Valteline.

Napoleon condemned the Grison league by default ; and as an arbitrator chosen by the two parties, and the representative of the Milanese government which had guaranteed the capitulations of the Valtelins, he pronounced his judgment in these terms, on the 19th Vendemiaire, year 6 (October 10th, 1797) :

" The inhabitants of the Valteline, Chiavenna, and Bormio, revolted against the laws of the Grisons, and declared themselves independent during last Prairial. The government of the Grison republic, after having employed other means to reduce its subjects to obedience, had recourse to the mediation of the French republic in the person of General Bonaparte, and sent to him as their deputy, Gaudanzio Planta.

" The inhabitants of the Valteline having also demanded the same mediation, the general-in-chief received the respective deputations at Montebello, on the 4th of Mestidor (June 22nd); and, after a long conference, accepted, in the name of the French republic, the office of mediator. He then wrote to the Grisons, and to the Valtelins, to send deputies to him as soon as possible.

" The inhabitants of the Valteline, Chiavenna, and Bormio sent punctually the required deputies.

" Several months have elapsed, and the Grison government has not yet dispatched any, notwithstanding the repeated requests of Citizen Comoyras, president of the republic at Coire.

" On the 6th of last Fructidor (August 23), the general-in-chief, seeing the anarchy in which the Valteline was plunged, caused a letter to be written to the Grison government, desiring them to send deputies before the 24th of Fructidor (September 10.)

" It is now the 19th of Vendemiaire (October 10), and the deputies from the Grisons have not made their appearance.

" Not only have they not appeared, but there is no doubt that, in contempt of the mediation accepted by the French republic, the Grison league has prejudged the question, and that the refusal to send deputies is the result of powerful intrigues.

" Consequently, the general-in-chief, in the name of the French republic:

" Considering—1st. That the good faith, the upright conduct, and the confidence of the inhabitants of the Valteline, Chiavenna, and Bormio, in respect to the French republic, obliges the latter to reciprocate these qualities, and to assist them.

" 2nd. That the French republic, in consequence of the request made by the Grisons, is become arbitrator and mediator between these two nations.

" 3rd. That there is no doubt that the Grisons have violated the capitulations which they were bound to observe in respect to the inhabitants of the Valteline, Chiavenna, and Bormio; and that, consequently, the latter have re-entered into the rights which nature has given all nations.

4th. " That one people cannot be subject to another, without violating the principles of public and natural law.

" 5th. That the wishes of the inhabitants of the Valteline, Chiavenna, and Bormio tend very decidedly to the Cisalpine republic.

" 6th. That the conformity of religion and of language, the nature of the locality, of communication, and of commerce, equally authorize this union of the Valteline, Chiavenna, and Bormio, with the Cisalpine republic, from which it was formerly separated.

" 7th. That since the decree of the communes com·
posing the Grison league, the proposal of organizing
the Valteline, as a fourth component part of the
Grison league, has been rejected; that, consequently,
the Valteline has no other refuge against the tyranny
of the Grisons, than by a union with the Cisalpine
republic;

" Decrees, by virtue of the authority with which
the French republic is invested, by means of the
request which the Grisons and the Valteline made for
its mediation, · that the Valteline, Chiavenna, and
Bormio are at liberty to unite themselves to the Cisalpine republic."

The question was thus decided.   Bursts of joy and
of enthusiasm animated the unfortunate inhabitants
of the Valteline; rage and humiliated pride produced
the contrary effects among the Grisons.

Immediately after this decree, the Valteline and
the Cisalpine republics began to negotiate their
union. The Grisons then perceived their fault. They
wrote to Napoleon, that their deputies were setting
out to defend their rights before him, thus pretending
to be ignorant of what had taken place. He answered
them, that it was too late; that his decision had
been given on the 10th of October, and that the Valteline was already united to the Cisalpine republic;
that the question, therefore, was set at rest for ever.

The justice which had thus been done to this little
nation, produced a favourable effect upon every
generous mind.

The principles upon which the judgment of Napoleon was founded, spread abroad throughout all Europe, and gave a mortal blow to the usurpation of the Swiss cantons, who had nations for their subjects. The aristocracy of Berne should have been enlightened by this example, and should have felt that the moment was come to make some sacrifices to the increasing light of the age, to the influence of France, and its justice. But prejudice and pride never listen to the voice of reason, of nature, or of religion. An oligarchy only yields to force. It was not till many years afterwards that the inhabitants of the higher Valais consented to regard those of the lower Valais as their equals, and that the peasants of the Pays de Vaud and of Aargau forced the oligarchs of Berne to acknowledge their rights and their independence.

CHAPTER VII.

PEACE OF CAMPO-FORMIO.

THE exchange of the ratifications of the preliminaries of Léoben took place at Montebello, on the
26th of May, between Napoleon and the Marquis de
Gallo. A question of etiquette arose for the first
time; the Emperors of Germany were not in the
habit of giving the alternative to the Kings of France,
and the cabinet of Vienna was fearful that the republic would refuse to recognise this custom, and
that, in imitation of its example, the other powers of
Europe would cease to allow the Emperor to assume
that kind of supremacy, which had always been conceded to the holy Roman empire since the days of
Charlemagne. It was in the first moments of his joyful
intoxication, at the acquiescence of the plenipotentiary of France in this ancient usage, that the representative of Austria renounced the idea of a congress

at Berne, consented to a separate negotiation, and
agreed not to open the congress of Rastadt, with a view
to the settlement of a peace for the empire, till the
following July.   In a few days, the contracting
parties came to an understanding on the terms of a
definitive treaty, on the following basis:—1st, the
Rhine to be the boundary of France; 2ndly, Venice
and the river Adige to constitute the boundaries of
the Austrian dominions in Italy; 3rdly, Mantua and
the Adige to be the limits of the Cisalpine republic.
The Marquis de Gallo declared, that by the next
courier he had no doubt of receiving powers *ad hoc*
to sign a treaty founded on these bases.   On the 6th
of May, Napoleon and General Clarke had received
the necessary authority from France.   The conditions
were more favourable to France than the directory
had dared to hope; and the peace, therefore, might be
considered as concluded.

At the time of the revolution, Clarke had been a
captain in the Orleans regiment of dragoons, and from
1789 he followed the party of Orleans.   In 1795, he
was called to the aid of the Committee of Public
Safety, and appointed to conduct the topographical
department.   Being specially protected by Carnot, he
was selected by the Directory, in 1796, to make overtures of peace to the Emperor, and for this purpose
went to Milan.   The real object of the journey was
not to open a negotiation, but to be present at head
quarters as the secret agent of the Directory, and to
exercise a species of *surveillance* over the General,

whose victories began to give some degree of umbrage.
Clarke sent notes to Paris with his observations upon
the leading persons in the army, which excited murmurs, and exposed him to disagreeable consequences.
Napoleon, convinced that government stood in need
of instruction, preferred confiding this secret mission
to a known man, to entrusting it to subaltern agents,
who are prone to collect in the wine-shops and ante-
chambers the greatest absurdities; he therefore protected Clarke, and employed him in various negotiations with the King of Sardinia and the princes of
Italy.   After the 18th Fructidor, he defended him
with warmth, not only because he had found means of
gaining his esteem, but also because he thought it
becoming his dignity to defend a man with whom he
had been long in habits of daily intercourse, and of
whom he had no ostensible reason to complain. Clarke
had not a military mind; he was a man of business,—
a careful and honourable worker, and a great enemy
to all knavery. He was descended from an Irish
family, which had accompanied the Stuarts in their
misfortunes.   Proud of his descent, he rendered himself ridiculous under the empire by means of genealo-
gical researches, which formed the strongest contrast
with the opinions which he had professed, the career
he had run, and the circumstances of the age in which
he lived; this was an absurdity. But this failing did not
prevent the Emperor Napoleon from entrusting him with
the portfolio of the war department, as he considered
him a good administrator, who ought to be attached

to his interests in consequence of the favours which had been heaped upon him. Under the empire he rendered very important services, by the integrity of his administration; and for the sake of his memory it must ever be a subject of regret, that at the close of his career he formed part of a ministry which must for ever bear the bitter reproach of France, for having made her pass under the *Caudine forks*, by disbanding the army which had been the glory of the nation for twenty-five years, and, to the astonishment of her enemies, delivering into their hands places which were still impregnable.

If, in 1814 and 1815, the royal confidence had not been placed in men whose souls were humbled by the force of circumstances, or who, being renegades to their country, saw neither safety nor glory for the throne of their master, except under the yoke of the Holy Alliance—had the Duke of Richelieu, whose ambition it was to deliver the country from the presence of foreign bayonets—had Chateaubriand, who had just rendered such eminent services at Ghent, been entrusted with the direction of public affairs, France would still have come forth powerful and terrible from these two great national crises. Chateaubriand had received the holy fire from nature; his works attest it, his style is not that of Racine, but that of a prophet; there was no man in the world, except himself, who could have ventured to say with impunity in the tribune of the Chamber of Peers, that *if Bonaparte's grey riding-coat and his three-*

*cocked hat were placed upon a stick on the coast
of Brest, it would cause all Europe to rush to
arms.* Should he ever come to the helm of affairs, it
is quite possible that Chateaubriand may fail, as so
many other great men have done; but it is certain
that everything which is grand and national ought to
harmonize with his genius, and that he would repel
with indignation all inducements to perform those
infamous arts by which the administrations of those
times disgraced themselves. Count Meerfeld, the new
Austrian plenipotentiary, arrived at Montebello on the
19th of June. The cabinet disavowed the Marquis de
Gallo, and persisted in not treating for a peace except
at the congress of Berne, and in conjunction with its
allies. Austria had evidently changed her system. Had
she become a party to a new coalition? Did she place
her confidence in Russian armies? Was it one of the
effects of Pichegru's conspiracy? Were hopes now
entertained that the civil war, which then desolated
the west of France, would spread over the whole
country, and the power fall into the hands of the conspirators?

The Austrian plenipotentiaries admitted that they
had no answer to make, when Bonaparte observed to
them that England and Russia would never consent
to the Emperor's indemnifying himself at the expense
of the ancient state of Venice; and that, to refuse to
negotiate, except in concert with these powers, was
in effect the same as to proclaim their intention of
once more having recourse to the chances of war.

The minister Thugut sent new instructions; he gave up the congress of Berne, and adhered to the principle of a separate negotiation.

The negotiations were opened at Udine on the 1st of July, at which General Clarke alone was present on the part of France. Napoleon announced that he would not join in the deliberations till he had seen from the minutes of the conferences that the Austrian ministers were really desirous of concluding a peace, and empowered to bring it to a conclusion. A few days afterwards, he left Montebello and proceeded to Milan, where he remained during the months of July and August. Austria was watching with anxiety the issue of the crisis which was agitating France, and these two months were passed in useless conferences. The 18th of Fructidor, however, destroyed all their hopes, and Count Cobentzel proceeded in all haste to Udine, armed with full powers from the Emperor, whose entire confidence he possessed. The Marquis de Gallo, Count Meerfield, and Baron Engelmann, took part in the negotiation, but really only figured there for mere form.

Napoleon went to Passeriano, and Clarke having been recalled, he found himself sole plenipotentiary for France. On the 16th of September, negotiations were commenced with Count Cobentzel. The conferences were alternately held at Udine and Passeriano. The four Austrian plenipotentiaries occupied the one side of a rectangular table, at the ends of which were seated the secretaries of legation, whilst the other side

was occupied by the French plenipotentiary alone.
When the conference was held at Passeriano, the
whole party dined with Napoleon, and when at Udine
they dined at the quarters of Count Cobentzel.
Passeriano is a charming country house, on the banks
of the Tagliamento, four leagues from Udine, and
three from the ruins of Aquileia. After the first
conference, Count Cobentzel disavowed all that his colleagues had been saying for four months past; he put
forward extravagant pretensions, and it was found
necessary to recommence that system of assumption
and bullying which had been exercised since the month
of May. The course to be pursued with such a negotiator was obvious; it was necessary to retire as far
from any just middle course on the one side, as he
continually did on the other.

Count Cobentzel was a native of Brussels; extremely agreeable in society, and of the most refined
manners, but obstinate and intractable in matters of
business. His reasoning was deficient in justness and
precision; he was conscious of the deficiency, and
attempted to supply the want by pomposity of expressions and imperious gesticulations.

The Marquis de Gallo, minister of Naples at Vienna,
enjoyed at the same time the favour of the Queen of
Naples and that of the Empress. He was insinuating
and supple in his manner, but honourable in disposition.

Count Meerfeld, colonel of a Hulan regiment, had
attracted notice, and succeeded in gaining the con-

fidence of Baron Thugut, the Austrian minister. Engelmann was a man of office and detail, of upright mind
and good intentions.

After the arrival of Count Cobentzel, the progress
of the negotiation was such as to leave no reason to
doubt that Austria was sincere in her desires for a
peace; that she had contracted no new engagements
with England or Russia. The Austrian negotiators
having arrived at the conviction, that a peace was not
to be concluded except by the adoption of the bases
which had been laid down in the preliminaries of
Montebello, it would have been immediately concluded
had not the directory changed its policy. The 18th
of Fructidor blinded its members as to their real
power, and they thought they could demand new
sacrifices from the nation with impunity. They
caused it to be insinuated to Napoleon, that it would
be well to break off the negotiations and to re-commence hostilities, at the same time that the official
correspondence was always dictated in the spirit of
the instructions of the 6th of May. It was evident,
they desired war, but wished to throw the responsibility of the rupture upon the shoulders of the
negotiator. When it was seen that this move was
completely unsuccessful, and they believed their power
to be consolidated, they sent their *ultimatum* in a
despatch, dated the 29th of September.

Napoleon received the despatch on the 6th of
October, at Passeriano. France was now unwilling
to cede to the Emperor either the territory of Venice

or the frontier of the Adige; this was equivalent to a declaratioa of war.

Napoleon, however, had fixed ideas of his own upon the degree of obedience which he owed to his government, in reference to the proper discharge of his military duties.   He did not consider himself bound to execute the orders of the government, except merely in as far as he thought them reasonable, and their success probable.   He would have regarded himself as guilty of a crime, if he had consented to execute a mischievous plan, and, in such a case, would have offered his resignation, which was, in fact, the course which he pursued in 1796, when the directory was desirous of sending a part of his army into the kingdom of Naples.

His ideas were not so completely fixed respecting the degree of obedience which he was bound to render as a plenipotentiary. Could he send in his resignation in the very midst of a negotiation, or compromise the issue of it, by executing orders with which he could not agree, and which were, in fact, equivalent to a declaration of war?   But his principal character at Passeriano was that of a commander-in-chief.   It appeared to him absurd to declare war in his character of a plenipotentiary, when he would, at the same time, feel himself constrained, as a general, to desert his office, in order not to commence hostilities, entered upon against his judgment.

The minister for foreign affairs delivered him from his anxiety. In one of his despatches, he informed him, that the directory, in determining upon its *ultimatum*, had been of opinion that the general-in-chief was in a condition to compel its acceptance by force of arms. He reflected long and deeply on this communication, and the result was, a conviction that he held in his hands the fate of France; that peace or war was dependent on the course which he chose to pursue. He decided upon adhering to the instructions of the 6th of May, and signing the peace upon the bases agreed to at Montebello, which had been approved of by the government before the 18th Fructidor.

The motives by which he was determined, were—
1stly. That the general plan of the campaign was faulty.
2ndly. That, not having received the *ultimatum* till the 6th of October, the war could not be re-commenced till the 15th of November, and that it would then be very difficult for the French armies to penetrate into Germany, whilst the season would be favourable for collecting a great number of Austrian troops in the plains of Italy. 3rdly. That the command of the army was entrusted to Augereau, whose political aspirations had been greatly exalted by the events of Fructidor, and his staff chiefly composed of Séids of the propaganda, intoxicated with the principles of 1793, which was an insurmountable obstacle to that agreement which must necessarily exist between two armies engaged in the pursuit of the same object.

Napoleon had expressed a wish that the command of the army of the Rhine should be given to Desaix, on the defection of Moreau. 4thly. Because he had requested a re-inforcement of 12,000 infantry, and 4000 cavalry, which had been refused; he had only in his army 50,000 troops of the line, and was, meantime, twenty days' march nearer Vienna than the army of the Rhine, having to contend against three-fourths of the whole Austrian forces, which covered Vienna on the side of Italy, whilst a mere corps of observation was opposed to the armies of the Rhine and Moselle, the Sambre and Meuse. 5thly. Because the directory, in its madness, in the despatch of the 29th of September, had announced its intention of refusing to ratify the treaty of alliance, offensive and defensive, which had been concluded with the King of Sardinia, on the 5th of April preceding. By the terms of this treaty, the king had engaged to furnish a contingent to the army of Italy, consisting of 8000 infantry, 2000 cavalry, and forty pieces of cannon. This refusal of the directory caused a general consternation in Turin; the court could no longer fail to see the design of the French government; it had nothing more to care for. It would be necessary, therefore, to weaken the army of Italy to the amount of 10,000 men, in order to reinforce the garrisons of Piedmont and Lombardy.

On the 21st of October, the directory caused it to be made known, that, in compliance with the wishes of the commander-in-chief in Italy, they had resolved to reinforce the army in that country by 6000 men drawn from the army of the Rhine; to modify the plan of the campaign according to his desire; and finally, to ratify the treaty of alliance, offensive and defensive, with the King of Sardinia; and that they had communicated their intentions to the legislative body on the same day—the 21st of October.

The treaty of Campo-Formio had, however, been signed three days before this despatch was written, and it did not reach Passeriano till twelve days after the signature of the peace. Had the directory adopted this resolution on the 29th of September, the day on which it decided on the terms of the *ultimatum*, Bonaparte would, perhaps, have decided on going to war, with a view of delivering the whole of Italy as far as the Isonzo, of which he was more desirous than any other person.

It was the interest of Napoleon to conclude a peace. The republicans, on their part, manifested extreme jealousy—" So much glory," they said, " is incompatible with liberty." Had he recommenced hostilities, and the French armies gained possession of Vienna, the directory, persevering and zealous in the spirit which had actuated its members since the 18th of Fructidor, would have made the greatest efforts to revolutionize the empire, and this would indubitably have led to a new war with Prussia, Russia, and the Germanic confederation. The republic, however, was ill governed; the administration was corrupt, and inspired neither confidence nor consideration. If he broke off the negotiations, the responsibility of the consequences would rest upon him; if, on the con-

trary, he gave peace to his country, he would add to
the glory of a conqueror and pacificator, that of being
the founder of two great republics; for Belgium, the
departments on the Rhine, Savoy and the county of
Nice, could not legitimately be incorporated with
France, except by means of a treaty of peace with the
Emperor, which was equally necessary for the consolidation of the Cisalpine republic. Covered with laurels,
and with the olive branch in his hand, he would then
retire with safety into private life, with a glory equal
to that of the most renowned heroes of antiquity; the
first act of the drama of his public life would be thus
terminated; circumstances and the interests of the
country would decide his subsequent career; glory, the
love and esteem of the French people, were the means
of arriving at everything.   France wished for peace.

The struggle of kings against the republic was a
struggle of principles; it was the Ghibellines against
the Guelphs—it was the oligarchs who reigned in
London, Vienna and Petersburg, struggling against
the republicans of Paris.   The French plenipotentiary conceived the idea of changing this condition
of things, which always left France alone against the
others combined—of throwing an apple of discord
among the allies; of changing the state of the question,
and creating new passions and new interests.   The
republic of Venice was completely aristocratical, and
the courts of St. James and Petersburg took a lively
interest in its fate; and the house of Austria, by

seizing on Venice and its territory, would excite their highest dissatisfaction and jealousy.

The senate of Venice had behaved badly to France, but very well to Austria. What opinion would the nations entertain of the morality of the cabinet of Vienna, when they saw it appropriate to itself the states of the Austrian allies—above all, the most ancient state of modern Europe, which maintained principles strongly opposed to those of the French democrats; and that under the pretext of convenience alone?

What a lesson would this be for Bavaria and the other powers of the second order; the Emperor would be obliged to deliver up to France the fortress of Mayence, which he only held as a deposit; he would appropriate to himself the spoils of the German princes, of whom he was the legal and constituted protector, and whose armies were fighting in his ranks. All this would exhibit to the view of Europe a bitter satire on absolute governments and European oligarchies—would make their old age obvious to all, and announce that the time of their decadence and dissolution had arrived.

Austria would be satisfied, for if she ceded Belgium and Lombardy, she received an equivalent, if not in revenue and population, at least in reference to geographical and commercial position. Venice was bounded by Styria, Carinthia, and Hungary. The league of the European oligarchy would be divided; France would avail herself of the opportunity to join issue hand to hand with England, in Ireland, Canada, and the Indies.

The different parties into which the Venetians were divided became immediately extinct; aristocrats and democrats united against the sceptre of a foreign nation. No fears could be entertained that a people of such mild manners would adopt any affection for a German government; that a great commercial city and naval power would sincerely attach herself to a monarchy foreign to the sea and destitute of colonies; and if ever the moment should arrive for calling the Italian nation into life, this circumstance would prove no obstacle. The years the Venetians would have passed under the yoke of the Austrian government, would lead them to receive a national government with enthusiasm, whatsoever it might be, a little more or a little less aristocratic, whether the capital was fixed at Venice or not.

The Venetians, Lombards, and Piedmontese, the Genoese, with the people of Parma, Bologna, and Bergamo; the Ferrarese, Tuscans, Romans, and Neapolitans, all required to be reduced to their first elements before they could be converted into one Italian state. It was necessary, so to speak, to recast them. In fact, fifteen years afterwards, in 1812, the Austrian power in Italy, the throne of Sardinia, those of the Dukes of Parma, Modena, and Tuscany; that of Naples itself, the oligarchies of Genoa and Venice, had all disappeared. The temporal power of the Pope, which in all past time had been the cause of the division of Italy, was no longer likely to be an obstacle. The grand duchy of Berg had still remained vacant, and was waiting for the court of King Joachim. "I require," Napoleon had said, in 1805, at the council of Lyons, " *twenty years to create the Italian nation.*" Fifteen years had sufficed; all was ready, and he only waited for the birth of a second son, to conduct him to Rome, crown him King of the Italians, confer the regency on Prince Eugene, and proclaim the independence of the Peninsula from the Alps to the Ionian Sea, from the Mediterranean to the Adriatic.

The court of Vienna, worn out with the bloody struggle which she had sustained for several years, no longer attached any importance to Belgium, which it was impossible for her to defend; she considered herself fortunate, after so many disasters, in obtaining indemnities for losses which were beyond recovery, and in contracting an alliance with France, which would guarantee to her advantages in the arrangement of German affairs. Although, however, a perfect understanding was arrived at respecting the *principles*, the contracting parties were far from being agreed on the *mode* in which the execution was to be effected. Count Cobentzel said, " He would have the Adda for a frontier, or nothing." He supported his pretensions on statistical calculations. " You wish," said he, " to re-establish the system of 1756; for that purpose it is necessary to give us an advantageous peace, which may be decided on, irrespective of the events of the war; both powers have had their glorious

days ; our armies ought mutually to esteem each
other; and a disadvantageous peace for one of the
powers, would prove nothing better than a truce.   In
consenting to this principle, how is it you refuse to
grant us a complete and absolute indemnity?   What
are the bases of power?   Population and revenue.
What losses does the Emperor my master sustain?
Belgium and Lombardy, the two most populous and
richest provinces in the world—Belgium, which is of
double value to you, because it ensures you the possession of Holland, and will enable you to close all the
ports against England, from the Baltic to the Straits
of Gibraltar.   We consent, moreover, to concede to the
republic, Mayence, the four departments of the Rhine,
Savoy, and the county of Nice.   What do we ask of
you in return for such extensive concession?   Four
millions of Italians—bad soldiers, but inhabiting, it is
true, a very fertile country; we have, then, a right to
look for the valley of the Adda as our frontier."

The French plenipotentiary replied, " It is an advantage to Austria to be relieved of Belgium, which
was a burthensome possession; England alone could
have an interest in her retaining possession of it.   If
you calculate what that province has cost you, you
will be convinced that it has always been an object of
expense to your treasury.   But in no case can it any
longer be of any particular value to us, because the
new principles which have changed the state of
France have been already adopted there.   To desire

to obtain in the very frontiers of Styria, Carinthia, and Hungary, an indemnity equal in revenue and population to a distant and detached province, is an exaggerated pretension; besides, by passing the Adige you will weaken yourselves, and neither you nor the Cisalpine republic will have a frontier."

These reasonings probably produced a conviction in the minds of the Austrian plenipotentiaries—however that may be, they reduced their pretensions to the line of the Mincio. "But," said Count Cobentzel, "that is our *ultimatum*, for were my master, the Emperor, to consent to give you up the keys of Mayence, the strongest place in the universe, without exchanging them for the keys of Mantua, it would entail dishonour and disgrace." All the official means of protocols, notes and replies, having been exhausted without any satisfactory results, recourse was had to confidential conferences; at last, however, nothing further could be gained or conceded on either side, and the armies were put in motion.

The French troops, which were cantoned in the districts of Verona, Padua, and Treviso, passed the Piave, and established themselves on the right bank of the Isonzo. The Austrian army was encamped upon the Drave and in Carniola. On their way from Udine to Passeriano, the Austrian ambassadors were obliged to traverse the French camp. They were received with the highest military honours, and the conferences were accompanied by the continual rolling

of drums.   Count Cobentzel, however, remained immoveable.   The carriages were ready, and he announced his departure.

On the 16th of October, the conferences were held
at Udine, at the quarters of Count Cobentzel.   Napoleon recapitulated, in form of a manifesto to be entered
on the minutes, the course of conduct pursued by
the French government since the signing of the preliminaries of Léoben, and at the same time renewed
his ultimatum.

The Austrian ambassador made a long reply, in
order to prove that the indemnities offered by France
were not equivalent to the fourth of what he had lost;
that the Austrian power would be considerably
weakened, whilst the French power would be increased
to such a degree, as seriously to threaten the independence of Europe; that with the possession of Man·
tua and the Adige as a frontier, France would in
reality unite the whole of Italy to the territory of the
Gauls; that the Emperor was irrevocably resolved to
hazard all the chances of a war, and to take refuge
even in his capital, rather than consent to such a disadvantageous peace ; that Russia offered him assistance, that her armies were ready to march to his aid,
and then it would be seen what Russian troops were;
that it was very evident, Napoleon had sunk his character of a plenipotentiary in that of a general, and
did not, therefore, wish for peace.   He added that he
would take his departure during the night, and that
all the blood which might be shed in this new struggle

would fall on the head of the representative of
France.   Then the latter, with great coolness, but
deeply offended by this outbreak, rose from his seat,
and took from a cupboard a small porcelain tray,
which Count Cobentzel liked, as having been a present
from the Empress Catherine; " Well!" said Napoleon,
" the truce is broken and war declared!   But remember, that before the end of autumn, I will break your
monarchy to pieces, as I now dash this porcelain into
fragments." As he said these words, he dashed the porcelain upon the ground, and its fragments were strewed
over the floor. He saluted the congress, and departed.
The Austrian plenipotentiaries stood speechless.   A
few moments after, they heard that whilst he was get-
ting into his carriage, he had dispatched an officer to
Prince Charles, to give him notice that the truce was
broken, and that hostilities would re-commence in
twenty-four hours.   Count Cobentzel, alarmed at the
prospect, sent the Marquis de Gallo to Passeriano,
carrying with him a signed declaration, that he consented to adopt the ultimatum of France.   On the next
day, the 17th of October, the peace was signed, at five
o'clock in the evening.   It was on this occasion, that the
secretary who framed the treaty, having inserted, as
the first article, " The Emperor of Germany recognises
the French republic," Napoleon said, " Put out that
article; the French republic is like the sun; he who cannot see it must be blind.   The French people are
masters at home; they have created a republic—to-
morrow, perhaps, it may become an aristocracy, and

the day after, a monarchy. This is its imprescriptiblé
right, and the form of its government is a question of
home, and not of foreign affairs." The treaty was
dated at Campo-Formio, a small village between Passeriano and Udine, which had been declared neutral by
the secretaries of legation for that purpose. It was
thought advisable to go there, although there was no
house fit to serve as a lodging for the plenipotentiaries.

By this treaty, the Emperor recognised to the
republic its natural boundaries, the Alps, the Mediterranean, the Pyrenees, and the ocean—consented to
the formation of the Cisalpine republic by the amalgamation of Lombardy, the duchies of Reggio, Modena,
and Mirandola—the three legations (Bologna, Ferrara,
and Romagna), the Valteline, the Venetian states on the
right bank of the Adige (those of Bergamo, Cremona,
and Polesina) and ceded the Breisgau, which removed
the hereditary states to a distance from the French
frontiers. It was agreed that the fortifications of Mayence should be put into possession of the troops of the
republic, after a military convention to be agreed
upon at Rastadt, where the French plenipotentiary
and Count Cobentzel were to meet. All the princes
deprived of their territories on the left bank of the
Rhine, were to receive indemnities on the right bank,
by the secularization of the ecclesiastical states. The
peace of Europe was to be settled at Rastadt. The
cabinet of the Luxembourg and that of Vienna were to
co-operate. The Prussian territory, on the left bank,
was reserved; and it was agreed, that it should be

ceded to the republic by the treaty of Rastadt, but
with an equivalent in Germany for Austria. Corfu,
Zante, Cephalonia, Santa Maura, and Cerigo, were
ceded to France, which, on its part, consented to the
Emperor's taking possession of the Venetian states
situated on the left bank of the Adige, which would
add more than two millions of people to the population
of the empire. By one of the articles, the property
possessed by the Archduke Charles, as heir to the
Archduchess Christina in Belgium was assured to
him; it was in consequence of this article, that the
Emperor Napoleon, at a later period, purchased for a
million of francs the chateau of Laeken, near Brussels,
which before the revolution constituted a part of the
property of the Archduchess; the other domains belonging to the Archduke in the Netherlands, were
obtained by the Duke of Saxe-Teschen. This stipula-
tion was a testimony of esteem which the French
plenipotentiary gave to the general against whom he
had just been fighting, and with whom he had kept
up relations honourable to both.

During the conferences at Passeriano, General
Desaix came from the army of the Rhine, to inspect
the battle-fields which had been rendered illustrious
and memorable by the army of Italy. Napoleon
received him at his head-quarters, and thinking to
astonish him, made him acquainted with the light
which the portfolio of Entraigues had thrown upon
the conduct of Pichegru. " I knew long ago," said
Desaix, smiling, " that Pichegru was a traitor :

Moreau found proofs of it in the papers of Klinglin, as well as the details of the corruption, and of the reasons by which his military manœuvres were regulated. Moreau, Regnier, and myself only were in the secret. I wished Moreau immediately to give an account of it to the government, but he refused. Pichegru," added he, " is perhaps the only example of a general who purposely allowed himself to be defeated." He alluded to the manœuvre by which Pichegru removed the principal part of his forces to Rassein on the upper Rhine, in order to cripple the operations before May-ence. Desaix visited all the battle-fields, where he was received with the greatest distinction. It is from this period that his intimate friendship with Napo-leon dates; he loved glory for itself, and France above everything. He was a man of a simple, active, and prepossessing character, and of extensive informa-tion; no man was more thoroughly acquainted than he with the theatre of war on the upper Rhine, Suabia and Bavaria. His death caused tears to flow from the eyes of the conqueror of Marengo.

About this time, General Hoche, the commander of the army of the Sambre and Meuse, died suddenly at Mayence. Many persons have supposed that he was poisoned, but the supposition has no foundation what-ever. This young general distinguished himself at the lines of Weissenburg in 1794, gave abundant proofs of his abilities in La Vendée in 1795 and 1796, and had the glory of pacifying, for a time, that dis-turbed province. Influenced by a noble patriotism, an ardent disposition, remarkable bravery, and an active, restless ambition, he did not know how to wait for the course of events, but always exposed himself by premature enterprises. By marching his troops to Paris at the crisis of the 18th Fructidor, he violated the constitution, and was very near falling a victim to his temerity. He attempted an expedition to Ireland; no one was more capable of promoting its success. On every occasion, he testified his attachment to Napoleon. His death, and the disgrace of Moreau, left both the armies of the Rhine, and the Sambre and Meuse, without commanders. The government united these two armies into one, and gave the command of the whole to Augereau.

Napoleon successively sent the principal generals to Paris with stands of colours, which at once served as a means of making the government acquainted with their persons, and of attaching them to their cause by suitable rewards. He commissioned General Berthier to be the bearer of the treaty of Campo-Formio, and wishing at the same time to give a proof of his respect for science, he associated with him, in the commission, Monge, who was a member of the commission of the arts and sciences in Italy, and who belonged to the old Academy of Sciences. The commander-in-chief took great pleasure in the very interesting conversation of this great geometrician and naturalist of the first order, who was a very zealous patriot, but always pure-minded, sincere, and truthful. Loving France and its people as if they were his own children, he regarded democracy and equality as the results of a geometrical demonstration; he was of an ardent mind, but, whatever his enemies may have said, an honest man; on the invasion of the Prussians in 1792, he offered to give his two daughters in marriage to the first two volunteers who should lose a limb in the defence of the territory of France, which offer on his part was sincere. He followed Napoleon to Egypt, and science is indebted to him for his excellent work on descriptive geometry.

The treaty of Campo-Formio took the directory by surprise; it was far from expecting such a result, and gave indications of its dissatisfaction. It is confidently said, that its members thought for a moment of not ratifying it, but public opinion was too clearly pronounced, and the advantages secured to France by the peace were too obvious to admit of such a course.

Immediately after the signature of the peace, Napoleon returned to Milan to put a finishing hand to the organization of the Cisalpine republic, and to complete the administrative measures of his army. He was then to proceed to Rastadt, in order to terminate the great work of a general continental peace, and he took leave of the Italian people in these words:

" Citizens,—Reckoning from the 1st of Brumaire, your constitution will be in full activity; your directory, your legislative body, your court of cassation, and other subordinate administrative departments, will be fully organized.

" You are the first example in history of a people who have become free without factions, without revolutions, without internal commotions.

" We have given you liberty; study to preserve it. After France, you are the most populous and the richest of all republics; your position calls upon you to play a distinguished part in the affairs of Europe.

" In order to be worthy of your destiny, pass nothing but wise and moderate laws.

" Cause them to be executed with energy and power.

" Favour the propagation of knowledge, and respect religion.

" Do not fill your ranks with outcasts of society, but with citizens who cherish the principles of the republic, and are intimately attached to its prosperity.

" You require to be deeply penetrated with a feeling of your power, and of the dignity which surrounds a free man.

" Divided amongst yourselves, and subject for ages to tyranny, you could not have regained your liberty; but, should you be left to yourselves for a few years, no power on earth will be strong enough to deprive you of its possession.

" Till that time, the great nation will protect you from the attacks of your neighbours. Its political system will be united to yours.

" Had the Roman people made the same use of power as the French people have done, the Roman

Eagle would still have been on the Capitol, and eighteen centuries of tyranny and bondage would not have dishonoured the human race.

" In order to consolidate your liberty, and with the sole view of promoting your happiness, I have accomplished a work, which only ambition and the love of power have hitherto prompted men to perform.

" I have made appointments to a great number of places, and been exposed to the danger of overlooking men of integrity, and of nominating intriguers; but there were still greater inconveniences in leaving you to make these nominations, before you were organized.

" I am about to depart in a few days. Only the orders of my government, and the imminent danger of the Cisalpine republic, will recall me to the midst of you.

" To whatever part, however, the service of my country may call me, I shall always take a lively interest in the prosperity and glory of your republic.

(Signed)   " BONAPARTE.

" Head-Quarters, Milan, the 22nd of Brumaire,
        year 6, (Nov. 12th, 1797.)"

Napoleon set out for Turin, where he alighted at the house of M. Ginguené, the French minister, on the 17th of November. The King of Sardinia wished to see him, and to give him some public evidence of his gratitude. The circumstances, however, were already such, that he did not think it right to accept these friendly demonstrations of the court. He continued his route to Rastadt, and crossed Mount Cenis; at Geneva he was received as he would have been in a French town, and with all that enthusiasm peculiar to the Genevese. On his entry into the Pays de Vaud, three groups of young and pretty girls came, at the head of the inhabitants, to compliment him; one of these groups was dressed in white, the second in blue, and the third in red. These young maidens presented him with a crown, on which was inscribed the famous sentence, in which the liberty of the Valteline had been proclaimed; a maxim so dear to the people of the Pays de Vaud; "*One people ought not to be subject to another people.*" He passed through several Swiss towns—among others, Berne—and crossed the Rhine at Bàsle, on his way to Rastadt.

The order of the day on his departure from Milan, contained the following address: "Soldiers! to-morrow I set out for Rastadt. Separated from the army, I shall sigh for the moment when I shall again be in the midst of it, ready to brave new dangers. Whatever post the government may assign to the soldiers of Italy, they will always prove themselves worthy supporters of liberty, and of the glory of the French name. Soldiers! in discoursing of the princes whom you have conquered, the people whom you have enfranchised, and the battles which you have fought in two campaigns, say to yourselves—*In two campaigns we will do more still !*"

On his arrival at Rastadt, Bonaparte found the

state-apartments of the palace prepared for him.
Treilhard and Bonniet, whom the directory had appointed as his fellow-commissioners in these negotiations with the Germanic body, had preceded him
some days. At this congress, the aged Count
Metternich represented the Emperor as the head of
the German confederated states, and Count Cobentzel
represented him as head of the house of Austria; there
were therefore two legations, opposed to each other
both in their interests and their instructions. Count
Lehrbach was the representative of the circle of
Austria in the Diet. Count Metternich supported the
character of pomp and parade—Cobentzel conducted
the business. After having exchanged the ratifications
of the peace of Campo-Formio, the plenipotentiaries,
in execution of the treaty, signed the convention for
the surrender of Mayence. The Austrian troops
were to march out of Mayence, and to leave behind
merely the troops of the elector, whilst, at the same
moment, the French were to invest and take possession
of the fortress. 2ndly, the French were to abandon
Venice and Palma-Nova, leaving behind Venetian
troops only, and the Austrians were to seize upon
these cities, as well as the whole country. Albini,
the minister of Mayence, uttered the most violent
complaints, and all the German princes gave way to
the loudest reproaches. "Mayence," said they, "does
not belong to Austria." They accused the Emperor
of having betrayed Germany for the promotion of his
interests in Italy. Count Lehrbach, as deputy from

the circle of Austria, was deputed to reply to all these complaints and protestations; he acquitted himself with all that power, arrogance, and irony, which were natural to his character.

Sweden sent a representative to Rastadt in her character of mediatrix, and as one of the guarantees of the treaty of Westphalia. Since the treaty of Teschen, Russia had arrogated to herself the same pretensions, but she was at this moment at war with France. Since the treaty of Westphalia, the condition of the states of Europe had undergone many changes; Sweden at that time exercised a great influence upon Germany; she was at the head of the Protestant party, and was resplendent with all the glory of the victories of the great Gustavus. Russia was not then European, and Prussia had scarcely an existence. These two powers had made a rapid advance; whilst Sweden was falling into decay, and was now sunk into a power of the third order. Its pretensions, therefore, were altogether unreasonable; and besides, this court had been foolish enough to appoint, on this occasion, Baron Fersen, as its representative at the congress of Rastadt. The favour which this Swedish baron had formerly enjoyed at the court of Versailles, his intrigues in the constituent assembly, and the hatred which he never failed to testify towards France, rendered him the most unsuitable person on whom their choice could have fallen; his selection might, in fact, be regarded as an insult to the republic. When, as a matter of etiquette, he was introduced into

the apartments of the French plenipotentiary, he
caused himself to be announced as ambassador of
Sweden, and mediator at the congress. Napoleon
told him he could not recognise any mediator, and
that, besides, his former opinions disqualified him from
exercising such an office between the republic and
the Emperor of Germany; and that he would not
receive him again. Baron Fersen was so completely
disconcerted, and the manner of his reception made
such a noise, that he left Rastadt the next day.

Immediately after the surrender of Mayence to the
French troops, Napoleon united in conference with
Treilhard and Bonniet, and after having shown
them that the instructions of the directory were insufficient, he declared his intention of not remaining
any longer at the congress, and that he was about to
set out. The business was more complicated at
Rastadt than at Campo-Formio; and it was necessary
to cut it short, in order to bring it to a conclusion.

The directory did not know what course to adopt;
they appointed new plenipotentiaries, who were to
join Treilhard and Bonniet. Bonaparte, already
dissatisfied with the foreign policy of France, determined to have nothing more to do with a negotiation
which would necessarily turn out badly. Moreover,
the internal condition of the country was presaging
the approaching triumph of the demagogues; and
besides, the same reasons which led him to decline
any public reception at the court of Sardinia, determined him to withdraw from the testimonies of ad-

miration heaped upon him by the German princes. He thought it best to bring to a close the first act of his political life, by the peace of Campo-Formio, and to retire into private life at Paris, as long as circumstances would allow. During his short sojourn at Rastadt, he caused the French plenipotentiaries to be treated with all that attention and respect due to the representatives of a great nation from the representatives of foreign powers, and from that crowd of petty German sovereigns who were present at the congress. Before his coming, the French plenipotentiaries had been treated with some neglect; the allowances which had been assigned them were altogether insufficient. He persuaded the government to place very considerable sums at the disposal of the negotiators, in order that they might appear in a manner consistent with their rank, and this step contributed to the manifestation of the consideration due to the republic.

CHAPTER VIII.

NAPOLEON IN PARIS AFTER THE CAMPAIGN
OF ITALY.

NAPOLEON departed from Rastadt, traversed France incognito, arrived in Paris without stopping, and alighted at his small house in the Rue Chantereine, Chaussée d'Antin. The municipal body, the administration of the department and all the public bodies, emulated each other in presenting him with tokens of the national gratitude. A committee of the *Conseil des Anciens* submitted a proposal to bestow upon him the estate of Chambord, and a magnificent *hotel* in Paris. The directory—it is not easy to say why—took alarm at this proposition: its confidential friends caused it to be withdrawn. By a decision of the municipality of Paris, more independent than the councils, the name of the Rue de la Victoire was given to the Rue Chantereine.

During the two years in which Bonaparte had been

in command in Italy, he had filled the world with the splendour of his victories, and now the coalition of the great powers was broken up.   The Emperor and the princes of the empire had recognised the republic. The whole of Italy was subject to her laws.   Two new republics had been created there on the French system. England alone remained under arms, but even *she* had manifested a wish for peace, and if the treaty had not been signed, it was wholly owing to the folly of the directory after the day of Fructidor.

In addition to these great results, obtained in reference to the foreign affairs of the republic, there were joined all the advantages which she had gained in her internal administration and her military power. In no period of the history of the country had the French soldier more strongly entertained the feeling of his superiority over all the soldiers of Europe.   It was owing to the influence of the victories of Italy, that the armies of the Rhine, and the Sambre and Meuse had been able to carry back the French colours to the banks of the Lech, where Turenne had been the first to raise our standards.   At the commencement of 1796, the Emperor had 180,000 men on the Rhine, and wished to carry the war into France.   The armies of the Sambre and Meuse, and of the Rhine, had no suffi-cient forces to offer resistance; their numerical in-feriority was notorious; and if the valour of so many brave men was a guarantee for an honourable defence, the hope of conquest could never have entered into their contemplation.   The days of Montenotte, Lodi, &c.,

carried alarm to Vienna; they obliged the Aulic council
to recall successively Marshal Wurmser, the Archduke
Charles, and more than 60,000 men from the German
armies, which restored the equilibrium on that side, and
enabled Moreau and Jourdan to take the offensive.

More than 120,000,000 of francs in the form of
extraordinary contributions, had been raised in Italy;
60,000,000 had been employed in paying, providing
for, and reorganizing the army of Italy, whilst the
other 60,000,000, sent to the treasury of Paris, had
been applied to the improvement of the internal
condition of the country, and to the service of the
army on the Rhine.   But at that time, the whole
system of the minister of finance was so vicious, the
administration so corrupt, and the treasury so badly
governed, that the armies derived very little advantage from this vast wealth.   Independently of this
important succour of 60,000,000, the treasury was
indebted to the victories of Napoleon for 70,000,000
of annual saving, a sum to which the support of the
armies of the Alps and of Italy amounted in 1796.

Considerable supplies in hemp and timber, and
vessels of various kinds, seized by conquest at Genoa,
Leghorn, and Venice, served to form a very necessary
relief to the naval yards at Toulon.   The national
museum was enriched with *chefs-d'œuvre* of the arts,
which had embellished Rome, Parma, and Florence, and
which were estimated at more than 200,000,000.

The commerce of Lyons, Provence, and Dauphiné
began to revive from the moment in which the free

passage of the Alps was opened to it. The squadrons
of Toulon rode triumphant in the Mediterranean, the
Adriatic, and the Levant. A new era of happiness
and prosperity dawned upon France, and it was to the
conqueror of Italy that the country was pleased to
owe these advantages.

After the arrival of Napoleon, the chiefs of all
parties presented themselves at his house; he refused
to receive them. The public was extremely curious to
see him; the streets and squares through which it was
thought he might pass, were thronged with people;
but he showed himself nowhere.   The *Institut*
having named him a member in the department of
Mechanique, he adopted the costume of the members
of the body. As a general rule, he received at home
only a few *savans*—such as Monge, Barthollet, Borda,
Laplace, Prony, and Lagrange; and some generals—
as Berthier, Desaix, Lefebvre, Caffarelli Dufalge,
Kleber; and a very small number of deputies.

He was received in a public audience by the directory, which had caused a great platform to be erected
for the purpose at the Luxembourg; the pretended
object was the formal acceptance of the peace of
Campo-Formio. He avoided speaking of Fructidor,
of the affairs in which the nation was at the moment
engaged, and of the expedition to England. His
address was simple, but at the same time contained
numerous remarks calculated to suggest various
reflections. The following observations fell from him
in various parts of his speech: " The French people,

in order to secure their liberty, have had kings to combat; and in order to obtain a constitution founded upon reason, they have had the prejudices of eighteen centuries to subdue. Religion, feudality and despotism, have successively governed Europe for twenty centuries; but from the peace which you have just concluded will date the era of representative governments; you are now to organize the great nation, whose vast territory is circumscribed by those boundaries alone which nature herself has prescribed.

" I place in your hands the peace of Campo-Formio, ratified by the Emperor. This peace secures the liberty, prosperity and glory of the republic. When the happiness of the French people shall be founded upon the best organic laws, the whole of Europe will become free."

During this ceremony, General Joubert and Brigadier General Andreossi carried the flag which the legislative body had given to the army of Italy, and which was covered with inscriptions in letters of gold. Some of these were as follow:—" The army of Italy has made 150,000 prisoners, taken 170 stand of colours, 550 pieces of heavy artillery, 600 field-pieces, five *équipages de pont*, nine ships of 64 guns, twelve frigates of 32 guns, twelve sloops and eighteen galleys. Armistice with the Kings of Sardinia and Naples, with the Pope, with the Dukes of Parma and Modena. Preliminaries of Léoben. Convention of Montebello with the republic of Genoa. Treaties of Tolentino and Campo-Formio. Given liberty to the states of Bologna, Ferrara, Modena, Massa-Carrara, Romagna, Lombardy, Brescia, Bergamo, Mantua, Cremona—part of the Veronese, of Chiavenna, Bormio, and the Valteline; to the people of Genoa, to the imperial fiefs, to the departments of Corcyra, the Ægean Sea, and Ithaca. Sent to Paris the *chefs-d'œuvre* of Michael Angelo, Guercino, Titian, Paul Veronese, Albano, the Carracci, Raphael, Leonardo da Vinci, and others. It has been victorious in eighteen pitched battles, and in sixty-seven partial engagements; 1. Montebello; 2. Millesimo ; 3. Mondovi ; 4. Lodi; 5. Borghetto; 6. Lonato; 7. Castiglione ; 8. Roveredo; 9. Bassano; 10. St. George; 11. Fontanaviva ; 12. Caldiera ; 13. Arcola; 14. Rivoli; 15. La Favorite; 16. Tagliamento; 17. Tarwis; 18. Neumarkt."

The directory, the legislative body, and the minister of foreign affairs, gave splendid *fêtes* to Napoleon. He appeared at them all, but remained only for a very short time. That of Talleyrand was characterized by the highest degree of good taste. A celebrated lady, determined to break a lance with the conqueror of Italy, addressed him in the midst of a large circle, and asked him, who, in his opinion, was the greatest woman in the world, dead or alive? He smilingly replied, " She who has borne the most children." The public crowded to the sittings of the *Institut* to see him, and there he was always to be found seated between Laplace and Lagrange—the latter of whom was sincerely attached to him. When he went to

the theatre he sat in a private box, and rejected deci-
sively the application of the managers of the opera,
who were desirous of giving him a grand representation.   Marshal Saxe, Lowendhal, and Dumouriez, had
all been present at such representations on their
respective returns from Fontenay, Bergen-op-zoom,
and Champagne.   When, on his return from Egypt,
on the 18th Brumaire, Napoleon appeared at the
Tuileries, he was still unknown to the inhabitants of
Paris, who exhibited the most eager desire to gratify
their curiosity.

The directory treated him with the greatest distinction; when they thought it their duty to consult
him, they sent one of the ministers to invite him to
be present at the council.   When there, he sat between two of the directors, and gave his opinion upon
questions of importance.

The troops, as they re-entered France, extolled him
to the skies in their songs, and proclaimed aloud that
it was necessary to drive away the lawyers, and make
him a king.   The directors affected the greatest
frankness, and went so far as to show him the secret
reports of the police, but they were unable completely
to conceal the annoyance and chagrin which they felt
at so much popularity.   Napoleon fully appreciated
the delicacy and embarrassment of such a situation.
The administration was badly conducted, and many
hopes were turned towards the conqueror of Italy.
The directory wished him to return to Rastadt, but
he refused, on the pretext that his mission in Italy

had been concluded with the peace of Campo-Formio, and that it was no longer suitable to his views to wield both the pen and the sword. Shortly after, he consented to accept the command of the army of England, in order to impose upon Europe, and to cover the design and preparations of the expedition to Egypt.

The troops composing the army destined for the invasion of England, were cantoned in Normandy, Picardy, and Belgium. Their new general was to inspect all the points, but he wished to traverse the departments *incognito*. These mysterious movements caused still greater uneasiness in London, and effectually masked the preparations going on in the South. It was on this occasion, on his visit to Antwerp, that he conceived the design of those great maritime establishments, which he caused to be put into execution under the empire. It was also on one of these journeys that he perceived all the advantages which St. Quentin would derive from the canal which was afterwards opened under the consulate, and settled his ideas as to the superiority of Boulogne for attempting an enterprise against England simply with pinnaces.

The principles which were henceforward to guide the policy of the republic had been laid down by Napoleon at Campo-Formio, without any regard to the instructions of the directory; the latter, in fact, had remained wholly ignorant of them; besides, the members could not govern their passions; every new incident influenced them. Switzerland furnished the

first example of this. France had had constant reason
to complain of the canton of Berne and of the Swiss
aristocracy. All the foreign agents, whose business it
was to agitate France, found a *point d'appui* in
Berne. The question was now discussed, whether it
would not be wise to take advantage of the great
influence which the republic had just acquired in
Europe, to destroy the preponderance of that aristocracy. Napoleon strongly approved of this feeling
of indignation on the part of the directory, and
thought with it, that the moment was now arrived to
secure the political influence of France in Switzerland,
but he did not think it necessary for that reason to
revolutionize the country. It was necessary to conform to the spirit of the treaty of Campo-Formio, and
to arrive at the accomplishment of the object designed,
with as few changes as possible. His wish was, that
the French ambassador should present a note to the
Helvetic diet, and that its contents should be supported by two camps, one in Savoy, and a second in
Franche-Comté; that in the note it should be declared,
that France and Italy thought it necessary for their
policy and safety, as well as for the dignity of the
three nations, that the Pays de Vaud, Argau, and the
Italian bailiwicks, should become free cantons, in all
respects independent, and equal to the others; that
they had reason to complain of the aristocracy of
certain families in Berne, Soleure, and Fribourg, but
that they would be disposed to forget all grounds of
complaint, provided that the peasants of these cantons

and of the Italian bailiwicks were restored to their political rights.

All these changes might have been effected without difficulty or having recourse to arms; but Rowbell, through the influence of Swiss demagogues, caused a different system to be adopted, and without regard to morals, religion, or the localities of the cantons, the directory determined to impose upon the whole of Switzerland a uniform constitution, similar to that of France. The small cantons were irritated at the loss of their liberty, and the whole country rose at the prospect of a change which destroyed all existing interests, and kindled universal resentment. It became necessary for the French troops to interfere and to conquer — blood flowed, and Europe took alarm.

On the other hand, the court of Rome, influenced by that spirit of infatuation by which it was characterized, and embittered rather than corrected by the treaty of Tolentino, persisted in its system of aversion to France. This cabinet of weak old men without wisdom, excited a great fermentation in opinion around them. It quarrelled with the Cisalpine republic, and was guilty of the great imprudence of appointing the Austrian General Provera to the command of its troops; this General played his part in promoting the general excitement, and a tumult broke out. Young Duphot, a General of the greatest promise, who happened to be at Rome as a traveller, was massacred at the gate of the French ambassador, whilst endeavouring

to allay the spirit of disorder. The ambassador retired
to Florence. Napoleon, when consulted, replied by
his usual adage: " *That it was not for events to
govern policy, but for policy to regulate events;*
that, however wrong the court of Rome might be, the
course of conduct to be pursued towards it was still a
very grave question; that it was necessary to correct,
but not to destroy it; that, by overturning the Holy
See and revolutionizing Rome, a war with Naples
would be the necessary result, which ought to be
avoided; that the French ambassador ought to be
ordered to return to Rome, to demand the punishment
of the ringleaders, and to receive a nuncio from the
Pope, who would express the regret of his Holiness;
to drive away Provera, to raise the most moderate
prelates to the head of the government, and to force
the Holy See to conclude a concordat with the Cisalpine republic that by these combined measures, Rome
would be tranquillized, and unable to cause further
uneasiness ; that the concordat with the Cisalpine
republic would moreover have the effect of preparing
the minds of the people of France for a similar measure. Laréveillère, surrounded by his theophilanthro-
pists, was decidedly of opinion that measures should
be adopted against the Pope.

" The time had now arrived," said he, " to make
this idol disappear. The words *Roman republic*
would be sufficient to fill with transport the ardent
imaginations of the revolution. The general of Italy
had been too circumspect in his time, and if any

disputes or quarrels now arose with the Pope, it was entirely his fault. But, perhaps, he had his particular views; in fact, his conduct towards the Pope, and his generous compassion for exiled priests, had given him in France many partisans, who were not friends of the revolution."

As to the fears expressed on the probability of such measures leading to a war with Naples, he treated that part of the question with great subtlety. According to him, France had a numerous party in Naples, and ought to entertain no fear of a power of the third rank. Berthier received orders to march with an army upon Rome, and to re-establish the Roman republic; which was done. The names of consuls and senate, and other offices and orders of ancient Rome, again greeted the ear. Fourteen cardinals assembled in the church of St. Peter, to chant a *Te Deum*, on the re-establishment of the Roman republic, and the overthrow of the throne of St. Peter. The people, intoxicated with independence, carried with them in their enthusiasm the greatest part of the clergy.

The hand which had hitherto guided and restrained the officers and administrators of the army of Italy, was no longer there, and in Rome they allowed themselves to fall into the most unpardonable excesses. The furniture of the Vatican was wasted and destroyed, the best works of art and rarities of every description were seized upon, and a general feeling of dissatisfaction was raised among the inhabitants. The soldiers themselves protested loudly against the conduct of some of their generals, whom they accused of exciting the disorder. This state of things was attended with the greatest danger, and there was the greatest possible difficulty in restoring order. It is said, with good reason, that the Romans were stimulated by the intrigues of Neapolitan, English, and Austrian agents.

Bernadotte had been appointed ambassador to the court of Vienna. This appointment was bad; for the disposition of this General was too excitable and warm; his head was not sufficiently calm; besides, a General could not be a very acceptable ambassador to a nation which had been constantly beaten. A civilian ought to have been sent, but the directory had not such a man at their disposal; men of this class were either too obscure, or had been alienated by the government. However this may be, Bernadotte suffered himself to be governed by his temper, and committed grave faults. One day, without any one being able to divine the reason of his conduct, he caused the national tricolor to be hoisted on the top of his hotel; he had been insidiously urged to this step by agents who wished to compromise Austria. In fact, the populace broke out into disorders, tore down the tricolor, and insulted Bernadotte.

The directory, in its rage, called upon Napoleon to support them by his influence upon public opinion. They made him acquainted with a message to be sent to the councils, in order to lead to a declaration against Austria, and with a decree, by virtue of which the command of the army destined for Germany was to be conferred upon him. This general, however, did not concur in the opinion of the government. " If you wish," said he, " to make war, you must prepare for it, quite independently of this incident respecting Bernadotte; you must not engage your troops in Switzerland, in the South of Italy, or on the coasts of the ocean.

" It will be necessary not to proclaim the intention of reducing the army to 100,000 men, which is not yet executed, it is true, but which is known, and operates as a discouragement to the troops. These measures indicate that you have reckoned upon the continuance of peace. Bernadotte has been essentially wrong, and by declaring war, you will play the game of England. It requires but a very small knowledge of the cabinet of Vienna, and its policy, to be certain, that if it had really wished for war, it would not have insulted you,— on the contrary, it would have caressed you, and lulled your suspicions, whilst the troops were being prepared for action; you would only have discovered its real intentions by the first fire of its artillery. Be assured, that Austria will give you satisfaction. To suffer a nation thus to be at the mercy of such casual events, is not to have, or to pursue, any great system of policy." The power of truth calmed down the indignation of the government, and the Emperor gave ample satisfaction. The conferences of Seltz took place, but the incident delayed the expedition to Egypt for fifteen days.

In the meantime, Napoleon began to fear, that in the midst of the storms which the vacillating course pursued by the government, and the nature of things, was every day accumulating, an enterprise to the East had become contrary to the true interests of the country. "Europe," said he, to the directory, "is anything but tranquil; the congress of Rastadt is not terminated—you are obliged to keep your troops in the interior to secure the elections, and some are necessary to keep down the spirit of insubordination in the departments of the West. Would it not be better to countermand the expedition, and to wait for more favourable circumstances?"

The directory took alarm, and fearing that Napoleon would place himself at the head of the government, it became the more ardent in urging on the expedition. It was not aware of all the consequences of those changes which had taken place in the political system within six months. According to it, the events in Switzerland, far from weakening France, gave it excellent military positions, and the Helvetic troops as auxiliaries. Affairs with Rome were settled, for the Pontiff had already withdrawn to Florence, and the Roman republic was proclaimed; the case of Bernadotte could not be attended with any further consequences, for the Emperor had offered to make reparation—the moment, therefore, was more favourable than ever for making attacks upon England in Ireland, and Egypt.

Napoleon then offered to leave Desaix and Kleber

behind; their talents might become useful to France. The directory refused them; it did not appreciate their merits. " The republic," said the directors, " is not dependent on these two generals, but could find a crowd of officers to cause the country to triumph, if it were in danger—soldiers are much more wanted than generals."

The government was on the very edge of a precipice, which it did not perceive. Its affairs were badly conducted—it abused the victory of Fructidor. It was not its good fortune to be able to rally around the cause of the country those who really did not belong to the faction of foreigners, but had merely been drawn away in its suite. It was thus deprived of the services of a very great number of individuals, who out of resentment threw themselves into the arms of the opposite party, although both their interests and their opinions naturally led them to attach themselves to that form of government. The directory found itself constrained to employ men without character; and hence a great degree of public dissatisfaction, and the necessity for maintaining large bodies of troops in the interior, with a view to secure the elections, and to keep down the spirit of revolt in La Vendée. It was easy to foresee that the new elections would lead to great agitation. The directory had no longer any system of administration, except in matters of foreign policy. It went on, from day to day, led by the individual dispositions of the directors, or by the various nature of a government consisting of five persons. It

neither foresaw nor anticipated anything, and had no
perception of the difficulties which seriously obstructed
its course.   When they were asked, "How will you
make the approaching elections?"   "We will provide
for that by a law!" replied Laréveillère.   The result
showed what the nature of the law was of which he
was thinking.   When it was said to them, "Why do
you not recall all the friends of the republic, who have
only been led astray in Fructidor?   Why do you not
recal Carnot, Portalis, Marcaire, &c., in order to form
a FASCES against foreigners and emigrants, of all those,
who possess enlightened and liberal ideas?"   They
made no answer—they could not conceive the nature
of their solicitude—they thought themselves popular,
and believed their government to rest upon a solid
foundation.

A party composed of influential deputies in the
two councils, the Fructidorians, who sought for a
protector, and the most observant and enlightened
generals, long and eagerly pressed Napoleon to make
a movement, and to put himself at the head of the
republic; but he refused.   His time was not yet
come.   He did not yet think himself sufficiently
popular to be able to stand alone.   With respect to
the art of governing, and to what was necessary for a
great nation, he entertained ideas very different from
those of the men of the revolution and of the assemblies, and he was afraid of compromising his character.
He resolved to set out for Egypt, but with the determination of re-appearing, as soon as circumstances

should arise to render his presence desirable or necessary, as he foresaw would certainly happen. In order to secure him the mastery of France, it was necessary that the directory should suffer reverses in his absence, and that his return should restore victory and success to our colours.

The government proposed to celebrate the anniversary of the execution of Louis XVI., and it was a subject of earnest consideration among the directors and the ministers, whether Napoleon ought to be present at this ceremony or not. It was feared, on the one hand, that it might injure his popularity if he did not go, and on the other, that if he went, people would forget the directory, and fix their attention wholly on him. It was, however, determined that, notwithstanding this, his presence was required by policy. One of the ministers was commissioned to arrange the affair. Napoleon, who was desirous of avoiding all participation in celebrations of this kind, observed that—" He filled no public office; that personally he had nothing to do at this proposed *fête*, which, from its very nature, could be pleasing to very few; that it was one of the most impolitic things to do, for the event which it commemorated was a catastrophe and a national misfortune; that he could very well understand why the anniversary of the 14th of July should be commemorated, because on it the people had won their liberty and their rights, but that they might have been gained without polluting themselves by the execution of a prince declared inviolable and irresponsible by the constitution itself; that he would not pretend to say, whether that event was useful or injurious, but he maintained that it was an unfortunate incident; that national *fêtes* were celebrated for victories, whilst men wept for the victims who lay dead upon the field of battle; that the celebration of the execution of a man, could never be the act of a government, but of a faction or a club; that he could not conceive how the directory, which had caused the clubs of Jacobins and of anarchists to be shut, and which was now in treaty with so many princes, did not perceive that such a ceremony made more enemies than friends to the republic; and that, instead of conciliating, it alienated—instead of softening, embittered—instead of strengthening, shook and weakened; and, finally, that it was altogether unworthy of the government of a great nation." The negotiator on this occasion employed all his means of persuasion. He attempted to prove that, " this *fête* was just because it was politic; that it was politic, because all countries and republics had celebrated, as a triumph, the fall and overthrow of absolute power and the murder of tyrants; that Athens had always celebrated the death of Pisistratus, and Rome the fall of the Decemvirs; and that, moreover, it was in accordance with the law of the land, and that every man owed it submission and obedience; and, finally, that the influence of the General of Italy upon public opinion was such that he ought to appear at this ceremony; and if he did not appear, his absence would be injurious to the interests of the republic."

After several interviews and conferences, a *mezzo-termine* was hit upon. The *Institut*, as a body, was to be present at the *fête;* it was agreed that Napoleon, as a member of the *Institut*, should appear amongst its *savans*, and follow the class to which he belonged, thus discharging a corporate duty, which he did not consider as a voluntary act. The affair thus arranged was very agreeable to the directory. When, however, the members of the *Institut* entered the church of St. Sulpice, some one who recognised Bonaparte pointed him out, and from that moment the whole public attention was fixed upon him. The thing which the directory feared really took place. Its members were completely eclipsed. At the close of the ceremony, the multitude allowed the Directory to retire unattended, waited for him who had been so anxious to conceal himself amongst a crowd, and made the air re-echo with the cries of—" *Vive le Général de l'armée d'Italie!*" so that these events merely served to increase the displeasure of the government.

About this time, another circumstance occurred which imposed upon Napoleon the disagreeable necessity of blaming, in no measured terms, the conduct of the directory. Two young persons, who frequented the Café Garchi, and dressed their hair after a particular fashion, were, under the pretext of a political movement, insulted, attacked, and assassinated. This

murder was committed according to the orders of
Sotin, the minister of police, and executed by his
agents.   The circumstances were now of such a nature
as to compel Napoleon, although living in as retired a
manner as possible, to direct his particular attention,
for the sake of his own safety, to measures of this
description. He loudly expressed his indignation.
The directory took alarm, and commissioned one of
their ministers to go and explain to him the motives
of their conduct.   They instructed him to say—
" That such events were common at critical periods;
that revolutionary times were not regulated by the
ordinary methods of proceeding; that it was in this
case necessary to place restrictions upon high society,
and to repress the boldness of the *salons;* that this
was one of that kind of crimes with which the ordinary
tribunals could not deal; that they could not, undoubtedly, approve of the *lanterne* of the constituent
assembly, but that without it the revolution never
would have made progress; and, finally, that it was
one of those evils which it was necessary to tolerate in
order to avoid greater."

Napoleon replied—" That such language might
have been just endurable before Fructidor, when
parties were drawn against each other, and the directory had been rather in the position of defending itself
than that of carrying on the administration; that
then, perhaps, such acts might have been defensible on
the plea of necessity; but that at present, the directory
found itself invested with full powers—no opposition

was offered to the due course of law—the citizens, if
not attached, were at least submissive, and such an
action had, therefore, become an atrocious crime, a
real outrage upon civilization; that wherever the
words *law* and *liberty* were named, all citizens became responsible for one another; that here, with this
employment of cut-throats, every man must feel himself struck with terror, and be ready to ask, where is
this to stop?"

These reasons were too cogent to need development
to a man of intelligence like the minister, but he had
a mission, and did his best to justify an administration, whose favour and confidence he was anxious to
continue to enjoy.

CHAPTER IX.

CONDUCT OF NAPOLEON AS CONSUL.

" As Consul, my first thought after the battle of Marengo, was to open negotiations with England, and had Fox lived, there can be no doubt that a permanent peace would have been made between England and France, because Fox knew the true interests of his country. It would have been easy to have inspired the two nations with the most friendly dispositions towards one another. The French have always esteemed the English and their national qualities; wherever esteem exists, there is only a step to friendship; and had suitable measures been adopted for the purpose, nothing would have been easier, than to have brought about this in the case of England and France. I have done England great mischief, and would have done her more had the war continued; but I have never ceased to esteem the English people, and would have made almost any sacrifices to be at peace with them, except such as would have involved or tarnished French honour. On the throne, I expressed a high opinion of the English nation—of its liberty, policy, independence, greatness, and generosity. A martyr to the crimes of its ministers, my esteem for the people still remains.

" In 1800, as First Consul, I wrote as follows to the King of England:

" ' Is the war, which has now desolated the four quarters of the world for eight years, to be eternal? Are there no means of bringing about an understanding? How is it that the two bravest, most powerful, and enlightened nations of Europe can sacrifice to ideas of vain glory, any longer than their safety and independence require, the advantages of commerce, internal prosperity, and social peace? How is it, that they do not feel that peace is the first of necessities, as it is of glories?'

" This honourable and conciliatory advance was repulsed; six months, however, had scarcely elapsed, when Lord Minto, the English ambassador at Vienna, sent a note, in which he expressed a desire, on the part of the cabinet of St. James, to enter, conjointly with Austria, into negotiations for peace with France. There was, however, great reason to believe that this overture was not sincere, and that England only wished to take part in the negotiations, with a view to embarrass and prolong their course, and to find a pretext for re-attaching Russia to the coalition. In

truth, had England wished for peace, there was nothing to prevent her from treating directly, and from
authorising Austria to conclude *directly* for herself.

" On presenting herself at Lunéville, and making
common cause with the court of Vienna, was England
ready to sacrifice a portion of her conquests beyond
sea, in order to purchase back the countries conquered
by France in Germany and Italy? The egotism of
the insular politics was too well known to allow any
one to deceive himself by such illusions; peace with
Austria could be easily concluded, because there was
a precedent in the recent treaty of Campo-Formio;
peace with England, on the contrary, was surrounded
by difficulties. The last arrangement was that of the
treaty of 1783; since that time everything had been
completely changed. To admit, therefore, a negotiator
from England at Lunéville, was to place the shuttle
and yarn in her hands, to enable her to weave a new
coalition. The cabinet of the Tuileries, however, in
order to be better convinced of the truth of its conjectures, proposed at once to open the negotiations of
Lunéville with the ministers of Austria and England,
on condition, that during the continuance of the
negotiations, hostilities should continue by sea and
land; which was strictly according to the usage in
such cases. The treaties of Westphalia, Utrecht,
Aix-la-Chapelle, &c., had been concluded in this
manner. The superiority of the French armies was
too well established to enable England, by her intrigues, to retard the progress of the negotiations.

Every new victory would have merely served as a stimulus to the allies to bring them to a conclusion; the proposition, therefore, was rejected. It was then proposed to admit the plenipotentiaries to Lunéville, and to continue the armistice by land, provided that it was also extended to sea, that both the allied powers should be on the same footing. Was it, in fact, right that Austria should demand the prolongation of the armistice in order to negotiate, and that England should be admitted to the congress without any cessation of hostilities? Had the English minister been sincere in his declarations, he would have found very little inconvenience in making some slight sacrifices as a compensation to France for the injury which she suffered by the prolongation of the armistice by land; and, finally, if this second proposition was rejected, it might then be proposed to treat separately, but at the same time, with Austria and England; with Austria by prolonging the armistice, and with England during the continuance of hostilities.

" The English minister showed great astonishment, and exclaimed against the strange proposition of a naval armistice! It was something new in the history of the two nations; but, at last, he admitted the principle. Count Otto, who was in London, as a commissioner to treat for the exchange of prisoners, carried on the negotiations with Lord Grenville. He soon perceived, however, that England, whilst conceding the principle, wished to refuse its consequences, and so to fetter the conditions of the armistice as to

Q 2

offer no advantage whatever to France. The three German cities which were invested, received supplies, and England consented to the adoption of the same course with respect to Belleisle, Malta, and Alexandria. The two last, however, were in no want of provisions, but could, on the contrary, furnish some to England. The only advantage which France could derive from a naval armistice, was, that it would enable her to renew her commercial intercourse with all the ports in her colonies. England refused to concede this in the case of Malta and Egypt. France finally proposed as her *ultimatum*, that instead of raising the blockade of Alexandria, six frigates, armed *en flûte*, should enter the harbour as cartel-ships; this would afford the means of sending an additional force of 4000 men to the army of Egypt, a very small advantage indeed compared with those obtained by Austria by the prolongation of the armistice, which enabled her to employ her vast English subsidies in raising new troops and strengthening her means of resistance.

" The negotiations for a naval armistice were broken off. The fortresses of Ulm, Philipsburg, and Ingolstadt, were surrendered by the Emperor to France, as the price of the prolongation of the truce for six weeks.

" A few months afterwards, the peace of Lunéville saved the house of Austria, and re-established a calm upon the Continent. And finally, shortly afterwards, the minister signed the preliminaries of London, by which the English oligarchy, baffled and confounded, acknowledged the democratic French republic, not only increased by the Belgian provinces, but by Piedmont, Genoa, and the whole of Italy.

" Fox came to France. His journey was a series of acts of homage rendered by all classes of the people. Fox was the model of a statesman, and his school, sooner or later, ought to rule the world.

" The void produced by the French revolution in the organic system of ancient Europe, was by no means filled in the eyes of the oligarchy, who felt, more strongly than ever, the dangers which threatened their political domination. The centre of action and *point d'appui* of all these plots against the new order of things in France, was in London; the exhaustion of the people had imposed upon the oligarchy the peace of Amiens; but a two years' truce was too long a tax upon the hateful and irreconcilable passions by which their hearts were filled; all the organs of the aristrocracy, therefore, were set to work to re-open the bloody arena, on which two great nations, made to be friends, were about to be condemned to a death-struggle for twelve years more.

" On the 20th of May, 1803, a proclamation, issued by the government, announced to France the rupture of the peace of Amiens:

" ' We are forced to make war to repel an unjust aggression; we will do so with glory.

" ' If the King of England is resolved to keep Great Britain in a state of war, till France shall recognise his right of executing or violating treaties at his pleasure, as well as the privilege of outraging the French government in official and private publications, without allowing us to complain, we must mourn for the fate of humanity.

" ' We assuredly wish to leave to our descendants the French name honoured, and without a stain.

" ' Whatever may be the circumstances, we shall, on all occasions, leave it to England to take the initiative in all proceedings of violence against the peace and independence of nations; and she shall receive from us an example of that moderation, which alone can afford any real security for social order and the happiness of nations.'

" On his part, the English minister made the King of England say, 'that he was about to place himself at the head of his people; that France had serious designs against the constitution, the religion, and the independence of the English nation; but that, through the measures which he was about to take, this same France would reap nothing from its project but defeat, confusion, and misfortune.'

" ' Is this indeed,' cried the First Consul, 'the language of the King of England, the chief of a nation which is mistress of the seas, and sovereign of India? Do those who adopt such language, forget that Harold, the perjured, also put himself at the head of his people? Are they ignorant that the *prestiges* of birth, the attributes of sovereign power, and the royal purple, are very fragile bucklers in those moments when death, traversing the ranks of the combatants, awaits the glance of the prince, and an unexpected movement, in order to choose the party which is to furnish his victims ? In the day of battle, all men are equal.

" ' The habit of fighting, superiority in tactics, the coolness and presence of mind of the commander, make the conquerors or the conquered. A Septuagenarian King, who should for the first time put himself at the head of his army, would only be an additional embarrassment on the day of battle, and furnish a new chance of success to his enemies.

" ' The King of England speaks of the honour of the crown, the maintenance of the constitution, of religion, laws, and independence. Would not then the peaceable enjoyment of all these blessings have been secured to the English people by the peace of Amiens ? What has the rock of Malta to do with the religion, the laws, and the independence of England ? It does not lie within the compass of human prudence to penetrate the secret means which the wisdom of Divine Providence will adopt for the humiliation of perjury, and the punishment of those who foster divisions and sow enmity between two great nations, and drive them to make war under the most miserable pretexts.

" ' Defeat, confusion, misfortune! all these menaces are absurd, and unworthy of the chief of a great nation, even were he an Alexander, Cæsar, or Frederick; for the more elated he might be by victories, the more unpardonable would he be to forget that the fate of war and the issue of a battle often

depend on very trifling events; to venture to predict
that the French army would meet with nothing on
the soil of England but defeat, confusion, and misfortune!'

" Two hundred thousand men covered, with their
camps, the coasts of France, from Ostend to the mouth
of the Somme. Measures were taken to concentrate all
the maritime resources of France, Spain, and Holland,
with a view of sweeping the channel, and facilitating
and covering the passage of thousands of gun-boats and
barges which were being built in all the dock-yards of
France and Holland, and which were to be collected
between St. Valery and Ostend for the embarkation of
the troops. On both sides of the channel, nothing was to
be seen but preparations for attack or defence. The
aged and venerable George III. left his royal residence,
to exchange his peaceful life for the fatigue of camps.

" The cabinet of St. James's omitted no means to
rouse that kind of apathetic indifference with which
the danger of England was viewed at the courts of
Vienna, Petersburg, and Berlin. La Vendée could
not have frankly laid down arms, and attempts were
made to raise the standard of insurrection in that
province. These attempts were useless; the concordat
had rallied the clergy around the government of
Napoleon; the Vendean peasant was weary of war,
enjoying with thankfulness the blessings of the pacification, and the gifts which the First Consul distributed with a liberal hand, to heal the wounds of the

war, by rebuilding the churches, and repairing or reconstructing their habitations.

" The cabinet of St. James's was led into numerous mistakes by the emigrants, who, deceived by the illusions of their own minds, had induced their protectors to engage in many troublesome expeditions. It had a great idea of the power and means of the Jacobins, persuaded itself that a great number of them were dissatisfied—that they were disposed to unite their efforts with those of the royalists, and would be seconded by generals jealous of the First Consul. It thought that by systematizing these efforts of parties opposed to each other, but united by a common passion, it might form one powerful enough to create an efficacious diversion.

" During the past four years, I had reunited all the parties into which France· was divided before my accession to power; the list of emigrants was closed; I had at first marked, then erased, and finally granted an amnesty to all those who wished to return to their country; all their existing and unsold property had been restored, with the exception of the forests, of which the law assigned them the revenues; there no longer remained on that list any names except those of persons immediately attached to the princes of the house of Bourbon, and who did not wish to take advantage of the amnesty. Thousands upon thousands of emigrants had returned, and been subjected to no other conditions than the oath of

fidelity and obedience to the republic. I thus enjoyed the most delightful consolation which a king
can enjoy, that of re-organizing more than 30,000
families, and of restoring to their country all that
remained of men who had made France illustrious in
different ages; even those who continued emigrants
frequently received passports to come and visit their
families. The public altars were rebuilt, the deserted
or exiled priests were restored to their functions, and
paid by the republic. These laws effected great
amelioration in public affairs. They, however, were accompanied by the inevitable inconvenience of embol-
dening, by their very mildness and indulgence, the
enemies of the consular government, the royalist
party, and the hopes of our foreign enemies.

"From 1803 till 1804, there were five conspiracies;
it is to this period that the death of the Duke of
d'Enghien belongs."

CHAPTER X.

THE DUKE D'ENGHIEN.

THE Duke d'Enghien lost his life because he was one of the principal actors in the conspiracy formed by Georges, Pichegru, and Moreau.

Pichegru was arrested on the 28th of February, Georges on the 9th, and the Duke d'Enghien on the 18th of March, 1804.

The Duke d'Enghien took an active part in all the intrigues which had been carried on from 1796 by the agents of England; this is proved by the papers seized in the cartridge-box of Klinglin, and the letters of the 19th of Fructidor, 1797, written by Moreau to the directory.

The king's speech, delivered to the English parliament in March, 1803, announced the commencement of a new war, and the rupture of the peace of Amiens. The French government indicated the design of carry-

ing the war into England. During the years 1803
and 1804, the whole sea-coast at Boulogne, Dunkirk,
and Ostend was covered with camps; formidable
squadrons were prepared in Brest, Rochefort, and
Toulon; the whole of the dock-yards of France were
filled with gun-boats, sloops, rafts, and pinnaces, and
thousands of men were employed in excavating and
enlarging the channel ports, to enable them to contain
these numerous flotillas. England, on her part, flew
to arms; Pitt relinquished the peaceful occupations
of the exchequer, put on a uniform, and thought
of nothing but warlike machines, battalions, forts,
and batteries; the aged and venerable George III.
forsook the quiet of his palaces, and was daily engaged in reviews; camps were formed on the heights
of Dover, and in the counties of Kent and Sussex; the
two armies were, in fact, in sight of one another,
separated merely by the straits.

At the same time, England neglected none of those
means calculated to rouse the continental powers; but
Austria, Russia, Prussia, and Spain, were either allies
or friends of France, which gave laws to the whole of
Europe. The attempts which were made to re-kindle
the war in La Vendée, were not more successful.
The concordat had rallied the clergy to Napoleon,
and the feelings of the inhabitants of the province
had undergone a complete change, for they contem-
plated with gratitude the progress of his administration. The great public works which he had decreed
gave employment to thousands of hands; it was de-

signed to connect the Vilaine with the Rance by a canal, which would enable the French coasters to pass from the coasts of Poitou to those of Normandy without the necessity of doubling Cape Ushant. A new city was springing up in the midst of La Vendée, and eight new public highways were about to traverse the west; and finally, considerable sums, in the form of insurances, were distributed among the Vendeans, in order to enable them to rebuild their houses, churches, and parsonages, which had been burnt or destroyed by order of the committee of public safety.

All the emigrants who were in the pay of England had received orders to form a junction in the Breisgau, and in the grand duchy of Baden. Massey, an English agent who corresponded with the government, Drake, and Spencer Smith had taken up their abode at Offenburg, and furnished in profusion whatever money was necessary for the execution of all these plots.

The minister, Decrès, who was desirous above everything of gaining the favour of his master, used every possible exertion, by means of smugglers, to ascertain what was going on in England, and was the first to give information respecting the plots which were being woven in Germany, and in which Spencer Smith and Drake were the chief instruments.

The First Consul made bitter complaints to the minister of foreign affairs, of the negligence displayed by the French diplomatic agents at the German courts; Monsieur de Talleyrand was excited to action, and required explanations from Baron Dalberg, *chargé d'affaires* of Baden, in Paris, and one of his most intimate acquaintances. Dalberg now saw an opportunity of making his fortune, and he judged correctly; for it was to this circumstance he was indebted for being created a duke, with a pension of 200,000 francs. He did not hesitate to reveal, even to the minutest details, all that he knew of the presence of the Duke d'Enghien at Ettenheim, and of the attempts of the English agents in Munich and Switzerland.

Marshal Moncey, inspector-general of the *Gendarmerie*, and Count Schee, prefect of Strasburg, confirmed by their reports the opinion that the Duke d'Enghien was the soul of the conspiracy, and had been invested with extraordinary powers to enter France in the character of Lieutenant-General of the kingdom, in the name of the Pretender, as soon as the conspirators had succeeded in assassinating the First Consul.

On receiving this intelligence, an extraordinary council was convoked at the Tuileries. The ministers and the chief dignitaries of the senate and of the legislative body were present, and all were of opinion that the safety of the republic demanded the adoption of extraordinary measures. The forcible capture of the Duke d'Enghien was decreed.

Caulaincourt, aide-de-camp of Napoleon, was bound to obey the instructions which Berthier and Talleyrand, the minister of foreign affairs, were desired to give him, for the accomplishment of the mission with which he was entrusted:

1st. To confound the plots which were laid by the English ministers on the right bank of the Rhine.

2ndly. To make sure of the persons and papers of the Baroness de Reich and her accomplices, who were busy at Offenburg in devising schemes for the overthrow of the consular government, and the death of the First Consul.

3rdly. To give explanations to the Court of Baden respecting the violation of their territory, as soon as Ordenner had seized upon the Duke d'Enghien.

Ordenner was bound to obey his orders, to pass the Rhine with 300 dragoons, and to carry off the prince; and a court-martial was bound to condemn him, if he was proved guilty. Innocent or guilty, Caulaincourt and Ordenner were bound to obey; if he were guilty, the court-martial was obliged to condemn him —if innocent, they ought to have acquitted him, inasmuch as no order could justify the conscience of a judge. There is no doubt, that if Caulaincourt had been appointed judge of the Duke d'Enghien, he would have refused; but being charged with a diplomatic mission, he was bound to obey. All this is so obvious, that nothing but folly, or the madness of party-spirit, can find anything to say against it. It is true that such party-spirit found it easy to attack an ancient name distinguished by new and honourable services, and was bent on calumniating Caulaincourt in this case. This hatred and injustice were among the causes of his favour. Caulaincourt, being entrusted before the time of the Empire with one of the departments

of service in the palace, had afterwards merely the title
of the functions which he had already filled.

The death of the Duke d' Enghien ought to be attributed to those who in London directed and commanded the assassination of the first consul, who
destined the Duke de Berry to enter France through
the district of Beville, and the Duke d'Enghien by
Strasburg. It ought to be attributed also to those
who, by their reports and conjectures, forced the
council to regard him as the chief of the conspiracy;
and it ought to be made a subject of eternal reproach
to those who, urged on by a criminal zeal, did not
await the orders of their sovereign before executing
the sentence of the court-martial.

The Duke d'Enghien fell a victim to the intrigues
of the time; and his death, which has been made a
matter of reproach to Napoleon, was injurious to him,
and of no political utility whatever. Had Napoleon
been capable of decreeing the commission of such a
crime, Louis XVIII and Ferdinand would not now
have been upon their thrones.

It is true that the Emperor, in his will, has taken
upon himself the responsibility of this act, which even
in his eyes was not justified by necessity, had not a
strange impression on his own mind excited him to
one of those passionate movements to which he sometimes yielded, as we shall see.

The Emperor had written and sealed up his will
about twelve days, when he first saw, in the European
papers, in relation to the death of the Duke d'Enghien,

an attack as unjust as it was virulent against two persons to whom no blame whatever attached. These were the Dukes of Vicenza and Rovigo—" Bring me my will," said he; and having broken the seal by a convulsive movement, he seized his pen, and wrote, in characters scarcely legible, " I decreed and determined the death of the Duke d'Enghien, because it was necessary for the safety, interest, and honour of the French people, when the Count d'Artois maintained sixty assassins in Paris. Under the same circumstances, I would act in the same manner." An hour after having performed this act, he called us, made us seal up the will and codicils, and place our own seals and signatures upon the envelopes.

Napoleon never committed crimes. What crime would have been more profitable to him than the assassination of the Count de Lille and the Count d'Artois? The proposition was often made to him, especially by * * * and * * *, and would not have cost him two millions. The Emperor rejected the proposal with contempt and indignation. During the whole of his reign, no attempt was ever made on the lives of these princes. When Spain was in arms in the name of Ferdinand, this prince, and his brother, Don Carlos, the sole heirs of the throne of Spain, were at Valencey, in the heart of Berry; their death would have put an end to the affairs of Spain. He was advised to adopt such a course, but he regarded it as criminal and unjust. Were Ferdinand and his brother, Carlos, put to death in France?

It would be easy to quote many other examples, but these two may suffice, as being the most striking and conclusive. Hands accustomed to gain battles by the sword, never tarnish themselves by the commission of crimes, even under the vain pretext of public utility; this pretext has, in all ages, been the frightful maxim of weak governments alone, which disavow all the obligations of religion, honour, and European civilization.

Napoleon attained the summit of human greatness by direct paths, without ever having committed an action which morality ought to disavow. In this respect his elevation is unique in history. David, in order to secure the throne, put to death the house of Saul, his benefactor; Cæsar kindled the flames of civil war, and destroyed the government of his country; Cromwell caused his master to be executed on the scaffold. Napoleon was a stranger to all the crimes of the Revolution. At the time in which he commenced his political career, the throne had crumbled into dust. The amiable Louis XVI. had perished, and factions were rending the country to pieces. It was by the conquest of Italy, and by the peace of Campo-Formio, which ensured the greatness and independence of France, that Napoleon commenced his career; and when he assumed the supreme power in 1800, he triumphed over anarchy. His throne was raised on the unanimous desires of the French people.

A dictation of the Emperor seems to me to be necessary to complete the foregoing reflections.

CHAPTER XI.

ON STATE-PRISONS.

THE aged Queen Caroline of Naples was living in Sicily, overwhelmed with vexation, and steeped in humiliations. The English had unworthily sacrificed her to their ambitious views upon Sicily. She was thirsting for vengeance, and her imagination—degraded by all the blood which she had caused to be shed, when the unskilfulness of the directory re-opened to her the gates of Naples—could not be restrained within any bounds, when she thought she saw a ray of hope.

The marriage of one of her daughters with the Duke of Orleans was made subservient to the policy of the moment. On the birth of the Duke de Chartres, she conceived the infernal idea of offering him up as a holocaust, in order to buy back the crown of Naples. "This child," she wrote to the Emperor, "will one day become a dangerous rival of your son; he will fully represent a principle of conciliation between interests which you have amalgamated in appearance, but which your death will separate anew. Restore to me the crown of Naples, and I will at the same time serve your cause, and satiate my hatred of the English, by new Sicilian Vespers, which will swallow up a whole race of rivals of your dynasty."

The Emperor was filled with indignation, and caused the bearer of this execrable message to be conveyed to a state-prison; there he would have long remained, had not the events of 1814 restored him to liberty.

It was such men who filled the state-prisons of the empire; and everything which has been said of imperial despotism is a calumny.

THE EMPEROR'S REPLY TO AN ENGLISHMAN WHO SPOKE WITH CONTEMPT OF LOUIS XVIII.

"You are badly acquainted with the course of events, and are unjust towards Louis XVIII. Neither he nor any of the princes of his family were deficient in courage during the events of the Hundred Days. It was on the first appearance of the Revolution in its early progress that they proved themselves wanting in courage. Like princes, they should have shared all the dangers of the Vendeans, in 1815. They did all they could do—the whole people repudiated them, and merely regarded them as kings of the emigrants. It was impossible for the Bourbons to have prevented the popular masses from carrying me off in triumph from

Cannes to Paris. Mark what took place at Lyons:
the troops deserted the Count d'Artois; remember
the case of Ney, at Besançon. At the cry of *Vive
l'Empereur*, his soldiers compelled him to recognise
the orders sent by me through my aide-de-camp St.
Yon, whilst he was dictating to his staff plans for
opposing me. Think of the Duchess of Angoulême,
at Bourdeaux—she was heroic in her resolutions, but
not a voice responded to her appeal; and yet Bourdeaux was the very city, which, ten months before,
had been the first to raise the shout of *Vive le Roi!*
Think of the Duke of Angoulême in the South, and
the Prince of Condé in La Vendée; the magic of his
name proved powerless against the impressions left
by my reign. The Vendean peasants said to him:
' We can do nothing against Napoleon: he has rebuilt
our churches and our houses, he has restored to us
our priests, and we can have no wish for civil war.'

" The Bourbons have proved powerless in stopping
the reaction provoked by the madness of some incorrigible emigrants, and the antipathy against them
became a complete epidemic, which seized upon all
classes of the nation. Do greater justice to the
Bourbons—they are a race of brave men—cowardice
among them is but a rare exception—their fault consisted in being only the representatives of superannuated interests; and they were, consequently, repulsed
by all the interests of new France."

" It has been said that the number of priests arrested

amounted to five hundred. The fact is, that there
never were more than fifty-three priests in detention,
on account of secret correspondence with Rome, and
they were legally imprisoned. Cardinal Piétro, because he was at the head of the correspondence with
the *petite eglise*, in order to establish vicars apostolic,
which was contrary to the principles of the Gallican
church, and dangerous to the safety of the state; and
Cardinal Pacca, because he signed the bull of excom-
munication, on account of which no ill will was exhibited towards the Pope, but the whole responsibility
of this act was thrown on the minister who signed it.
The intention was, if any person was assassinated at
Rome in consequence of this bull, to inflict punishment
on the Cardinal. The bull, however, excited universal
contempt, which was an extremely fortunate circumstance for the Roman cardinals and prelates. D'Astro,
vicar of Paris, kept up a correspondence with Cardinal
Piétro; he had received, and clandestinely hawked
about bulls unknown and not received in France,
which was contrary to the principles of the Gallican
church, and characterized as a criminal offence by the
penal code.

" How was it possible that 500 priests should have
been arrested for affairs connected with the church,
when the whole number of persons, at that time confined in the eight state-prisons, only amounted to 243
individuals, which was composed—1st, of priests who
were imprisoned for the reasons assigned above; of
emigrants, whose names were still retained on the list,

for having borne arms against the nation; of agents of England or foreign powers, who had violated their oaths, and who, if they had been judicially tried, would have been immediately condemned to death; a degree of severity which there was no desire to exercise. 2ndly, of Chouan chiefs, or promoters of civil war, condemned to death, but not executed, because they had given useful information to the government, and whose knowledge was important, either to identify new Chouans who might be arrested, or to furnish accounts of localities and past events which it was desirable thoroughly to understand; 3rdly, of emigrants, who had received an amnesty, but were still under the inspection of the police, for having been engaged in conspiracies against the state and the government. They, also, if subjected to a judicial trial, would have been condemned to death, but their trial would have contributed to keep alive the public feelings with respect to the danger to which France was exposed, of losing her chief; moreover, some of these plots, such as that of the Baron de la Rochefoucauld and of Vaudricourt, commissioner of war of the army of Condé, at the same time that they were criminal, were so stupid, that it was quite sufficient to keep their advisers and abettors in a state prison till the peace; 4thly, of men of a lower class, loaded with crimes cognizable by the inferior courts, but belonging to still existing associations and societies, whom the jury, though persuaded of their guilt, would not have dared to condemn, for fear of their accomplices. Their

detention was founded upon an order signed by the
judge who had presided at their examination, and who
testified the facts, supported by an order signed by
the Prefect and the Council of the Prefecture, and which
required that these persons should not be set at liberty,
but kept in prison as being dangerous to public tranquillity. Such were the persons who made up the
number of 243, confined in the eight state-prisons of
a country containing 40,000,000 of inhabitants, and
emerging from the evils of a horrible revolution,
which had shaken the foundations of the whole social
system of an empire long agitated by civil discord, and
continually harassed by foreign wars. There is no
similar case to be found in the history of nations, for
there is no country in Europe which does not contain
a greater number of persons pining in prisons, under
the warrant of various authorities, and under forms
approved by the laws. These 243 individuals, the
number of whom continually diminished, were detained
in eight prisons, of which Vincennes was one; each,
therefore, one with the other, contained from thirty to
forty persons.

" These state-prisons were established by virtue of a
decree of the council of state, of the date of the 3rd
of May, 1810; it was a liberal regulation, and a
beneficent act of the administration, but which, from
being ill-understood, gave rise to the strangest ideas
in foreign countries. Sir Francis Burdett, at a meeting in Westminster, accused me of having established
six Bastilles. The decree was couched in the following
terms :

" We, Napoleon, Emperor of the French, King of Italy, protector of the confederation of the Rhine, mediator of the Swiss confederation, &c., &c.

" On the report of our minister of general police, considering that there is a certain number of our subjects detained in state prisons, whom it would neither be convenient to bring to trial before the ordinary tribunals, nor to set at liberty—that several of them, have at various periods, made attempts to disturb the public peace—that they would necessarily be condemned to death by the public tribunals, but that superior considerations prevent their being sent to trial—that others, after having been conspicuous as chiefs of revolutionary bands in the civil wars, have been again seized in open rebellion, and that motives affecting the general interest, are equally opposed to their being brought to trial—that many are either notorious public robbers or men addicted to crime, whom our courts have not been able to condemn, although convinced of their criminality, but whose enlargement would be injurious to the interests and safety of the public—that a certain number, having been employed as agents of the police in foreign countries, and failed in their fidelity, can neither be set at large nor brought to trial without compromising the security of the state—and, finally, that some belonging to different united countries, are men who cannot be brought to trial, because their crimes are either political or anterior to the union, and that they could not be set at liberty without compromising the interests of the state. Considering, however, that it is due to our justice to be well assured that such of our subjects as are confined in our prisons of state, are confined for just reasons affecting the public well-being, and not from any private considerations or personal causes—that it is proper to establish legal and solemn forms, for the examination of each particular case, and by such examination every year, to review the decisions of the privy council and the causes of detention, and to ascertain the propriety of its being prolonged, thus equally providing for the security of the state and that of its citizens—by the advice of our privy council, have decreed, and do hereby decree, as follows:—

" CHAP. I. — FORMALITIES TO BE OBSERVED FOR THE DETENTION OF STATE PRISONERS.

" Art. 1. No person shall be kept in any state prison, except by virtue of the decision of the privy council, founded upon a report of our chief judge, minister of justice, or our minister of police—such privy council being constituted according to the Act of the 16th Thermidor, year 10, chap. x., art. 86.

" 2. The detention authorised by the privy council, shall in no case be extended beyond a year, unless authorised by a new decision of the privy council, in the manner about to be explained. 3. In the month of December in each year, the list of all state prisoners shall be laid before us, at a special privy council. 4. The list shall contain the names of all the prisoners, together with their Christian names, age, residence, profession, place of imprisonment, its period and causes, together with the date of the decision of the privy council or councils, by which it has been authorised.   5. The column for observations shall contain an analysis of the reasons for putting an end to, or prolonging, the detention of each prisoner. 6. Before the first of January in every year, the decision of the privy council affecting each prisoner, forwarded by the minister of state, and certified by the minister of justice, shall be sent to the minister of police, and to the attorney-general of the court of appeal of the district.   7. The minister of police shall send to the commandant of every state prison, a formal document, certified by himself, and containing the decisions of the privy council concerning each of the prisoners.   8. Each of these decisions shall be copied in a register kept for that purpose, according to the forms prescribed by law and notified to every prisoner.

" CHAP. II.—OF THE INSPECTION OF STATE PRISONS.

" Art. 9. Each prison shall be inspected at least once in every year, previous to the report of the privy council, referred to as above.   Such inspection shall be made by one or more councillors of state, appointed by us for that purpose on the recommendation of our minister of justice, and shall take place before the first of September in each year.   10. Our commissioners shall visit every part of such prison, in order

to be well assured, that no one is detained contrary
to the prescribed forms, and that the means of safety,
order, cleanliness, and health are carefully maintained.
11. They shall hear the complaints of each prisoner
apart, his observations on the change of circumstances
which may affect his case, and his demands either to
be brought to trial or set at liberty.   12. They shall
set at liberty all persons detained contrary to the provisions required by chap. i.   13. They shall make a
report of their mission, and give their opinion on the
case of each prisoner.   14. These opinions shall all
be laid before the privy council referred to in chap. i,
art. 3.   15. Before the 15th of February in each
year, the attorney-general of the imperial court of the
district, by means of one of his deputies or imperial
attorneys under his orders, shall verify such reports,
and see that no persons are detained in the state
prisons within his jurisdiction, in opposition to the
forms above prescribed, and that the registers are
regularly kept.   A minute of this visit shall be drawn
up, which shall be forwarded to our minister of
justice, and in case of any contravention of this
decree, or of any detention either illegally enforced or
prolonged, the commissioner charged with the duty of
such visitation shall set all such persons at liberty.

" CHAP. III.—OF PERSONS KEPT UNDER SURVEILLANCE.

" Art. 16. The list of all persons under surveillance
shall be laid before us by the minister of police, at
the annual special council, referred to in art. 3.

17. This list shall be drawn up in the form prescribed for prisoners of state, in art. 4; and instead of the decision of the privy council required in the case of state prisoners, the authority by which the surveillance has been commanded shall be mentioned.
18. The prolongation or cessation of the surveillance shall be decided on by the privy council.

" CHAP. IV.—OF THE ADMINISTRATION OF STATE PRISONS.

" SECT. 1.—*Of the Inspection of Prisons.*

" Art. 19. The superintendence or administration of every state prison, shall be entrusted to an officer of *Gendarmerie*, who shall have the command of the party appointed for guarding the prison, and shall determine all such measures of safety or precaution as may be necessary to prevent escape. 20. There shall be a jailor for the interior superintendence, and the keeping of the registry. The jailor shall have under his orders a sufficient number of keepers. 21. The military commandant shall be selected by us, on the recommendation of our minister of police, to whose office shall exclusively belong everything relating to the administration of state-prisons, the maintenance of the buildings, the food, clothing, and safe keeping of the prisoners. 22. The jailor shall be nominated, and his nomination revocable at pleasure, by our minister of police. 23. The commandant, jailor, and keepers, shall be each of them responsible for the safe keeping of the prisoners, as far as his own department

is concerned.   24. If from negligence, or any other
cause whatsoever, a prisoner be suffered to escape,
they shall be deprived of their situations and prose-
cuted as the law requires. . . .

     " Sect. 2.—*Of the Relations of the Officers.*

" 25. The jailor shall be subordinate to the commandant, and   receive   his instructions from him.
26. The commandant shall   correspond with   the
minister of police, and the councillor of state of the
arrondissement, and be under the surveillance of the
prefect.

     " Sect. 3.—*Of the Interior Regulation.*

" 27. The governor shall keep an exact register of
the prisoners admitted and discharged, and copies of
the orders by virtue of which they are kept in confinement.   28. No order for the discharge of a prisoner
can be executed, without a notification to the commandant of the decision of the privy council, by which
such discharge has been ordered.   29. Any governor
or keeper who shall be found guilty of having favoured
the clandestine correspondence of any prisoner, ordered
to be kept *au secret*, shall be deprived of his situation,
and punished by six months' imprisonment.   30. The
commandant shall not, under any pretext whatsoever,
allow the prisoners committed to his charge to go out,
either with himself, the governor, or any of the
keepers.   31. In case of the sickness of a prisoner,
the commandant shall immediately give notice to the
officer of health, who shall visit and treat the patient.
32. Every prisoner who shall require the same, shall

be entitled to receive the sum of two francs daily, or the common allowance, in aid of his support. 33. Prisoners shall retain the disposition of their property, unless otherwise specially ordered. 34. With this view, they shall give, under the surveillance of the commandant, all the necessary powers and receipts. And whatever sums they receive shall only be given them in his presence and under his authorisation.

" Art. 35. There shall be no state prisons-except in the places hereinafter mentioned. 36. No state prisoner shall be confined, except temporarily or in transition, in any other state-prisons than those appointed by us. 37. State-prisons shall be established in the Castles of SAUMUR, HAM, IF, LANDSKRONA, PIERRE-CHATEL, FENESTRELLE, CAMPIANO, and VINCENNES. 38. Our ministers of justice, war, police, and finance are commanded, each in his department, to carry this decree into effect; a copy of which shall be inserted in the *Bulletin des Lois.*"

" The whole people of France would have been filled with indignation, had I attempted or wished to re-establish *Lettres de Cachet;* the forty magistrates composing the council of state, would not even have entertained such a proposal; I should besides have been insane, if, having any design to interfere with the civil liberties of the people, I had commenced, as I actually did, by proclaiming and causing to be inserted in the *Bulletin des Lois*, regulations which were guarantees for individual liberty, and opposed to all our constitutions, even to that existing before 1789, and maintained by the parliaments.

" Under the convention, the laws against suspected persons and against emigration, had given birth to a great number of state-prisons; there were more than 2000 of them, containing as many as 60,000 persons; during the early part of the reign of the Directory, this number was greatly diminished, and all these prisons successively ceased to exist. The number of prisoners of state was gradually reduced to 3000; they were removed into the ordinary prisons, and their superintendence was in the hands of the administration, and especially of the police. The commissioners of police and the minister were magistrates of the public safety, and had authority to cause names to be enrolled in the jailor's books. A special article of the constitutions of that period conferred this right on the minister of police or on the administration, in case of any plots or conspiracies against the well-being of the state. The number of prisoners was augmented in 1799, after the revolution of Prairial, by the execution of the law of the hostages. There were 9000 prisoners at the time of the 18th Brumaire; these were, for the most part, set at liberty, and in the period of the empire scarcely 1200 remained belonging to these classes.

" The police was accustomed to exercise the most deplorably arbitrary rule. It was consequently found necessary to transfer the surveillance of the prisons to the tribunals, to authorise the imperial attorneys general to visit and examine them. and to set all those at liberty, who were not actually in the hands of justice. The police of the prisons was conferred on the tribunals; the police was no longer allowed to detain persons in the common prisons; the prisoners of state, to whom we have already referred, were placed under the immediate administration of the police, with power to the imperial attorneys-general to visit and examine the list even of the state prisoners, and set all those at liberty who had not been arrested by virtue of a decree of the privy council, countersigned by the minister of justice. From that moment. liberty was ensured in France. Every prisoner could at once address himself to the magistrates; the minister of police and his agents were despoiled of that frightful power which enabled them to arrest any man at their discretion, and to keep him in their hands without his being thereby, *ipso facto*, amenable to the law or under its protection. Thus, instead of a committal emanating from a mere commissary of police, a deliberative resolution of the privy council became necessary, in order to retain a prisoner in the hands of justice. This privy council, over which I presided, was composed of five high dignitaries and of two ministers, besides the ministers of police and justice, of two senators, two councillors of state, the first president, and the imperial attorney-general of the court of cassation. In all, there were sixteen persons of the highest dignity and character in the empire, who were ap-

pointed to decide on cases of personal arrest. Was
a better guarantee ever given to the citizens of any
country? This decree declared, that no prisoner of
state could be kept in confinement beyond the term
of a year, and that at the termination of the year he
was to be set at liberty, if the privy council did not
prolong the term of his captivity by a new resolution.
For this purpose, the prisons were visited each year
by two councillors of state; their reports, recommend-
ing charge or discharge, were carefully examined, and
measures, in accordance with the opinion of the
minister of justice, adopted by the privy council.
The privy council delivered their votes, commencing
with that of the president of the supreme court of
cassation.

" This decree, then, was a real benefit—a liberal law
—a diapason to establish the harmony of society, by
means of which nothing arbitrary was left in the
hands either of the magistracy, the administration, or
the police, and a complete guarantee was given to the
citizens. There was no councillor of state, appointed
as an inspector of prisons, who did not regard it as
an honour to be instrumental in releasing as many
persons as possible. All those who were present at
meetings of the privy council, can attest that these
councillors always acted as if they had been the
advocates of the prisoners. The prisons would have
disappeared with the circumstances to which they
owed their origin, with that race of brigands which
had been called into existence by the civil wars.

The intriguing priests of the *petite église*—the men who were exasperated by the revolution, by the losses which they had suffered, and their prejudices, were continually engaged in devising assassinations or weaving plots for the overthrow of the state. There were 200,000 individuals in France who had emigrated, or been transported, or figured in the civil wars, to whom I had restored their country and their property, but under the condition of their being subjected to special surveillance. It was from this class of men that the state prisoners were drawn; and the right of surveillance was legalized conformably to the liberal spirit of justice, by which all the acts of the council were animated.

" Whenever the fourth part of the privy council were of opinion that a prisoner might be set at liberty, he was immediately discharged. Prisoners thus arrested, independently of the right of recourse to the privy council, and to the council of state, had also a constitutional guarantee in the committee of the senate for the protection of individual liberty; none of them neglected to apply to the committee; the committee deliberated, and asked for explanations from the minister of police. This body was the means of setting many at liberty; it was necessary to pay attention to its demands, because, when its members had once given their opinion, if the administration failed to listen to it, they immediately made a report to the senate. Although this committee for the protection of individual liberty never made much

s 2

noise, never delivered long harangues, nor exhibited any desire to draw public attention to itself, yet it was of the greatest utility. Had the state prisons, like a Bastile, contained citizens who were merely the victims of the intrigues or dissatisfaction of the prince, this intervention alone would have been sufficient to put an end to the abuse. It is equally erroneous to suppose that the legislative body had no share in the formation of the laws; the legislative committees discussed the substance of them with the councillors of state, and formed projects of new laws; their influence was not tumultuous, but it was not the less real.

" An event which occurred at Dantzig caused me to reflect upon the decree respecting state prisons. An old man had been confined for fifty years in the castle of Weichselmunde, and had lost his memory; it was no longer possible either to know who he was, or the reasons for which he had been imprisoned.

" I was anxious for the strict execution of the law, which prescribed, that in all ordinary cases, persons should be placed before a magistrate within twenty-four hours after their arrest; that in extraordinary cases, according to the nature of the circumstances, there should be no greater exception to this rule than the space of a year; and that in all such cases, the sentence of detention should be pronounced by a privy council of sixteen persons, and on the report of the minister of justice. This regulation may have excited foolish complaints. In public societies, people talk idly, without any knowledge of the question. The title, perhaps, was not well chosen; and it would have been better to have called these houses, *prisons for the confinement of persons subjected to general surveillance.*

" No people ever enjoyed a larger share of civil liberty than those of France under my reign; there is no state in Europe which has not had a greater number of individuals arrested and cast into prison under various titles or forms, or who are not actually engaged in suits pending before the tribunals. A country in which the insolence and injustice of the press upon its quays and public places, is authorised by law, ought not to boast of enjoying true civil liberty. Such liberty does not exist for the common people in England, however real it may be in the case of the higher classes. If the criminal legislation of England be compared with that of France, who can doubt the superiority of the latter, and the comparative abuses and imperfections of the former? As to the criminal legislation of Austria, Russia, Prussia, and the other states of Europe, suffice it to say, that there is neither publicity nor confrontation of witnesses. My laws are highly esteemed by the Italians, and there is no country into which they have been introduced, whose inhabitants have not petitioned for their continuance as a favour.

" Misfortune brings with it good as well as evil; it makes us acquainted with the truth. It reduces convictions to errors, and transforms consequences into

the condition of fantastic dreams. Now that my head
no longer bears the heavy burthen of a crown, I can
reflect, like a philosopher, on the times in which my
faults were the work of Providence; I recognise the
influence of chance in the destinies of man, and in
those events which are decisive of the fate of empires.
The favours which I bestowed were most frequently
merely happy accidents for those on whom they were
bestowed. And yet, what king is there who can
say more conscientiously than myself, that he has
been anxious to disregard all intrigue, and to render
justice to his subjects? Intrigue, however, is so skilful, and merit so awkward and timid, extremes so
nearly meet, and the atmosphere of courts is so murky,
that do what one will, it is impossible always to proceed on the true course. A good choice is a mere
lottery in the case of a sovereign, and intrigue is
constantly at work to undermine the path under the
feet of merit. Any errors which I may have committed in the bestowal of favours, have not, in fact,
been voluntary, but the results of a vice inherent in
the very existence of royalty, and of governments of
every description, by whatever name they are called.

"When I began to form a court, I sought among the
high officers of the army for names which, by their
recent and glorious celebrity, might worthily replace
those which were the most illustrious of the ancient
court. Some old names presented themselves to me;
the Duchess of Montmorency, the Countess of Remusat, the Count of Bearn, and Count Ségur, who

had formerly been ambassador at Petersburg: it was,
however, absolutely necessary to engraft these names
upon names in the army, and which were connected with
the revolution, in order to avoid provoking discontent
and want of confidence among the people. I was
also desirous of having done with the *reasoners* in the
army of the Rhine, by rallying around my person the
most brilliant amongst them. Caulaincourt had long
served under Moreau, and he was entrusted with the
task of sounding the feelings of his old comrades. Col.
Préval, formerly an adjutant-general, and a very
distinguished officer, was one of those whom I was
desirous of having about my person. He belonged to
a military family, and his fitness and abilities recommended him to my attention above all others. I was
told that he rejected the proposition with contempt.
I was not astonished, for such, in fact, was the
feeling by which all the faithful friends of Moreau
were at that time influenced. Well, nothing could
be more untrue!

"Ten years afterwards, General Préval, whose personal qualities were so worthy of admiration, was
brought into immediate relation with me, and I found
that he had never refused, but would have been
delighted to have become a member of my household.
It is a subject of regret both for him and for me, that
he was prevented from becoming what I desired.
He is an officer of great merit, and had he not been
kept at a distance from me, I should certainly have
made him minister of war; but I should have had to

begin by conferring upon him dignity and rank. Under my reign, it was not so easy to find a suitable minister. No man in France understood the organization and mechanism of armies as well as General Préval. His military conduct at Frankfort was something perfect in policy, and on that occasion, he furnished me with the standard of what might be expected from a general who was as intelligent as he was brave. But I am looking for examples of the effect of intrigues. Have I not, by such means, been deprived, in the course of years, of the services of Macdonald, Dalmas, Lecourbe, Carnot, and Dessoles? With respect to the last, however, I have nothing to regret, since his treason in 1814. In short, let it be proved to me, that any sovereign has shown himself more anxious than myself to do justice, or has better understood how to identify himself with the interests of his people, and then I shall repent of not having done more. I am, however, conscious that whilst on the throne, I constantly made it my first thought and desire to realize my motto: '*Everything for the French people.*' "

CHAPTER XII.

BRIEF VIEW OF THE CONSULAR PERIOD.

" THE 1st of January, 1804, completes the magnificent picture of the progress of the prosperity of France during the consular government.

" The legislative body, through the medium of their president, sent me the following address:

" ' The representatives of France offer you their thanks, in the name of the French people, for all the useful works planned and executed in France, and for the improvements in agriculture and industry, which the war has not interrupted.

" ' The custom of entertaining great ideas sometimes causes superior minds to neglect the details of administration. Posterity cannot reproach you with this fault. The idea, and the practical carrying out of it, have always been co-existent during your government.

" ' Everything is improving; hatred is being ex-

tinguished, opposition is giving way, and under the
victorious influence of a spirit which bends all to its
will, the circumstances, the systems, and even the
men who appear most opposed to one another,
approach and unite, and together serve to promote
the glory of their common country.

" ' Former customs and present customs are beginning to agree; everything is preserved which should
maintain the equality of civil and political rights;
everything is resumed which may tend to increase
the splendour and the dignity of a great empire. All
these advantages have been brought about in four
years. Those rays of our national glory, the
brightness of which had been diminishing for five
years, have regained all their splendour under your
government.'

" It has always been considered possible to have
effected a landing in England, and when this landing
was once effected, the question was reduced merely to
a second battle of Austerlitz or of Jena. Did Hannibal
look behind him when he crossed the Alps? Did
Cæsar, when he landed in Epirus, look back? London
is only a few days' march from the coast of the channel;
the army and the militia of England were extended
over a very wide space; as for the coast-guards, it
would have been impossible for them to have united
at the point of disembarkation, or to reach London
quickly enough to protect it. The place chosen for
the landing was only known to myself. I concealed
it from those most in my confidence; none of the

generals of the army knew it; nothing could give
any idea of where it would be. It might be Hastings,
Torbay, or some point at the mouth of the Thames.
It was quite necessary, therefore, to guard an extent
of coast more than thirty leagues long, and four days
would be necessary to collect forces for that purpose;
whilst, in two, or three at the most, the French army,
once disembarked, might have arrived in London with
a van-guard of 50,000 men.

"The flotillas were only to be the means of disem-
barking from 160 to 200,000 men, in the space of a
few hours, and of taking possession of all the maritime
places. They were to cross over, under the protection of a numerous squadron, assembled at Martinique,
and coming with all speed to Boulogne; and if this
fleet should miss its object one year, it might succeed
another time. Fifty, sixty, eighty, or a hundred sail
of the line, could sail from Toulon, from Brest, from
Rochefort, L'Orient, Cadiz, and unite at some common
rendezvous ; this fleet would then appear in the
English Channel like a dreadful tempest, whilst the
English squadrons were engaged in scouring the seas
for the protection of the East and West Indies. Had
not the squadron of Toulon, although encumbered by
500 transport vessels, been able to gain Egypt, in
spite of the English squadron under Lord Nelson?
At Paris, in the Faubourg St. Germain, every one
laughed at the project of a landing; Pitt, however,
did not laugh at it in London. He seems to have
conceived almost all the extent of the danger. He

therefore managed to clog France with a coalition, at the very moment when she was about to execute her purpose: the English oligarchy was never in greater danger.

" I should not have entered London as a conqueror, but as a liberator; I should have acted over again the part of William III., but with more generosity and disinterestedness. The discipline of my army would have been as strict in London as it was in Paris. No sacrifices, no contributions even, would have been exacted from the English. My troops would not have behaved like conquerors, but like brothers, who had come to restore them to liberty and to their rights. I should have told them to assemble, and themselves to work at their regeneration; I should have told them that they were our elder brothers in matters of constitution and of political legislation; that we only wished to take a part in the work of their regeneration; and I should have kept my word faithfully and strictly. Thus, only a few months would have elapsed, before the two nations, so bitterly opposed to each other, would have become completely identified in their principles, their maxims, and their interests; and I should only leave England in order to complete, from north to south, the work of European regeneration under monarchical forms. This system might have been as liberal as the republican system. Both aimed at the same object. Never was a more vast idea conceived in the interest of the progress of civilization, nor brought nearer to realization; it might have been executed with firmness, moderation, and good faith. And it is worthy of remark, that of the obstacles which caused it to fail, none took their origin from men: they were all caused by the elements. In the south, it was the sea; in the north, the burning of Moscow and the frost; thus, the water, the air, the fire—all nature, and nothing but nature was the opponent of a regeneration commanded by nature itself! The problems of Providence are not to be solved.

" If, by events difficult to comprehend, the French army had been obliged to stop at the Medway, it would have done, in all the ports of the Thames and in the roadstead of Portsmouth, what the English did at Toulon; the arsenals of Portsmouth and Chatham would have been left in ruins, and for at least twenty years, the maritime power of England would have given no annoyance to France."

CHAPTER XIII.

GENERAL CONSIDERATIONS ON THE POLICY OF FOREIGN
GOVERNMENTS, AND ESPECIALLY OF THOSE OF
ENGLAND AND AUSTRIA.

THE incessant quarrels with Sir Hudson Lowe, and
perhaps also his conversation with Lord Amherst,
had led the Emperor's mind to reflect on his gigantic
struggle with England, and the constant efforts which
he had used to induce the English ministers to see that
it was the interest of both nations to come to a
good understanding with one another. During the
whole day, the Emperor appeared to be labouring under a sort of moral and physical depression.
He had scarcely quitted his sofa or the fire-side, for
a moment, and his valet-de-chambre had remarked
that he had only taken a little soup and the wing of a
chicken for his dinner. Towards midnight he caused
me to be sent for, and asked me, with a smile, if I was
in a humour to spend the remainder of the night with.
him. He then led me into the drawing-room, and

giving free course to the impulse of his mind, he dictated to me the following note, as materials for that chapter of his memoirs which might treat of his negotiations with England:

" When deplorable weakness and endless versatility manifest themselves in all the acts of power; when yielding, sometimes to the influence of one party and sometimes to that of another, and living from day to day without any fixed plan, or any definite object in view, its possessors have exhibited the clearest evidence of their incapacity, and the most moderate citizens are compelled to agree, that the state is not governed; when, finally, to the incapacity of the administration at home, it is guilty of the greatest error which it is possible to commit in the eyes of a proud nation—viz., degradation in the opinion of foreign nations—then a vague restlessness begins to pervade the whole mass of society. It is deeply agitated by the fear of the loss of national reputation and honour; and turning its eyes upon itself, it appears to seek for a man capable of effecting its deliverance.

" Such a tutelary genius is always to be found within the bosom of a populous nation, but sometimes he is slow to appear, and, in fact, it is not enough that he exists, he must be known by others, and know himself, too. Till this happens, all attempts are vain, all intrigues powerless; the inaction of the multitude protects the nominal government, and, in despite of its incapacity or even its treasonable betrayal of the national interests, the efforts of its enemies do not prevail against it. But no sooner does this deliverer, so impatiently expected, appear, and give symptoms of his existence, than the national instinct divines it, and calls him to his post: obstacles disappear before him, and the whole of a great people unite, with one accord, and seem to say—' This is the man!'

" Such was the state of the public mind in France, when the nation confided its destiny to my hands.

" Peace, without having been gained in the field of battle, would have ruined the republic. War was absolutely necessary to maintain energy and unity in the state, as long as its administrative machinery did not work perfectly. Peace would have brought, in its train, a reduction of taxation and a discharge of a part of the army. Many men had been under arms since the levy *en masse*, in 1792, and were only raised for the defence of the country. To have detained them in service, when the republic was at peace with the Continent, would have been to abuse their patriotism, and provoke dissatisfaction and discontent amongst a great number of families; and, under all circumstances, it would have been necessary to give them their discharge. The consequence would have been that France, after two years of peace, would have found herself in a notorious and dangerous inferiority in the presence of the whole of mon-archical Europe, which as necessarily would have continued to be allied against her republican institutions.

" I owed it, however, to public opinion to open negotiations for peace; and the majority of the nation wished ardently for it, and circumstances appeared favourable to its conclusion.

" The cabinet of Berlin had just given evidence of a very pacific disposition. Count Haugwitz, the first minister, had said to the minister of France—' The revolution with you has been accomplished from below upwards, and by a succession of the most frightful storms; it will proceed more slowly among us, but will come, sooner or later, and from above downwards. The king is a democrat, after his fashion. He is an enemy to the privileges of the nobility, and has been born in the school of philosophers; and in a few years, the law will be in Prussia what it has become, by means of the revolution of France, equal for all. Have patience, then, and, believe me, we shall be your allies by the force of events, and that will be the day on which your government shall offer us guarantees of stability.' At the same time, however, a Prussian *corps d'armée* was assembling on the Lower Rhine, and threatening the department of the Roer.

" Duroc was sent to Berlin; the king and the queen showed him the most marked attention, and gave him various proofs of their regard. The Prussian troops quitted the banks of the Rhine, and returned to their usual quarters, but the cabinet still remained in an expecting attitude.

" After the 26th of December, 1799, the First Consul wrote to King George. This unusual step produced very different effects in England. The aristocracy merely regarded it as a violation of royal etiquette; the people, weary of the sacrifices which the war imposed upon them, were displeased with the insulting reply of Lord Grenville. This minister wrote to Monsieur de Talleyrand, that peace was impossible as long as France was governed by a system, subversive of all social order, and as long as the house of Bourbon was not restored to the throne—an event which would restore her colonies to France, as well as the friendship of all Europe. This arrogant minister allowed his passion to impel him so far as to say to parlialiament, ' To cease from fighting against a nation which is an enemy to all worship, all morality, and all government, is not to labour for the common good, but it is rather to grow weary of resisting evil. It is necessary, then, to carry on the war with vigour against a nation which is desirous of subjecting the world to its ravages. I declare, in the presence of Europe and of England, that I would prefer war and all its horrors, as long as France shall persist, as she has hitherto done, in the maintenance of those opinions and principles which have led to and effected the revolution: they were Jacobins, and they are so still. France proclaims war against kings; she regards nothing as sacred, and is faithless to her treaties.' The courageous efforts of the Whigs were unavailing to defend the First Consul from the furious assaults of the Tories, and to prove to them that to refuse peace was, in fact, to deny the history of their country, and to fight in order to trammel the progress of civilization. The cabinet of Vienna was in the pay of England, and its refusal to treat on the basis of the treaty of Campo-Formio served the policy of Napoleon. The battle of Marengo replaced France in the position, without which no treaty of peace could have any permanence.

" Italy being lost—Vienna menaced—Austria asked for peace. Lieut.-General Count St. Julien arrived at Paris on the 21st July, 1800, as the bearer of a letter from the Emperor of Germany to the First Consul. He announced himself as a plenipotentiary, commissioned to negotiate, conclude, and sign the preliminaries of a peace. The Emperor's letter was precise, and contained full powers: 'You may place,' observes the writer, 'full confidence in everything which Count St. Julien may say on my behalf, and I will ratify all that he may do.' I commissioned Monsieur de Talleyrand to negotiate with this plenipotentiary, and in a few days the preliminaries were arranged. I asked ·nothing which had not been already decided upon by the treaty of Campo-Formio, for I agreed to the Emperor's receiving indemnities in Italy for his losses in Germany. I only required that the two armies should remain in their respective positions till a definitive peace was signed.

" The Emperor's letter could leave no room to doubt respecting the ratification of the preliminaries. It, however, proved otherwise; the cabinet of Vienna disavowed Count St. Julien. Baron Thugut wrote that

the Emperor, his master, was bound to England by
treaties of peace, which rendered it impossible for him
to ratify the treaty, but that he was, nevertheless, disposed to open new negotiations; and he communicated
the contents of a letter, in which Lord Minto explained the grounds on which the English ministry was
equally well disposed to concur in promoting a general
peace.

" The changes thus effected in a few months were
very gratifying to the self-love of France. Not long
before, France had made the first efforts to obtain a
peace, to which Lord Grenville replied by torrents of
abuse. Suffering himself to indulge in the most extraordinary insinuations, he had expressed his desire
that the princes of that race of kings should be restored
to the throne of France, without which peace was impossible; and now it was the same Lord Grenville
who asked to treat with the First Consul, and even to
buy the opening of a negotiation at the price of a
naval armistice, which was wholly to the advantage
of France.

" The best thing which the republic could have done,
would have been to recommence hostilities. I was
anxious, however, to overlook no opportunity of re-
establishing peace with England, and for the attainment of that object, I suppressed the resentment
which I felt in consequence of the insult offered to the
French republic by the cabinet of Vienna, and made
no allusion to it in my reply. My minister of foreign
affairs wrote to Baron Thugut, that the First Consul

was ready to accept the proposal for a double negotiation and the admission of an English plenipotentiary to the conferences at Lunéville, on condition of an armistice by sea as well as by land; and that hostilities should recommence by land, if England refused to acquiesce in a naval armistice.

"At the same time a courier was sent to Monsieur Otto who was then in London, acting as French commissioner for an exchange of prisoners. I directed him to write, that my wish was that my ships and neutral vessels should be allowed to convey succours and provisions to Malta and Alexandria, in the same manner as the fortresses of Ulm and Ingolstadt were to be provisioned and reinforced by the Austrians. On the 24th of August, M. Otto addressed a note to Lord Grenville, in which he informed him of the contents of the communication made by Lord Minto, the English ambassador in Vienna, in which he signified the desire of the English government to take part in the negotiations which were about to be opened between Austria and France for the re-establishment of peace, and stated that the First Consul was willing to admit an English plenipotentiary to the negotiations, but that in this case, the conclusion of a peace would become more difficult, the interests to be discussed more numerous and complicated, and the negotiations prolonged, so as to be injurious to the cause of the French republic, unless some compensation were given for the prolongation of the armistices of Marengo and Sarsdorff, by a naval armistice with England.

"Lord Minto's despatches had not arrived in London.

"Lord Grenville was astonished at the receipt of this note, and sent to request M. Otto to communicate to him the whole of the letter of which he had sent a part; the latter immediately complied. In the meantime, Lord Minto's courier arrived in London, and Lord Grenville said to M. Otto, that the idea of a naval armistice was something new in the history of nations —that, nevertheless, the British ministry acceded to the principle, and would send Mr. Thomas Grenville as plenipotentiary to the place appointed for the opening of the negotiations. For this purpose, he requested M. Otto to furnish him with the necessary passports to enable him to enter France and reach his destination.

"This was evidently a mere elusion of the question, in order to gain time and to enable Austria to repair her losses before the resumption of hostilities. It was now the end of August, and M. Otto requested a categorical reply before the 3rd of September, because the armistice with Austria expired on the 10th of that month.

"On the 4th of September, Lord Grenville confined himself to asking for a written plan, as he was at a loss precisely to comprehend what France intended by an armistice applicable to naval operations.

"M. Otto immediately forwarded his plan, the principal features of which were: 1st, that the ships of war, and the trading vessels of both nations, should enjoy free navigation without being subjected to search or visitation ; 2ndly, that the squadrons blockading Toulon, Brest, Rochefort, and Cadiz should return to English ports; and, 3rdly, that Malta, Alexandria and Belleisle should be placed on the same footing as the fortresses of Ulm, Philippsburg, and Ingolstadt; and consequently, that all French and neutral ships should have free access to these ports.

" On the 7th of September, Lord Grenville replied, that his Britannic Majesty admitted the principle of a naval armistice; although contrary to the interests of England, it was a sacrifice which she was willing to make in favour of peace, and of her ally, Austria; but that none of the articles of the French scheme were admissible; and he offered to negotiate the following counter-scheme as a basis:

" ' 1st. Hostilities shall cease by sea; 2ndly, supplies shall be granted to Malta, Alexandria, and Belleisle for a fortnight at a time, according to the number of men which the garrisons respectively contain; 3rdly, the blockade of the harbours of Brest, Toulon, and other harbours belonging to France or her allies shall be raised, but no vessel of war which shall be in any of the said harbours shall go to sea during the continuance of the armistice, and the English squadrons shall remain in sight of these ports.'

" On the 16th of September, the French commissioner replied that his government proposed to his Britannic Majesty, that the negotiations should be opened at Lunéville, that the English and Austrian

plenipotentiaries should be admitted to a joint negotiation, and that in the meantime, the war should continue by sea and land, or that there should be an
armistice with Austria alone, and a negotiation with
Austria alone; and that, in the latter case, negotiations could be carried on between France and England,
either in Paris or London, without any interruption of
the naval war.

" The prolongation of the armistice by land would
give Austria time to re-organize her armies, seriously
injured at Marengo and Maestricht, would efface the
impressions produced upon the minds of the Austrian
soldiers by those two great victories, and enable the
King of Naples to put himself in a condition to interfere in the affairs of Italy; levies *en masse* were
already in the course of organization in the Apennines,
and the March of Ancona.

" A suspension of hostilities had only been conceded
to Austria, on her formal promise of concluding a peace
without delay, and by means of negotiations independent of her treaties with England. The First Consul,
therefore, felt himself perfectly authorised to resume the
offensive, both on the Rhine and in Italy, on the 10th
of September; General Moreau did not, however, put
his advanced guard in motion till the 19th, and he
stopped almost immediately, on the request of the
Austrian general, and the offer made to him, by the
court of Vienna, of placing the fortresses of Ulm,
Ingolstadt, and Philippsburg in his hands as a pledge
of the sincerity of its desire for peace.

" The First Consul acceded to this proposal, and a prolongation of the armistice for forty days was granted, reckoning from the 30th of September. At the same time, he consented to modify his first proposition respecting England, and on the 20th of September, M. Otto wrote to Lord Grenville, that 1st, the French government agreed that the French or allied squadrons should not leave their positions during the continuance of the naval armistice; 2ndly, that only such communications with Malta should be authorised, as were necessary to convey supplies every fifteen days, at the rate of 10,000 rations per diem; but that Alexandria not being invested by land, and having an abundant supply of provisions, it required that six French frigates sailing from Toulon should be allowed free ingress and egress to and from Alexandria without being disturbed by the English fleet, on the single condition of having on board an English officer with a flag of truce.

" The only advantages which the republic could have obtained from a suspension of hostilities by sea, were, that these six frigates armed *en flute*, would have been able to convey from 3 to 4000 men as reinforcements to Egypt, as well as such materials of war for the artillery, as it might stand in need of. As soon as the principle of negotiation was admitted, Lord Grenville authorised M. Amman, his under-secretary of state to confer with M. Otto, with a view of coming to an understanding. At their first interview, the under-secretary proposed to M. Otto, the evacuation

of Egypt by the French army, as a consequence of the
convention of El' Arish, concluded on the 24th of
January preceding, but broken on the 18th of May
following, in consequence of England not having
agreed to its ratification. Such a proposition could
not for a moment be entertained ; M. Amman perceived the difficulty, and relinquished the point. A
few conferences sufficed to bring the parties to a perfect understanding on all the points, except that of
sending six frigates to Alexandria. It was found impossible to come to any agreement on a point which
so nearly concerned England and her views upon
Egypt, and on the 9th of October, the English commissioner declared the negotiations at an end.

" These events led to serious complications; Malta
capitulated towards the beginning of September, and,
on the other side, a general rising was organized in the
Apennines, ready to break out on the arrival of 10,000
English under General Abercrombie, and of a Neapolitan division which was to pass the frontiers of the
kingdom, as soon as they were certain of the landing
of the English corps.

" In a state of things so dangerous to France, it
became necessary to conclude a peace at any cost.

" The opportunity appeared so much the more
favourable, as a change of ministry had just taken
place in Vienna. Baron Thugut was replaced by
Count Cobentzel, the negotiator of the peace of Campo-
Formio, who regarded it as an honour to be called
a man of peace. His first act was to announce in

Paris, that Count Lerbache was about to set out for
Lunéville without delay. Shortly after he himself set
out for Paris; his secret purpose was to gain time.

" The First Consul gave him a most distinguished
reception, but on the next day the veil was torn off.
On being requested by the minister of foreign affairs to
show his credentials, he hesitated, and alleged that the
etiquette required the respective parties to make a
regular exchange of powers at Lunéville. The First
Consul had appointed his brother Joseph, as his plenipotentiary at this congress, whom he now ordered to
set out forthwith for Lunéville, and requested Count
Cobentzel to proceed thither without delay. The
minutes of the proceedings were opened on the 6th of
November, and an exchange of powers took place, but
at the first sitting, the Austrian plenipotentiary· declared, that he could not treat without the concur-
rence of an English plenipotentiary, and as an English
plenipotentiary could not be admitted without the
consent of England to the last conditions proposed by
France, in the question of the naval armistices, such a
declaration was equivalent to a rupture. On the 17th
of November, hostilities recommenced on the Rhine,
and in Italy; but as the minutes were still open, the
French plenipotentiaries at Lunéville were ordered to
propose to Count Cobentzel to sign a separate peace
with the Emperor, which, in case of need, might be
kept secret, till negotiations were definitively broken
off with England. This peace was to embrace the
following conditions:

" ' The Mincio as the boundary between the Cisalpine republic and the Austrian states in Italy; the duchy of Tuscany for the Infant Duke of Parma; the legations for the Archduke Ferdinand; the restitution of Piedmont to the King of Sardinia, with the Sezio for its boundary on the side of the Cisalpine republic; the Alps and the Rhine as the frontiers of France. On these conditions hostilities were again to cease.'

" Austria refused. It was not until the French head-quarters were established at St. Piotten, and the advanced guard within four leagues of Vienna, that she determined to renounce her alliance with England. On the 19th of February, 1802, she signed the peace of Lunéville, which was ratified by the Emperor in Vienna on the 7th of March following.

" A very grave question was at this time agitated —the right of search.

" In the month of December, 1800, a mutual engagement was entered into by Sweden, Denmark, Russia and Prussia, to lend assistance each to the others against the pretensions of the English admiralty, which arrogated to itself the right of visiting and searching all vessels sailing under a neutral flag.

" This treaty called the quadruple alliance, laid down, and was formed to support, the following principles:

" ' 1st. The flag covers the merchandise.

" ' 2ndly. All vessels under convoy of the ships of a neutral state, are *ipso facto*, free from visit or search.

" ' 3rdly. Munitions of war alone are contraband, and subject to seizure.

" ' 4thly. The right of search is not to be employed, except in cases where munitions of war are on board.

" ' 5thly. Neutrality is established in all cases in which the captain and the half of the crew are natives of the country under whose flag the ship sails.

" ' 6thly. Ships of war belonging to the contracting powers, shall be considered entitled to convoy merchant vessels not only of their own, but of each of the four powers reciprocally.

" ' 7thly. A Russian, Danish, and Swedish squadron shall be continually at sea, to protect the commerce of the contracting nations, and to cause the principles laid down in this treaty to be respected.'

" This question had led to a complete division between the cabinets of France and England, and involved the necessity of war between these two great rivals for the supremacy of the sea. The treaty of Amiens had decided nothing on this point; the First Consul was desirous of peace, and his plenipotentiaries had orders not to embarrass or entangle the negotiation by the discussion of questions whose solution was not indispensable to the interests of the moment.

" During the ages of barbarism, the right of nations was the same by sea and land. Individuals belonging to hostile nations were seized and made prisoners, whether they were taken with arms in their hands, or not, and were kept in bondage till an adequate ransom was paid. Their property in money and goods was confiscated in whole or in part. The influence of civilization, however, had effected a complete change in this respect among nations at war by land, without having produced the same effect in cases of vessels at sea; so that matters are regulated by two different rights, as if there were two kinds of reason and justice. The right of nations in war by land no longer justifies the spoliation of individuals, nor any change in their personal condition. War only applies to governments; thus property does not always change hands; stores of merchandise remain intact; personal liberty is guaranteed. Those alone are considered as prisoners of war, who are taken with arms in their hands, or who form a part of the military force. This change has effected a vast amelioration of the evils of war, rendered the conquest of nations more easy, and war less bloody and disastrous.

" A conquered province takes an oath of submission and obedience, and, if the conqueror requires it, gives hostages, surrenders its arms, and pays the usual taxes to the credit of the conqueror, who, if he deems it necessary, has and exercises the right of imposing an extraordinary levy, either for the support of his army, or as an indemnity for the expenses of the war. This contribution, however, has no regard to the value of merchandise; it is only a *pro rata* increase of the ordinary contributions to a greater or less extent, nearly equal to a year's revenue, and is imposed upon the whole body of the people, so that it never involves the ruin of individuals.

" The right of nations which regulates maritime war has still continued to remain the same as it was in ages of barbarism. The property of individuals is confiscated, and persons not engaged in actual hostilities are made prisoners. When two nations are at war, all vessels belonging to either one or the other, whether at sea or in port, are liable to be seized and confiscated, and the individuals on board to be made prisoners of war. Thus, by a manifest contradiction (supposing France and England to be at war) an English ship which should be found in the port of Nantes, for example, at the moment at which the war was declared, would be confiscated, and the crew made prisoners of war, although not engaged in hostilities; whilst goods in the same city, belonging to an English merchant would not be sequestrated or confiscated, and the merchant himself travelling in France would receive the necessary passports to enable him to leave the country. An English vessel at sea, captured by a French ship, would be confiscated, although the cargo belonged to private individuals, and the crew would be made prisoners of war although not taken in arms, whilst a convoy of a hundred waggons of merchandise belonging to an Englishman, and traversing France at the time of a declaration of war between the two powers, would not be seized.

" In a war by land, even territorial properties possessed by foreign subjects are not confiscated; they are, at most, placed under sequestration. The laws therefore which regulate war by land are much more conformable to the spirit of civilization, and individual safety and well-being, than those which prevail in naval affairs, and it is greatly to be desired that a time may come, when the same liberal ideas shall be extended to naval wars, and that the great belligerent powers may carry on warlike operations against each other, without the confiscation of merchant ships, or treating their crews as legitimate prisoners of war; and commerce would then be carried on, at sea, between the belligerent parties, in the same way as it is carried on by land, in the midst of the battles fought by their armies.

" According to common rights, the sea is the domain of all nations; it extends over three-fourths of the globe, and forms a medium of intercourse among the different inhabitants of the earth. A ship laden with merchandise, and at sea, is still subject to the civil and criminal laws of the country under whose flag she sails; she may, perhaps, be considered as a floating colony, inasmuch as all nations are equal sovereigns upon the sea. If merchant vessels belonging to belligerent powers were allowed to navigate the ocean freely, much less would there be any reason for exercising any right of search in case of neutrals; but as it has become a principle that merchant vessels belonging to the states of belligerent powers are liable to capture and confiscation, the result necessarily is, that all ships of war should have the right of satisfying themselves with respect to the genuineness of the flags of neutral ships with which they fall in at sea, for if, in any case, she proved to be an enemy's vessel, she would be liable to seizure, hence the right of search, recognised by all the great powers of Europe in various treaties; hence vessels of war have a right to send out their boats, and order an officer to go on board neutral vessels, to require the captain to produce his ship's papers, and thus to assure themselves of the country to which the ship belongs. The exercise of this right is recognised by all treaties, but at the same time, the greatest delicacy is expected and enjoined in the manner of its exercise; it is usual for the armed ships to remain beyond the range of cannon-shot, and for only two or three persons to go on board the vessel visited, in order that all appearance of force or violence may be avoided.

" The principle has been recognised, that a vessel belongs to the nation under whose flag she sails, when she is furnished with proper papers, and the captain and one-half of the crew are citizens of the nation to which the vessel claims to belong. All civilized powers have agreed in forbidding their neutral subjects to carry on a contraband trade with powers which are at war. All such articles as powder, balls, shells, guns, saddles, bridles, or other munitions of war whatsoever, are reckoned contraband, and vessels with such articles on board are supposed to have transgressed the laws of their own country, because every sovereign binds himself to forbid his subjects to carry on trade in such articles, and therefore all such articles are liable to seizure and confiscation.

" The visit made by a cruiser is not merely a simple visit to ascertain the genuineness of the flag under which the ship visited sails, but the commander of the cruiser, in the name of the sovereign whose flag the vessel bears, exercises a new right of search to ascertain whether the vessel has any contraband articles on board.

" Should there be any soldiers on board, they too are regarded as contraband, and this right does not at all derogate from the principle, that the flag covers the merchandise.

" There is still another case, that in which vessels belonging to neutral powers proposed to enter ports in a state of siege, and blockaded by an enemy's squadron, such vessels being laden not with munitions of war, but with provisions, timber, wine, or other merchandise, which might be useful to the besieged, and enable them to prolong their defence. After long discussions among the powers, it was finally agreed and determined by several treaties, that in every case in which a port is really blockaded so that there would be manifest danger to a vessel attempting to enter the harbour, then the commander of the blockading squadron is empowered to interdict neutral vessels from entering the port, and to capture the ship, provided she makes an attempt to violate the blockade, and to sail into the port either by force or stratagem.

" Thus maritime laws are based upon these principles: 1st. The flag covers the merchandise; 2ndly, a neutral vessel must submit to be visited by ships of war belonging to belligerent nations, to ascertain whether she is *boná fide* a vessel belonging to the country whose flag she bears, and that her cargo does not include contraband articles; 3rdly, contraband is restricted to munitions of war; and, 4thly, neutral vessels may be prevented from entering any harbour which is really blockaded, so that there would be manifest danger to any vessel attempting to enter such port or harbour. These principles form the code of maritime law for neutral vessels, because the different powers have freely, and by various treaties, bound themselves to the observance of them, and to enforce that observance upon their subjects in all cases of necessity.

" The different maritime powers—Holland, Portugal, Spain, France, England, Sweden, Denmark, and Russia, have at different times, and in various treaties, successively bound themselves, each to the others, by the formal recognition of those principles which have been established and published in general treaties of pacification, such as those of Westphalia in 1649, and of Utrecht in 1712.

" England in the war with America, in 1778, pretended: 1st, that all merchandise for ship-building, such as wood, hemp, pitch, &c., were contraband of war; 2ndly, that a neutral vessel had the right to proceed from a friendly to an enemy's port, but that she could not be allowed to trade between one enemy's port and another; 3rdly, that neutrals could not sail from the colonies of a belligerent power to the mother country; 4thly, that neutral powers had no right to send their merchantmen under convoy of ships of war, or in such case, that they were still liable to the right of search.

" No independent power would acquiesce in these unjust pretensions ; for the sea being the common domain of nations, no one power can have the right to regulate and establish a law for what takes place there.   If the right of search be permitted in the case of neutral vessels, it is because the various sovereign nations have recognised this right for common convenience, and by special treaties.   If munitions of war are contraband, it is because treaties have made them so.   If belligerent powers can seize them, it is because the sovereign under whose flag the neutral vessel sails, has bound himself not to allow such a description of trade. The list of contraband articles cannot, however, obviously be extended at discretion, as was objected to the English claim, and no nation has bound itself to forbid trade in naval munitions, such as ship timber, hemp, pitch, &c.

" With regard to the second claim—it is contrary, it was said, to recognised usage: you cannot intermeddle with the commerce of neutral nations, further than to ascertain the genuineness of the flag; you have no right to know what a neutral ship is doing on the high seas, because such a vessel is on her own rightful element, and beyond your authority.   She is not protected, it is true, by the batteries of her country, but she is so by the moral power of her nation and of her sovereign.

"The third pretension has no better foundation. A state of war can, and ought to have, no effect upon neutrals. They ought to be able to do in war what they can do in peace. In a state of peace, there is nothing to prevent a vessel belonging to one country from trading between another country and its colonies. If foreign vessels are permitted to trade in this way, this permission is not founded upon the law of nations, but on municipal regulations; and in all cases in which a nation is disposed to confer this privilege on foreign vessels, no other nation has any right to interfere.

"With regard to the fourth pretension, it was replied, that as the right of search was instituted merely in order to ascertain the genuineness of the flag, and whether the cargo was composed of articles contraband of war, an armed vessel under the commission of the sovereign of a neutral nation is a much better assurance of the genuineness of the flag, and of the cargoes not being contraband of war, than can result from any search whatever; and it would be a consequence of such a pretension, that a fleet of merchant vessels, under convoy of eight or ten ships of the line, would be liable to have the right of search enforced by a brig of war, or a privateer of a belligerent power.

"During the American war (1778), Monsieur de Castries, then minister of Marine in France, published,

and caused to be adopted, a regulation relative to the
commerce of neutral powers. This regulation was
drawn up in conformity with the spirit of the treaty
of Utrecht, and of the rights of neutral nations. The
principles above mentioned were therein declared to
be inadmissible, and that their observance was only
to continue for six months, after which, they should
cease to be regarded by neutral nations which should
not have made their rights known by England.

" This course was both just and politic. It satisfied all the neutral powers, and threw a new light
upon this question.

" The Dutch, who then carried on the largest trade,
annoyed by the English cruisers, and the decisions of
the English Admiralty, caused their merchant ships
to be convoyed by vessels of war, hoping that this
course would at least protect them against the exercise
of the right of search. A convoy, escorted by several
Dutch ships of war, was, however, attacked, taken,
and carried into an English harbour, an event which
filled the Dutch with indignation, and shortly after,
Holland and Spain declared war against England.

" Catherine, Empress of Russia, took such a part
in these great questions as the dignity of her flag and
the interests of her empire demanded. The trade of
Russia principally consisted in articles employed in
ship-building, and this led her to resolve to unite with
Sweden and Denmark in forming an armed neutrality.
These powers declared their determination to make
war upon any belligerent power which should violate

the following principles. which they assumed as the basis of their union: 1st, that the flag covers the merchandise (contraband excepted); 2ndly, that the right of search exercised by a ship of war upon a neutral vessel, should be exercised with the greatest possible delicacy; 3dly, that munitions of war alone, such as cannon, powder and ball, are contraband; 4thly, that every power has a right to convoy merchant ships; and that in this case, the declaration of the commander of the ship of war is sufficient to protect the flag and cargoes of the ships under her convoy and protection; 5thly, that a port cannot be regarded as blockaded by a squadron, except where there is manifest danger of entering such a port—and that a ship is not to be prevented from entering a port previously blockaded by a force no longer before it, from whatever cause the absence of the blockading squadron may have taken place, whether from stress of weather or from the want of provisions.

" The armed neutrality of the northern powers was announced to the belligerent powers on the 15th of August, 1780. France and Spain, whose principles were thus recognised, hastened to express their adherence to these conditions. England alone testified extreme dissatisfaction, but did not venture to brave the new confederation. She contented herself with the non-enforcement of her own principles, and thus virtually renounced them. Fifteen months afterwards, the peace of 1782 put an end to the maritime war. The war between France and England commenced in

1793; England very soon became the soul of the first
coalition. Whilst the armies of Austria, Spain,
Russia and Piedmont invaded our frontiers, she
employed all possible means to ruin our colonies.
The taking of Toulon, where our squadron was
destroyed by fire, and the rising of the west, in which
a great number of sailors perished, annihilated our
marine, and England no longer set any limits to her
ambition.   Thenceforth mistress of the seas, and
without a rival, she thought the moment was come, in
which she might without danger, revive her former
pretensions, which she had tacitly renounced in the
war of 1780—that is to say, that materials for ship-
building are contraband; that neutral powers have
not the right to convoy their merchant ships by ships
of war, and thus protect them from the right of
search; and that a blockade is to be respected not
only when the blockading squadron is present, but
when it is absent from stress of weather or other
reasons. She, however, went still further, and put
forward three new pretensions: 1st, that the flag
does not cover the merchandise, but that the property
of an enemy is liable to be seized and confiscated even
in a neutral bottom; 2ndly, that neutrals have not a
right to carry on trade between the colonies and the
mother country of a belligerent nation; and, 3rdly,
that a neutral vessel may enter an enemy's port, but
not proceed from one enemy's port to another.

" The assassination of Paul I. left England com-

plete liberty of action to maintain. with greater force
than she had ever yet displayed, her pretensions to
the absolute dominion of the seas. The quadruple
alliance was dissolved, and Denmark cruelly punished
for having dared to measure her strength with England in a naval engagement.

"Pitt had at this time retired before the ascendant of France; the signature of the treaty of the
quadruple alliance, the occupation of Hanover by
Prussian troops, and the necessity to sign a peace
imposed upon Austria by the defeat at Hohenlinden,
had deprived him of all hope of success in his scheme
of preventing any serious approximation to peace
between France and England. Lord Hawkesbury had
replaced Lord Grenville in the foreign office, and
hastened to renew the negotiations with Monsieur
Otto. There was some reason to hope for success on
this occasion, but on the arrival of the news concerning the events which had just taken place at Petersburg, the demands of England proved that peace
would be impossible until some new events should
constrain its adoption.

"It became necessary, at all costs, to alarm the
hearts of the citizens of London; considerable armaments were ordered to be got in readiness on the
whole coast of France, from the Gironde to the
Scheldt; all the French dockyards were put into a
state of full activity in order to construct a flotilla for
the conveyance of troops across the channel. The

English on their side raised troops, threw up entrench-
ments at the mouth of the Thames, and gave many
other proofs of their fear of an invasion.

"The interviews between M. Otto and Lord Hawkesbury had never been discontinued, and the pretensions
of the cabinet of St. James's, inadmissible as they were,
had still continued to be discussed, in the expectation
of the occurrence of some events favourable to peace,
when the First Consul, at the propitious moment,
caused a counter-project to be submitted through
M. Otto to the following effect:

" 1stly. Restitution of Egypt to the Grand Seignor,
Port Mahon to Spain, Malta to the Knights of St.
John of Jerusalem, and the recognition of the Ionian
republic.

" 2ndly. Ceylon to England, and the restoration of
the Cape of Good Hope to Holland.

" 3dly. Restoration, by England, of the colonies
in the West Indies, taken by her during the war.

" 4thly. Restoration to Portugal of the province of Olivenza, occupied by a Franco-Spanish
army.

" Lord Hawkesbury replied, that England was disposed to restore the Island of Malta to the Knights of
St John; that she considered the Indian question
settled by the acquisition of Ceylon—that as to the
question of the Antilles, she was ready to restore
Martinique, but must retain possession of Trinidad
and Tobago, and require that Demerara should
be a free port. After long discussions, all these

points were admitted, on condition that Spain should retain the province of Olivenza in lieu of Trinidad On the first of October, 1801, the preliminaries of peace were signed by M. Otto on these bases.

" The joy consequent on the announcement of this peace, was still greater in England than in France. Lauriston, the First Consul's aide-de-camp, who was sent to England as the bearer of the ratifications of the treaty, signed by M. Otto, was received with the most enthusiastic ovations, and Mr. Addington, the prime minister, said to him: " This is not an ordinary peace; it is an act of reconciliation between the two most powerful nations in the world."

" Conferences for a definitive peace were opened at Amiens. Lord Cornwallis was the representative of England; the interests of Spain were entrusted to the Marquis d'Azara; Herr Schimmelpenynck appeared on behalf of Holland; and the First Consul selected his brother Joseph for France. On the 27th of March, 1802, the peace was signed.

"From this day forth, the great object of the English Tories was a rupture of the treaty; and in this they were aided and abetted by the criminal device of a body of *emigrés*, who marched under the banner of the Count d'Artois. The French government had nothing wherewith to reproach itself. It did everything possible, consistent with French honour, to preserve the peace.

" The cabinet of St. James's, by violating the peace

of Amiens, involved Europe in a mortal struggle against the French republic, at the very moment in which it offered, through M. Malhouet, an *emigré*, formerly minister of Louis XVI., to place at my personal disposal 30,000,000 of francs, and the whole moral assistance of England, to induce me to proclaim myself king of the French, on the sole condition of ceding to England the rule of the Mediterranean, which would ensure the markets of the Levant for her manufactures, and sooner or later open to her the way to India by the Euphrates or the Red Sea.

" The reply to be given to this proposal required no hesitation; I gave it myself to Lord Whitworth, the English ambassador, in the following terms; ' I wish to owe nothing to strangers or to their interference; if ever the French nation places the royal crown upon my head, it shall be of its own free accord.'

" During the war in Italy, Austria had already sought to work upon my ambition by her insinuations; the Marquis de Gallo, the ambassador of Naples in Vienna, offered me, on the part of the Emperor, a sovereignty in Germany; but then, as always, my device as well as my life has been TOUT POUR LA FRANCE.

" In 1805, Napoleon, when conqueror of Austria, wrote anew to the King of England: ' Is not the world large enough to hold our two nations; and has not reason power sufficient to suggest means of reconciliation, if both parties earnestly desire it? Peace is the wish of my heart, though war has never been unfavourable to my arms. I conjure your Majesty, not to deny yourself the happiness of giving peace to the nations.'

"Pitt made war to the death upon the French revolution, because he regarded it as a species of mutual struggle for the English aristocracy. In 1806, however, before the battle of Jena, he would have accepted the pacific offers of the Emperor of the French, when the latter said to Lord Lauderdale :

"'You would do better to persuade your government to peace, for in a month I shall be master of Prussia. Prussia and Russia, if united, might offer some resistance, and perhaps with some hopes of success; but Prussia cannot do that alone. The Russians are three months' march distant from the first battle-field. The plan of the Prussian campaign is to defend Berlin, instead of retiring behind the Oder, and there awaiting the Russians before risking a battle. The Prussian army will be destroyed, and I shall be in Berlin before the advanced guard of the Russians shall have passed the Vistula. Make peace, therefore, whilst the moral power of the Prussia of Frederick the Great aids you with its friendship.'

"The Emperor of Austria offered to interpose, in order to decide his allies. ' The English,' said he, in the interview granted him at Austerlitz—' the English are merchants ; they set fire to the Continent, in order to secure the commerce of the world for themselves ; and France is right in her quarrel with England.'

"Pitt's death in 1806, brought Fox to the head of

affairs, and rendered peace possible. It might have been expected that the ancient rivalry of two great nations, worthy of mutual love and esteem, would have been extinguished; but the day of reconciliation had not yet arrived. Fox died, and the shade of Pitt protected the Tory ministry, which returned to power. The English cabinet, by following Pitt's principles, endeavoured on all hands to find new enemies for France. It sent a squadron to the Tagus to draw Portugal into the war; threatened the Ottoman Porte to compel it to enter into the coalition; intrigued with Russia, with a view to change her pacific intentions; and excited Prussia against France, by persuading her that she would lose Hanover, which France had suffered her to occupy, but which she would not guarantee, except on the condition of making common cause in compelling England to accept a peace. As long as Fox directed the negotiations, they were carried on in an honourable and frank spirit, with the view of re-establishing peace; after his death, the only object was to break them off, by all possible means to elude the responsibility of the rupture, and to give the war a spirit of greater violence than before, in hopes that a new coalition would be all in favour of the allies of England, and would be for her merely an account current at the Treasury; and finally, that France would be exhausted, and finish by succumbing in this incessant struggle against the whole of Europe.

" The decrees of Berlin and Milan were nothing but

just reprisals upon England for the course which she had pursued. The continental system appeared like the mere swagger of a diseased mind; no one comprehended its bearings, and it was even necessary to have recourse to force to ensure its execution. The tree, however, soon bore fruit, and time will do the rest.

" Had it not been for the treachery of 1814, the face of commerce would be now changed, as well as the route of industry; the impulse was immense, and our manufacturing interests and property were increasing immeasurably; the progress of knowledge was gigantic; ideas were everywhere being rectified, and science becoming popular in France. " I have been careful," said Napoleon to his minister of commerce, " not to fall into the errors of men of system, of preferring myself, and my own ideas, to the wisdom of nations. True wisdom is the result of experience; the economists who preach up freedom of trade, constantly quote the commercial prosperity of England as a model for imitation; but England is the country of prohibitions, and, in some things, she is right, for protection is always necessary to encourage rising industry, and, in such cases, the value of this protection cannot be replaced by customs—smuggling destroys the object of the law. Men in general fall far short of the truth in the solution of all these questions, so vital to national prosperity. The truth, however, will be more and more approximated by taking, as the basis of our reflections upon this subject, the classification which

I have always adopted in agriculture, industry, and commerce—objects which are distinct, and form a real gradation:

"1stly. Agriculture is the soul, the foundation of all national prosperity.

"2ndly. Industry—the ready money and prosperity of the people.

"3rdly. Internal trade—the profitable employment of the products of agriculture and industry.

"4thly. Foreign trade—the profitable employment of the surplus of the national products, the superabundance of property, but of much inferior interest to the others, to which it is subservient, and not they to it.

"It was the whole plan of the imperial administration to promote these diverse interests according to their national rank, but it was never successful in satisfying them all. Time will tell what they owe to it; the national resources which it has created, and the deliverance which it has effected for them from the bondage of the merchants of the city. It is now time to make known the secret of the treaty of commerce of 1783. The English, imposed it under threats of recommencing the war, and this was what they wished to on repeat the rupture of the peace of Amiens; but Napoleon was possessed of gigantic power, and *felt* that he was so; he replied, that he would persist in refusing, even if their armies were on the heights of Montmartre. He has been blamed, and that justly, for conceding *licences;* but this arose from the necessity of the moment, and was only a temporary resource, as the whole continental system was merely an arm of war. It would have been easy to come to an understanding concerning a peace, by a system of reciprocity in customs, in accordance with the interest of the two great commercial prosperities of England and France.

" During the interview with Alexander in Erfurt, in 1808, the Emperor induced him to join in a new attempt at reconciliation.

" Finally, in 1812, when Napoleon was in the apogee of his power, he made a fresh offer of peace to England, in concert with the Emperor of Austria and the King of Prussia, who went to Dresden expressly to visit him, and to give him a splendid proof of the sincerity of their alliance. The English ministry, and the libels of all the oligarchs in the world may say what they will, the Emperor Napoleon always wished for peace with England, because he regarded a general peace as the first condition of the regeneration of Europe.

" The cabinet of Lord Castlereagh, as well as that of the Venetian aristocracy, suffered itself to be ruled by old women. The great Lord Chatham said—' If England were to act with justice towards France, for twenty-four hours only, she would run to her ruin.' England is indebted to Lord Castlereagh for all the embarrassments of her situation, and the crisis which threatened her. A man must have been blinded by an absurd respect for the opinions of Lord Chatham, or by a more absurd vanity of disinterestedness, worthy

of a new Don Quixote, to have acted as Lord Castlereagh did at the congress of Vienna, at a time
when Austria acquired 10,000,000 of people; Russia
8,000,000; Prussia 10,000,000; and even Holland,
Bavaria, and Sardinia, obtained extensions of territory.   England would not have asked too much
as an indemnity for the almost incredible and impossible efforts which she had made, if she had
demanded and required the establishment of small
maritime independent states put under her protection, such as Hamburgh, Bremen, Lubeck, Stralsund,
Dantzig, Antwerp, Genoa, and Venice, to serve as
an *entrepot* for her manufactures, with secret stipulations, which should ensure her the means of extending
her trade with a moderate competition. A still graver
fault, however, was committed, by suffering Russia to
obtain the crown of Poland.   It would have been a
hundred times better to have given it to the King of
Prussia or to the Emperor of Austria; nor should the
Emperor of Russia have been allowed to usurp the
protectorate of the four provinces on the Danube.
Russia is aggressive by nature—sooner or later she
will make an irruption into Europe; and this, in fact,
is her duty for advancing the progress of civilization
among the four-fifths of her population.   Such an
irruption would be a powerful and seductive means of
consolidating her rule over the numerous and valiant
races who dwell on her frontiers.   They would be
drawn towards her by the fabulous tales of the pleasures of Europe; all would successively be grouped in

the ranks of the Russian light troops. The attractions
of the plunder of a city like Paris are much more than
sufficient to induce all the barbarians of the north
to unite in a predatory incursion into Europe. These
nations have all the elements of success; they are
brave, active, and indefatigable, insensible to changes of
climate; they subsist upon very little, and submit to
discipline like brutes. Should Russia succeed in destroying the nationality of Poland, and acquiring the
fraternity of the Poles, she will then be without a
rival. She will keep England at bay by threatening her
possessions in the Indies, and hold Austria in check by
the great moral superiority of her troops, and the assistance of the members belonging to the Greek Church,
who are so numerous in Hungary and Gallizia. According to all appearances, a Greek Patriarch will one
day officiate in St. Sophia, and from that moment
England will be deprived of India, and Europe at the
mercy of the knout.

" Another fault, perhaps not less grave, committed by the English ministry, was that of having
united Belgium with Holland; because Holland never
will be strong enough to prevent France from seizing
upon Belgium when she pleases, and because Holland,
not having the manufactures of Belgium, would again
become, in her own interest, the *entrepot* for the most
important products of the English manufactures.   It
would have been much better for England to have
restored Belgium to the Emperor of Austria.

" In short, the cabinet of Lord Castlereagh is re-

sponsible for all the evils and all the disasters which
threaten England, for having failed to take advantage
of the opportunity of ensuring immense commercial
advantages to his country, and of rendering his nation
the richest and the most powerful in the world.   He
signed the treaty of Paris, and conducted himself at
the congress of Vienna, as if England had been conquered. From being the directing power of the coalition, as she really was, he transformed her into a mere
auxiliary; happy in being able to pick up a few
crumbs at the banquets of kings, instead of speaking
like a master, he placed himself in the wake of the
chanceries of Vienna, Petersburg, and Berlin, which
for twenty years had all been in the pay of the
treasury in London.   He left his country oppressed
by an immense debt, contracted mainly for the interest of one family—the Bourbons—and of that Holy
Alliance, now so forgetful of all that England did for
them, that they already begin to close the markets of
the Continent against her manufactures, with no less
rigour than was done by the Emperor of the French
himself.

   " The debt of England is a gnawing worm—the chain
of all those embarrassments which will affect her
future course; for, in order to sustain this immense
weight, it will be necessary to continue, during peace,
the levy of those extraordinary taxes imposed during
the war ; this will, necessarily, lead to an increase in
the price of provisions, and insensibly bring the people
to the most frightful misery.   One of two things must

happen : either the wages of labour must increase proportionably, and then the products of English industry will no longer be able to compete with the productions of other nations in the continental markets, and the manufacturers will suffer; or, the wages of labour will remain stationary, to the advantage of the manufacturers, and in this case the labouring class will not be able to gain the means of providing for the most necessary wants.

" The first element of the well-being of a nation consists in a just equilibrium between the amount of taxes imposed for the maintenance of the public revenue, and the surplus of the price of its labour; unfortunately, however, the taxes are not productive till they reach the masses of the people, and whenever they affect the bread of the people they engender misery and all those scourges which it brings in its train.

" It is imperative on England to endeavour to combat this devouring monster—her debt—by all positive and negative means—by the reduction of her expenses and the increase of her commerce with the whole world. In making reductions, she must be unsparing; it is necessary to cut to the quick, when mortification threatens. In the case of sinecures, salaries, and the expense of her land-armies, reforms must be sweeping. The political greatness of England consists in her navy, and not in those small armies which she has sent to the Continent in the train of the large armies of Russia, Austria and Prussia.

" It is equally necessary for her to have recourse to

a wise reform of innumerable abuses, connected with ecclesiastical property, the position of farmers in reference to their landlords, the administration of Ireland, as respects the mother country, and that kind of social interdict which is imposed upon nearly one-third of the population of Great Britain in consequence of their religious faith; and, finally, by a free admission of all those really interested to the rights and privileges of electors. The present state of the electoral franchise is nothing more than a brilliant deception, which places the majority of parliament in the nomination of the aristocracy and the crown. As to Ireland, she possesses merely the fiction of a representation in parliament; but it is true, that she is, in fact, a conquered country. It would have been, in reality, much better for her to have been treated as a conquered country, and then she would, at least, have had the advantage of not seeing her national debt doubled by fusion with that of England.

"In England the aristocracy are absolute masters, and the moment that any reform threatens to touch their power or privileges, they have recourse to the habitual cry—' *The foundations of the constitution—touch the foundations, and the whole edifice will fall into ruins—and the liberties of the nation be destroyed.*' It is true, that, in spite of its monstrous defects, when viewed in connexion with the civilization of the age, the English constitution presents the curious phenomenon of a magnificent result; and it is the blessings of this result which make the people afraid of risking their loss; but how much more would these advantages be felt, if wise reforms were employed to facilitate the motions of this grand and beautiful machine!

"In her foreign policy, she must know how to dare to exercise, in case of necessity, those rights of sovereignty by sea, which the sovereigns of the Continent exercise for the protection of the industry of their subjects; dare to oblige them to open their markets to English products, under pain of establishing a tariff upon the rights of navigation, as a compensation for their burthensome or prohibitory duties on English commerce. Can it be that a King of Denmark has any better right of sovereignty over the Sound than a King of England has over the Channel or the Straits of Gibraltar? Is it that the protection of the English marine is of no value to the trading vessels of most of the Continental states? There is, in fact, no want of sufficient reasons for establishing the right of search under any pretext whatever. In speaking to the imagination of philanthropists of all colours, there is no longer any public right to invoke, when the equilibrium is destroyed; and at present the dominion of the sea belongs, in fact and incontestably, to England—consequently, she has a right to say to the Continental states—' Your merchandise shall not be allowed to pass over my seas, without the payment of the same amount of customs which you impose on your Continent—freedom of trade for my

merchandise—amen; but customs with you, and not
with me—no.'

"This, it may be said, would be war, but upon
whom? Spain has not three ships fit to put to sea;
Holland has not four; Naples one or two; Denmark
has none, since the burning of her fleet at Copenhagen; Russia—but it would require only the smallest
effort on the part of England to shut up the Russian
fleet in her ports, and burn her ships. As to France,
what will her navy be for twenty-five years to come?
The hundred ships which were built under the
empire, the treaty of Paris has taken from her!—poor
France!

"The Continent, such as it has been made by the
treaties of 1814 and 1815, will submit to the law—
bow to the tariffs and open its markets; for England
can make war upon whom she will with impunity,
whilst no continental power can go to war without
experiencing great losses in her commerce; and this
state of things will continue till France has again
assumed her proper rank of a great nation, with a
hundred ships of the line, as she had under Napoleon
and Louis XIV., and 500,000 troops on her frontiers.
The disinterestedness of England, in the division of
the spoils of the French empire, would be explicable,
if she had designed to establish her empire on the
Continent by the gratitude of the people, or if she
had been seated in a congress of kings as the natural
protectrix of constitutional institutions. What would
the poor Poles, the poor Spaniards, and the poor

Italians, not have given to escape being placed under the iron yoke of the czar, or the inquisition! What a noble character! What a glorious opportunity did the morning after the battle of Waterloo afford for opening the markets of the whole of Europe to English commerce! What better could the cabinet of St. James's have done than to give its hand to those noble means of modern regeneration, which sooner or later will be effectual, and against which kings, by right divine, and the oligarchy, by assumption, may exhaust all their efforts in vain! It is the rock of Sisyphus which they keep raised above their heads, and which will fall and crush them when the arm is no longer able to sustain its weight. Napoleon has planted the seeds of liberty with a bountiful hand, wherever the civil code has been introduced.

" The English ministry which shall put itself at the head of the liberal ideas of the Continent will receive the blessings of the universe, and all the heartburnings felt towards England will be forgotten. Such a course would have been quite in the spirit of Fox. Pitt would not have undertaken to pursue it. In the case of Fox, his heart warmed his genius, whilst in that of Pitt, his intellect withered up his heart.

" Whenever England shall undertake the regeneration of Europe, she will rest her efforts upon a foundation as deep as the earth; Napoleon's foundation was upon sand. The institutions of England are those of ages; England reigns over things established and immoveable. Napoleon had the immense task of

establishing them—of purifying a terrible and unexampled revolution. He succeeded in subduing anarchy
—in binding into a bundle the scattered elements
produced by the work of the republicans, but he was
constantly obliged to surround this bundle with his
powerful arm to save it from the attacks from without, whilst Europe was incessantly in arms to conquer
the principles which his crown represented within.
Factions attacked him with the most opposite views;
he was libelled in the time of the directory for his
concessions; he would have been the object, and
France the victim, of a *contre Brumaire*. In France,
the people are by nature so restless, so busy, and so
gossiping, that there would be twenty revolutions, and,
consequently, as many constitutions, all ready in the
portfolios of political constitution-mongers, of whom
there are as many in France, as there are bill-discounters
under the pillars of the exchange in Amsterdam.

" The conduct of the English ministry at the Congress of Vienna, and the negotiations of the treaty of
1815; its forgetfulness of all duty and patriotism, can
only be explained on the supposition of a secret
design, the object of which was to reduce the English
people under the yoke of military power; to forge
chains to fetter all their liberties; to reduce their
constitutional institutions to the shadow of their
former selves, and to cover them with the mantle of
despotism, all which would be in perfect accordance
with those principles which Prince Metternich wished,
and wishes, to triumph as the rule of European organiza-

tion born at the Congress of Vienna. The liberty
of England is a subject of continual alarm in Vienna
and Petersburg. When the English people feel the
royal yoke too heavy to bear; or when their distress
becomes insupportable—the grape-shot or the cord of
the executioner are the implements of justice. This is
possible as long as the evil has not penetrated to the
marrow of the masses; but when it has touched the
vitals, then those who were only a mob in the deluded
eyes of power, become a nation; and then it is seen
when too late, that it is indeed the masses which constitute the people, and not a few nobles or *millionaires;*
for the rabble no sooner gains the ascendancy than it
changes its name, and calls itself the nation. If conquered, a few wretches are seized—they are denomi-
nated rebels or robbers; and thus the world goes.
Mob, robbers, rebels, or heroes, according to the
chances of the strife. Poor humanity!"

CHAPTER XIV.

GENERAL POLICY OF SPAIN TOWARDS FRANCE DURING THE REIGN OF FERDINAND.

ABOUT this time the newspapers informed us that a proposal had been made to bring back the Emperor to Europe, and to change the damp residence of Long-wood for the fine air of Naples. We hastened to carry this news to the Emperor; but he shook his head and said: "It is impossible; as long as the men who formed the Congress of Vienna are in power, the sight of my shadow would suffice to strike them with terror; the best plan for the English government would, doubtless, be to come to an understanding with me, and to receive my promise not to leave Malta, without the Prince Regent's consent, for ten years; after the expiration of which period, I should be hospitably received in England; this plan would save eight or ten millions a year, a sum which I uselessly cost the government here; but I repeat, spare yourselves the pain of hope deceived. We have nothing to hope for from the oligarchs, unless danger opens their eyes, and proves to them that I alone had the power to keep the entrance-door of revolution closed, as well in the interest of kings as in that of the people."

Sir Hudson Lowe had now left us for some days in tranquillity. The Emperor had resumed his habit of taking exercise, and worked a great deal. Some news which he received from his brother Joseph led him to speak of Spain; he told me that during the hundred days, the most influential chiefs of the Cortes of Cadiz, the guerillas and the army, had communicated with him, and assured him that an aid in money would enable them to bring back King Joseph to Madrid, and to effect in Spain what the landing at Cannes had produced in France; so deeply had an immense majority of the Spaniards become aware, since the return of Ferdinand, of all the benefits to Spain contained in the constitution of Bayonne. "In any other circumstances," added the Emperor, "I would have assisted them, but I did not wish to render my position more complicated by interfering in the affairs of others, before having finished my own. I could not forget that the misfortunes of 1813 and 1814, proceeded from my intervention in the affairs of Spain. It was the events of Bayonne which destroyed my morality in Europe, divided my forces, multiplied my embarrassments, and opened a school to the English army; I committed, besides, great faults in the choice of my instruments, for the fault lies much more in the machinery than in the principle.

" Spain had long been the subject of my meditations; its manners; its territorial divisions; its old customs, on which all Castilian honour hangs; the ignorant superstition of the population; all were so many obstacles which it would be necessary to overcome, in order to regenerate the Spanish nation, which would be grand and powerful under the empire of constitutional institutions; but it was impossible not to occupy myself with its affairs.   In the crisis in which France then stood, in the struggle of new ideas, in the great cause of the age against old Europe, Spain could not be left behind in the social re-organization; it was absolutely necessary to carry it forward, *nolens volens*, in the movement of France; the fate of France demanded this, and the code of the safety of nations is not always that of individuals; and besides, Spain justified this necessity by her conduct during the war with Prussia and with Poland; when she at that time considered Napoleon in peril, she had deserted the alliance which her old king had sworn to him; the insolent proclamation of the Prince of the Peace; the sudden embarkation of the 25,000 men belonging to the corps of La Romana, could not be forgotten.   The injury ought not to have remained unpunished; it merited a declaration of war; and it was a great misfortune that the Emperor did not take this open and honourable step on his return from Tilsit.   The issue could not be doubtful; but France had need of repose; the war with Spain had cost it great sacrifices.

"The nation despised its government, and cried aloud for the blessings of regeneration; hopes might be entertained of accomplishing it without shedding any blood; the dissensions in the royal family authorised this hope, to which the events of Bayonne gave all the appearance of certain realization.

"A constitution had been freely accepted and sworn to by all orders of the nation, the new king had met with nothing, on his route from Bayonne to Madrid, but homage and demonstrations of satisfaction from the people, who were grateful for their deliverance from servitude under superannuated institutions, and proud of the respect which the Emperor of the French testified for Spanish nationality; in fact, King Joseph was the only Frenchman among them; he was surrounded entirely by Spaniards; his ministers, courtiers, and guards, were all Spanish.

"The constitution of Bayonne was but a work of circumstances; everything contained in it which was contrary to the interest of the mass of the people would have disappeared from it in time; Spain, like Poland, Germany, and Italy, would have been governed by the principles of the French civil code. Men of talent of all conditions would have been appointed to the first offices in the kingdom, and to all public employments, without distinction of birth. The choice of dynasties is, and ought to be, but a secondary question: family bonds are, doubtless, of some value; but this value is so

transient, and so often belied by history, that it did
not at all influence the Emperor in the choice of his
brothers as kings of Holland, Westphalia, and Naples;
for in crowning them, he considered them, in his own
mind, as viceroys—agents of his policy, whom he would
recall into the French ranks, according to the
exigencies of the definitive arrangements of a general
peace, or the re-organization of the Continent of
Europe.

" It was the mean intrigues of the princes of Spain,
their family quarrels, their betrayal of all the interests
of their country, and not the ambition of placing the
crown of Spain on the head of one of the Emperor's
brothers, which brought on the events of Bayonne.

" It was at Fontainebleau, after the peace of Tilsit,
that the first idea of an intervention in the affairs of
Spain was suggested to the Emperor.

" Whilst serious dissensions were arising between
the king, Charles IV., and his son, the Prince of
Asturias, negotiations were being carried on with
Monsieur Izquierdo to bring about the eventual partition of Portugal, in order to punish the house of
Braganza for its submission to the orders of the
cabinet of St. James.   The Prince of the Peace endeavoured to avail himself of this circumstance to realise
the ambitious dream of the Duke of Alba, and to
obtain for himself the small sovereignty of Algarve, as
a recompence for the devotedness which he then testified towards France.   This was the knot of the negotiation.   Izquierdo, who was much more the agent of

the favourite than that of the old king, sacrificed
everything to gain this end. The negotiation ma·le
his wishes easy of attainment; the agreement was
signed on the 27th of October. Prince Talleyrand informed Count Elma, the Portuguese minister at Paris,
of the conclusion of this treaty; it commenced the era
of treason. The court of Lisbon prepared itself for
everything; a second treaty, consequent upon the first,
was also signed at Fontainebleau on the 27th of October; it settled the respective forces which were to be
employed in the campaign against Portugal. A French
corps, consisting of thirty thousand men, was to enter
Spain, and march direct to Lisbon, in concert with a
Spanish division, 10,000 strong; a reserve of 40,000
French was to be in readiness to follow the movement
in case the English should interfere.

"At the same time that France was thus treating
with Spain, and endowing the prime minister of
Charles IV., Prince Talleyrand, who, as the minister
of foreign affairs, had just been carrying on the
negotiations and signing the treaty, reminded the
Emperor of the more than equivocal conduct of the
cabinet of Madrid, in the year 1806, and of the famous
proclamation of the Prince of the Peace, dated the 3rd
of October, 1806. He drew up a memorial containing
the causes of complaint of France against Spain, and
proposed to the Emperor to take decisive measures
towards that power.

"'There is but one reigning branch of the Bourbons
remaining—that in Spain; if left in our rear when we

turned against the powers of Germany, this branch
would always occupy a threatening position, in case of
any wars which France might have to sustain, either
in the north or in Italy; it would paralyse a part of
our forces, and it would be a continual object of uneasiness; accessible as it is to the intrigues of England,
and always ready to open its ports to English merchandise and troops, it would render the whole system
of peace and war incomplete. The moment is come
for declaring that the last branch of the house of
Bourbon has ceased to reign.

"'Let a prince of the Imperial house occupy the
throne of Spain, and the system of the empire will be
complete: Prussia subdued, Russia enfeebled in men
and money by an unfortunate war, the confederation
of the Rhine consolidated, the kingdom of Italy
secured, the bonds of friendship with the east drawn
closer, leaving nothing to be feared from the malevolence of Austria. Your majesty has now before you
time sufficient for attempting and concluding an
enterprise which will only require one campaign and
the employment of an army of 30,000 men; an army
which, it having been stipulated by the treaty of the
27th of October, will be levied and pass the frontier
without exciting any suspicion. Spain, taken entirely
by surprise, will offer no serious resistance; disgusted
with her government, prepared for necessary innova-
tions, she will welcome your Majesty's troops as libe-
rators.'"

This theme became the subject of the evening conferences between the Emperor and Prince Talleyrand; the latter was urgent, and the Emperor, who was as well pleased to talk of this as of anything else, did not look upon the project of conquering the Peninsula, with 30,000 men, in a serious light. He applied his reasonings and calculations to the eventual cases of a possible execution; he even sent for Marshal Moncey who had conducted the war in the Pyrenees, and questioned him on the different points of stratagem, of which he had made use in 1794.

The inhabitants of the castle knew nothing of what was passing; they only remarked the length of the Emperor's conversations with his minister of foreign affairs, which were sometimes prolonged to a late hour in the night; every one formed his own conjectures.

Another minister, who was roused by jealousy, and whose position gave him pretensions to, and means of, knowing everything—viz., the minister of police—became uneasy at these new confidences to which he had not the key; he at last thought he had discovered it, and his error gave rise to a very singular incident.

Fouché imagined that the subject of their conferences must be projects of divorce, and formed a plan in his own mind for cutting short the question on which they so long deliberated, feeling assured that this service would add to his credit, at the expense of a rival ambition.

He went directly to the Empress Josephine. He enlarged upon the interests of France, which called for a successor to the empire; he represented to the

Empress the glory which would exalt her above all other women, if she made this magnanimous sacrifice. Aided by the natural supposition that a minister would not dare to make such overtures without being authorised, Fouché so far succeeded in persuading Josephine, that he ventured to bring her the draft of a letter which she was to write to the president of the senate, in which she offered to the country the relinquishment of her position as an empress and a wife. The Empress, who feebly combated his reasons, put off signing the letter till the following morning.

One of the ladies of the court, Madame de Remusat, a woman of spirit, who had no notion of descending from her position as the favourite of an empress, to that of lady of honour to a fallen princess, made up her mind to act decidedly. She waited for the moment when the Emperor, having left his cabinet, was entering his bedchamber. It was one o'clock in the morning. She gave her name; the Emperor was going to bed; she was at an equivocal age, and found it very difficult to obtain admittance: she, however, insisted upon it, and said that in the morning it would be too late. The Emperor's curiosity was excited, and the door was opened. The thing was, in fact, curious enough: the Emperor learned that it was all about causing his wife to divorce herself. He immediately hastened to her, undeceived her, and gave her the assurance that if reasons of state should ever cause him to dissolve their marriage, she should receive the first intimation of it from himself alone. He kept his word.

Prince Talleyrand, who let no opportunity escape of giving the Emperor pledges of his unbounded devotedness to his dynasty, and who had already advised him to seat one of his brothers on the throne of Naples, perseveringly urged his project of dethroning the Spanish dynasty of the Bourbons, which would complete the work of extinguishing the last branches of the elder line of Bourbon, and he vainly entreated that his plans should be put into execution. But instead of marching into Spain at the head of 30,000 men, the Emperor set out for Venice, without even answering the letters written to him by the princes of Spain, imploring his intervention; these letters are remarkable:

" St. Laurent, 29th of October, 1807.

" SIRE AND BROTHER,—At a moment when I was entirely occupied in devising means to aid in the destruction of our common enemy—when I had hoped that all the plots of the late Queen of Naples were buried with her daughter—I saw with horror that the spirit of intrigue had penetrated even into the bosom of my palace. Alas! my heart bleeds in reciting so fearful an attempt!—my eldest son, the presumptive heir of my throne, had formed the horrible design of dethroning me; he had gone so far as to make attempts against the life of his mother. Such a fearful attempt must be punished with the most exemplary rigour of the laws. The law which called him to the throne must be revoked; one of his brothers will be more worthy to supply his place in my heart and on the throne.

"I am at this moment seeking for his accomplices, in order to make stricter inquiry into this plot of the blackest dye, and I have not lost a moment in sending this information to your majesty, praying you to aid me with your counsel and knowledge.

"I pray God, my good brother, to have your majesty in his holy keeping.

(Signed) "THE KING."

"From the Escurial, Oct. 11th, 1807.

"The fear of interrupting your imperial and royal majesty in the midst of the more important exploits and affairs which incessantly surround you, has hitherto prevented me from gratifying directly my most heartfelt desire, that of expressing, at least by writing, the sentiments of respect, esteem, and attachment which I cherish towards a hero who outshines all his predecessors, and who has been sent by Providence to save Europe from the total overthrow which menaced it, to steady its tottering thrones, and to restore nations to peace and happiness.

"Your majesty's virtues, your moderation, your kindness even towards your most implacable enemies, all these united to make me hope that the expression of these sentiments would be received by you as the effusions of a heart filled with the sincerest admiration and friendship.

"The position in which I have long stood, and

which cannot have escaped your majesty's penetrating
eye, has been another obstacle which arrested my pen
when on the point of expressing my wishes to you;
but, filled with the hope of finding in your imperial
and royal majesty's magnanimous generosity the most
powerful protection, I determined not only to express
the sentiments of my heart towards your august
person, but to pour my griefs into your bosom as
into that of a tender father.

"I am very unfortunate in being obliged by circumstances to conceal as a crime an action so just
and laudable, but such are the fatal consequences of
the extreme goodness of the best of kings.

"Filled as I am with respect and filial love for him
to whom I owe my existence, I can scarcely dare to
say to your majesty, that these very qualities, so esti-
mable in themselves, but too often serve as instruments to artful and wicked persons to hide the
truth from the eyes of the sovereign, although such
truth is so analogous to characters like that of my
revered father.

"If these persons, who unhappily exist here, would
allow him to know your majesty's character as I
know it, with what ardour would he not desire to
draw closer those ties which should unite our houses,
and what means would be more proper for this object,
than to demand of your majesty the honour of forming
an alliance between a princess of your august family
and myself? this is the unanimous desire of all my
father's subjects; and I doubt not that it would also

be his, notwithstanding the efforts of a few malcontents, as soon as he should be informed of your
majesty's wishes; this is what my heart desires, but
it is not the plan of the perfidious agents who besiege
him, and they may in the first moment surprise him;
such is the ground of my fears.

"Your imperial and royal majesty's answer can alone
unravel their plots, open the eyes of my well-beloved
parents, make them happy, and at the same time
complete the happiness of the nation and mine.

"The whole world will more and more admire your
majesty's goodness, and you will always have in me a
most grateful and devoted son.

"I therefore implore with the greatest confidence
your majesty's paternal protection, and that you
would not only deign to grant me the honour of an
alliance with your family, but would remove all the
difficulties and obstacles which may oppose the fulfilment of this wish of my heart.

"This act of kindness on the part of your majesty
is so much the more necessary to me, as I cannot
make the least effort myself, since this would be taken
as an insult to paternal authority; I am, therefore,
reduced to one course—namely to refuse, as I constantly do, to form an alliance with any other person
without the consent and approbation of your majesty,
from whom alone I await the choice of a wife. This
is a happiness which I hope from the goodness of your
majesty, and pray that God may preserve your precious
life for many years.

" Written and signed with my own hand, and sealed with my seal, at the Escurial, October 11th, 1807.

" From your majesty's most affectionate
servant and brother,

" FERDINAND."

The Emperor set out without having seen Fouché, but he sent him a message, enjoining him to interfere no more in any affairs but those of his office, and to silence the reports of divorce which he had spread in Paris.

The French troops, under the command of Prince Murat, crossed the Pyrenees and entered Spain, conformably to the treaty of Fontainebleau, without the Emperor's having come to any decision concerning the memorial which had been submitted to him by his minister of foreign affairs; but events suddenly changed the face of things; the French ambassador at Madrid sent information that the Prince of the Peace was advising the King Charles IV. to retire first to Seville, and then to Mexico, and to give up the Peninsula to England. This advice could not be explained, except by being attributed to an infernal combination.

The French ambassador at Madrid, soon afterwards announced the revolution of the palace which had placed the crown on the head of Ferdinand, and forwarded the protest of the old king, together with the letter in which he implored the Emperor's aid, and called for the punishment of a parricide on the Prince of Asturias.   Charles IV. wrote from Aranjuëz, March 21st, 1808.

"SIRE AND BROTHER,—You have, no doubt, received information of the events of Aranjuëz, and of their results. Your majesty will not look without some interest on a king, who, forced to abdicate his crown, comes to throw himself into the arms of a monarch his ally, placing himself entirely at his disposal, which alone can bring happiness to himself, his family, and his faithful subjects.

" My declaration of abdication in favour of my son was forced from me by circumstances, and by the arms and clamours of a rebellious guard, which plainly showed me that I must choose between life and death; and my death would have been followed by that of the queen.   I have been forced to abdicate, but being now reassured, and full of confidence in the magnanimity and genius of a great man, who always showed himself my friend, I took the resolution of putting myself entirely at your disposal, leaving in your hands my fate, that of the queen, and of the Prince of the Peace.

" I address to your imperial and royal majesty a protest against the events of Aranjuëz, and against my abdication.   I refer to it, and confide entirely in your majesty's goodness. I pray God to have you in his holy keeping.

" Your majesty's affectionate brother and friend,
" THE KING."

" PROTEST.

" I hereby protest and declare that my decree of the 19th of March, by which I abdicated the crown in favour of my son, is an act to which I was forced in order to prevent greater misfortunes, and the shedding of the blood of my well-beloved subjects; it is consequently to be regarded as null and void.

(Signed) " THE KING.

" Aranjuez, March 21st, 1808."

On the 29th of March, the Emperor wrote as follows to the Grand Duke de Berg:

" SIR,—I fear that you have deceived me with respect to the situation of Spain, and that you were deceived yourself: the affair of the 20th of March has singularly complicated matters; I am in great perplexity.

" Do not imagine that you are about to attack a disowned nation, and that your troops have but to show themselves to subdue Spain. The revolution of the 20th of March, proves that the Spaniards possess energy. You have to do with a new people; they will have all the courage and all the enthusiasm which are met with in men who have not worn out their political passions.

" The aristocracy and clergy are masters of Spain; should they become alarmed for their privileges and their existence, they will raise against us levies which might *eternize the war*.

" I have partisans in Spain; if I present myself in the character of a conqueror, I shall have them no longer.

" The Prince of the Peace is detested, because he is accused of having given up Spain to France; this is the grievance which has aided Ferdinand's usurpation; the popular party is the weakest.

" The Prince of Asturias possesses none of the qualities requisite for the chief of a nation; this will not prevent his being made a hero of, for the purpose of opposing him to us. I do ·not wish any violence to be exercised towards the members of this family; it is never of use to render oneself odious, and to inflame hatred. Spain has more than 100,000 men under arms. This is more than is requisite for maintaining an interior war with advantage; these forces, separated into various divisions, and placed at different points, might bring about the rising of the whole monarchy.

" I now present to you at one view, the obstacles which are insurmountable; there are others which you will yourself perceive.

" England will not neglect this opportunity of adding to our embarrassments; she daily sends information to the forces which she maintains on the coasts of Spain and on the shores of the Mediterranean; she is enrolling regiments of Sicilians and Portuguese.

" The Royal Family not having quitted Spain for the Indies, it is only a revolution which can change the state of this country. This is perhaps the country of Europe, which is the least qualified for it; those who perceive the monstrous vices of this government, and the anarchy which has supplanted legal authority are the smallest number; the majority profit by these vices and this anarchy

" I can, in accordance with the interests of my empire, do much good to Spain. What are the best means to take for this end?

" Shall I go to Madrid? Shall I act as great Protector, by pronouncing between the father and son? It seems to me that it would be difficult to establish Charles IV. on the throne; his yoke and his favourite are become so unpopular, that they could not maintain themselves for three months.

" Ferdinand is an enemy to France; it is for this reason that he has been made king. To place him on the throne would be to serve the factions which for twenty-five years have desired the annihilation of France. A family alliance would be but a weak tie; the Queen Elizabeth and several other French princesses perished miserably, when an opportunity was afforded of sacrificing them with impunity to some other vengeance.

" My opinion is that we must not be precipitate; that we must take counsel from the events which follow. We must strengthen our army, keep it on the frontiers of Portugal, and wait.

" I do not approve of the plan which your highness has pursued, in taking possession principally of Madrid.

You should have kept the army at a distance of ten leagues from the capital. You could not be sure that the people and the magistracy would recognise Ferdinand without any resistance. The Prince of the Peace must have partisans among the public officers. There is besides a kind of attachment of habit to the old king, which might produce some results. Your entry into Madrid, by alarming the Spaniards, powerfully served the cause of Ferdinand; I have ordered Savary to go to the old king, and see what is passing; you will concert measures with him, I will ultimately resolve on the line of conduct which I shall pursue; in the mean time, this is what I judge suitable to prescribe to you.

" You will not arrange that I shall have an interview in Spain with Ferdinand, unless affairs appear to you in such a position that I ought to recognise him as King of Spain.

" You will treat the king, the queen, and the Prince Godoy well; you will exact for them and pay to them the same honours as formerly; you will act in such a manner, that the Spaniards shall not be able to conjecture what line of conduct I shall pursue; this will not be difficult, as I have not yet determined on it myself.

" You will give the nobility and clergy to understand, that should France interfere in the affairs of Spain, their privileges and immunities will be respected. You will tell them that the Emperor desires to perfect the political institutions of Spain, in order to put that country on an equality with the actual state of civilization in Europe, and to free it from the rule of favourites; you will tell the enlightened magistrates and citizens that Spain needs a regeneration of its government; that it needs laws which shall secure the citizens, from the arbitrariness and usurpations of feudality, and institutions which shall revive industry, agriculture and the arts.

" You will describe to them the state of tranquillity and ease which France now enjoys, notwithstanding the wars in which she is always engaged; the splendour of her religion which owes its re-establishment to the concordat which I signed with the Pope; you will demonstrate to them the advantages which they may draw from a political regeneration; interior order and peace, exterior respect and power. Such must be the spirit of your conversation and of your letters; precipitate no step; I can wait at Bayonne; I can cross the Pyrenees, and, strengthening myself on the side of Portugal, carry on the war in that direction.

" I will take care of your private interests; give no thought to them yourself. Portugal will be at my disposal; let no personal project occupy you and direct your conduct; that would injure you still more than it would me.

" You go too fast in your instructions of the 14th. The march which you prescribe to General Dupont is too rapid, on account of the events of the 19th of March. There are some changes to be made in your instructions to the generals. Make new arrangements; you will receive instructions from my minister of foreign affairs.

" I desire that the strictest discipline may be observed; no pardon for any fault, however small; the inhabitants will be treated with the greatest consideration; the churches and convents will be especially respected.

" The army will avoid any rencounter, either with divisions of the Spanish army or with detachments. No bait must be offered either on one side or the other.

" Allow Solano to pass Badajoz—have him well watched; trace out the marches to be followed by my army, in such a manner as always to keep it at a distance of several leagues from the Spanish divisions. *Should the war be kindled, all would be lost.*

" It is for policy and negotiators to decide the fate of Spain; I recommend you to avoid an explanation with Solano, as well as with the other generals, and the Spanish governments.

" You will send me two expresses daily; in case of any more important event, you will dispatch an officer of ordnance to me. You will immediately send back the chamberlain Cournan, who brings you this despatch, committing to him a detailed report.

" I pray to God to have you in his holy keeping.

"NAPOLEON."

What took place at Bayonne is well known:

Charles IV. gave up all his claims to the Emperor Napoleon, Ferdinand renounced his, a junto was formed for deliberating upon and voting a constitution, and Joseph Bonaparte, being raised to the throne, entered Spain, accompanied by the grandees who had accepted the offices of his court.

Prince Talleyrand, who had long been impatient under the superiority of rank accorded to two citizens like Cambacères and Lebrun, had exchanged his office of minister for the honour of being reckoned among the great dignitaries of the empire, retaining at the same time the office of chamberlain, a household office, but with a salary which was not to be despised. He approved what had been done at Bayonne, offered his castle at Valençay, and when the princes of Spain had been sent to him, conceived, and offered with the most meritorious zeal to execute, the project of making them swear allegiance to the Emperor.

After the conferences at Erfurt, at which the Emperor Alexander left the south of Europe entirely at the disposal of Napoleon, the latter quitted Paris for the purpose of placing himself at the head of his army in Spain. He crossed the Pyrenees with 60,000 veteran troops, composed of the corps of Marshals Lannes, Soult, and Ney, and the guard; but before arriving at Madrid, which resisted for two days, he had to fight, and gain the battles of Tudéla, Espinosa, Burgos, and Somnassiésa.

These victories produced very various sensations at Paris. The more easy the seizure of Spain had

appeared to Prince Talleyrand, when he drew up the
memorial at Fontainebleau, the more sure a presage
did this obstinate resistance now seem to him of a
future disastrous to the Emperor. His old rancour
rejoiced at this prospect, and his re-awakened ambition
busied itself with calculations of the advantages which
it might draw from these disasters and from the errors
of public opinion.

" The Emperor," said he, " will not return from
Spain;" and from that moment his resolution was
taken.   He transformed into a grave wrong what ·
might be considered as a fault, and the echoes of his
saloons constantly repeated that an insatiable ardour
for combats and power had repulsed the best counsels;
that he had predicted to the Emperor what was now
happening to him, and that the reward of his prudent
and devoted skill had been his being obliged to resign
his office of minister of foreign affairs, which he had
done the more willingly as he had perceived the im-
possibility of preventing the Emperor from hastening
to his destruction. The intriguers of the saloons
formed the opinions of the coteries, and the coteries
that of the capital.

After having re-organised the government at Madrid,
and subdued the northern provinces, the Emperor
was preparing to march towards the south, when he
learned that the English army, under General Moore,
was advancing from the Taragno towards Valladolid,
for the purpose of interrupting our line of operations,
and cutting off our communication with France;

the Emperor quitted Madrid on the 24th of November.

On receiving information of his march, General Moore began his retreat. The French who had been delayed twenty-four hours in their passage of the Guadarama by a storm, rested every night at the place which the English had quitted in the morning.

The Emperor, on his arrival at Astorza, received a despatch there, on the 2nd of January, informing him that the Austrians were forming magazines, and were collecting troops on the shores of the Im, in order to attempt an aggression unforeseen and favoured by his absence. He was, at the same time, informed of the intrigues of the vice-elector, which had already assumed the appearance of flagrant usurpation.

Conventicles had collected a certain number of influential members of the senate. A ministry had already been organised. Laplace, Trais, Garot, were at the head of the list. Clement de Ris omitted no detail in his report; he gave the names of all the persons who were to compose this ministry. All measures had been taken for attempting then what was afterwards executed in 1814.

On receiving this news, the Emperor soon took his resolution; he left to Marshal Soult the mission of driving the English into the sea at the mouth of the Carogna; and set out, on the 3rd of January, for Valladolid. As early as 1805, England had incited Austria against us, in order to ward off the invasion with which she herself was threatened; the same means were put into operation in 1809, in order to effect a diversion in favour of Spain. The Emperor, who had intended to pass from the Corogna into Portugal, and to return by Cadiz to Madrid, after having subdued the whole Peninsula, was now obliged to renounce this wise project. After having passed a few days at Valladolid, for the purpose of making the necessary preparations for his absence by organizing the army, and placing it in a position in which it could await his return, he set out suddenly for Paris, and arrived there a day before the express announcing his departure from Valladolid.

"On Sunday, the 23rd of January, the first Sunday after his return, he received at his grand levee, the high dignitaries and officers of the crown, the ministers, the high chancellor of the legion of honour, the officers of the senate, &c. Before this numerous assembly, he addressed himself to the high chamberlain.

He reminded him of the memorial of Fontainebleau, of his endeavours and urgent entreaties to persuade him to commence the war with Spain. He told him that he did not reproach him with this as with a fault, because he had afterwards followed this advice given at an inopportune time. He then added: "You have changed your opinion. When you thought you foresaw a change of fortune, you made a merit of giving me advice exactly opposed to that which you had urged upon me for six weeks, and turned it into a fault on my part not to have followed it. I know all; I can forget all; but when a person creates for himself interests opposed to mine, and acts against me, he ought to have the modesty to resign an office so nearly attached to my person."

The high chamberlain, who had remained silent, understood that he was already displaced; and it was, in fact, the case: M. de Montesquieu had for two hours had his nomination to this high office of the crown in his pocket.

The disasters of the campaign of Moscow made it necessary to recall the armies of Spain to the Rhine. The minister of foreign affairs, the Duke of Bassano, proposed to the Emperor, in order to put a term to two affairs now become very dangerous, to restore the Pope to Rome, which would appease the religious order, and to send back Ferdinand to Spain, which would paralyse the powerful action of the Cortes, and would remove all subject for fear on the side of the south, until the conclusion of the struggle in which the Emperor was now engaged with the north.

The Emperor at first only admitted the first clause of this advice. He signed the concordat at Fontaine-bleau, January, 1813. He could not resolve to renounce the great results which he might expect from the immense sacrifices which had been making in Spain since the year 1809.

Spain was, doubtless, conquered, when the hostile demonstrations of Austria obliged him to leave the government of that country to King Joseph and his marshals. In less than three months, four Spanish armies, amounting together to 160,000 men, had been

defeated and dispersed. Madrid and Saragossa had
fallen into the hands of the French. The English
army had been forced to re-embark, after having suffered immense losses. But a change had, since then,
come over the affairs of the Peninsula. England had
made incredible efforts to rekindle the war; she had
lavished armies and treasures on this object. Spain
was surrounded on three sides by the sea; the English
squadrons easily and suddenly landed fresh troops at all
the various points of the coast; in Catalonia, in Biscay,
in Portugal, in the kingdom of Valencia, and at Cadiz.

The error committed in Spain, after Napoleon's departure, was not that of proceeding too quickly, but
of proceeding too slowly; if he had remained there a
few months longer, he would have taken Lisbon and
Cadiz, conciliated parties, and pacified the country.
The guerillas were not formed till a year after
Napoleon's departure, and then solely through the
effects of the pillage, disorders, and abuses, of which
the marshals set the example, in contempt of the
Emperor's most decisive and strict commands.

The corps under the command of Marshal Suchet,
which occupied the kingdom of Valencia, never suffered
a want of anything; the country, being well governed
by the marshal, supplied all the necessities of the
army; the contributions were regularly paid, and
war was carried on, as it would have been in Germany,
and all this because the marshal set an example of
severe probity, and maintained discipline among his
troops. Had all the other marshals done the same,

the war would have been reduced to the chances of a battle. Spain was lost after a five years' struggle against not only the population of a large and valorous kingdom, but also against the Anglo-Portuguese army which had become as skilful in manœuvres as that of the French.

It is difficult to find an explanation of these false manœuvres, of the faults of strategy, which brought on the disasters of Talavera, Salamanca, and Vittoria. One cannot help calling to mind on this occasion, the disgraceful causes of the affair of Beleme. The want of fortresses is a false argument; the French had taken them all. The true cause is this, that the Spaniards offered the same resistance to the French as they had done to the Romans. Conquered nations can only become subjects of the conqueror by a mixture of policy and severity, and by an amalgamation with the army. Things failed in Spain. If the French had amused themselves with making establishments on the Ebro, instead of marching over the Samo-sierra, and against Madrid and Benevente, for the purpose of expelling the English after the victories of Vittoria, Espinosa, Tudéla, and Burgos, they would have had 200,000 English, Spanish, and Portuguese troops against them, and their army would, in two months, have been driven beyond the Pyrenees.

After the Emperor's departure, the pursuit of the English army was executed without vigour; having forced the English to re-embark, the French general ought to have marched against Lisbon, Cadiz, and

Valencia; political means would then have done the
rest. No one can deny that if the court of Austria
had not declared war, and had thus allowed Napoleon
to remain four months longer in Spain, all would have
been brought to a termination. The presence of the
general is indispensable; he is the head, the guiding
star of an army; it was not the Roman army which subdued Gaul, but Cæsar; it was not the Carthaginian
army at the gates of Rome which made the republic
tremble, but Hannibal; it was not the Macedonian
army which overturned the empire of Persia, but
Alexander; it was not the French army which carried
the war to the banks of the Weser and the Im, but
Turenne; it was not the Prussian army which defended
Prussia for seven years, but Frederick the Great.

After the fatal events of Leipzig, it was of great
importance to the French to put an end without delay
to the dangers created by the affairs of Spain. The
Duke of Bassano received instructions to send the
Duke of San Carlos to Valençay, with proposals to
Ferdinand to return to his kingdom; Count Lafarest,
who was living on his estate in the neighbourhood of
Tours, received at the same time orders to go secretly
to Valençay, under the name of Don del Basca, and
negotiate the treaty which should restore the Prince
of Asturias to liberty and his crown.

Ferdinand had always shown the greatest aversion
to the Cortes. The Spaniards long regretted the constitution of Bayonne; had it triumphed, they would
no longer have had an ecclesiastical jurisdiction in

secular affairs, no more feudal service, no interior barriers. Their national domains would not have remained uncultivated and useless to the state and nation. They would have had a secular clergy—a nobility enjoying no feudal privileges or exemptions from contributions and public expenses; they would now be a different people.

Ferdinand had often said that he preferred remaining at Valençay to reigning in Spain with the Cortes; nevertheless, when Napoleon proposed his remounting the throne, in 1813, he did not hesitate. Count Lafarest was sent to him to negotiate this affair. The treaty was soon drawn up; no conditions were imposed on Ferdinand; for the engagement which he entered into to ratify the sales of national domains made during his absence, and not to call any of the persons who had held public employments to account, cannot be regarded as a condition. Ferdinand at this time loudly manifested his resolution of taking things in Spain as he found them, and reigning like a constitutional king. As soon as the treaty was concluded, he again proposed to contract, by a marriage, a closer alliance with Napoleon; this request was neither refused nor accepted. The reply given was, that the moment for agreeing to it was not yet come; that when Ferdinand was reseated on his throne, if he renewed his request from Madrid, it should then be received as it ought to be.

The treaty of Valençay had been negotiated with the greatest secrecy; it was important that it should not come to the knowledge of the English; they would have thwarted a proceeding, the result of which was to be to leave the army free to arrive in the plains of Champagne in time for the campaign of 1814.

The events which were being brought about at Paris settled things otherwise. The party which was struggling to overthrow Napoleon, succeeded in discovering this secret negotiation; they attempted to persuade him that a regard for his. glory ought not to suffer him to renounce Spain, and to secure his rejection of the treaty of Valençay.

Not having succeeded in their purpose, they published the existence of the treaty, and employed all the resources of intrigue to delay Ferdinand's departure, and thus retard the return of the army to France. Ferdinand was to have quitted Valençay in the course of November, 1813, and yet he did not cross the Pyrenees till the month of March, 1815.

While this negotiation was being opened with Ferdinand, Mons. Fallat de Beaumont, former archbishop of Bourges, received instructions to go to Fontainebleau, with full powers to treat with the pope respecting his return to Rome.

In the meantime, the intrigues of the former high chamberlain, to whose counsels fate willed that the Emperor should again listen, effected a change in the cabinet. The report of Count St. Aignous, on his arrival from the head quarters, was the occasion and pretext of this change; the office of minister of foreign affairs was entrusted to the Duke of Vicenza.

The Emperor, however, by a formal and unusual exception, left to the Duke of Bassano the care of pursuing the two negotiations which he had opened. The treaty of Valençay was signed on the 8th of December, 1813, and the pope, although he would not subscribe to any written engagement, was restored to his states. One thing alone was reserved to Ferdinand, who demanded the hand of one of the Emperor's nieces. It was agreed that this demand should be listened to when it was renewed from Madrid. It had been calculated that the first columns of the veteran army of Spain might be drawn up in line on the 1st of March.

The secret of the treaty was now known to all enemies at home and abroad. Constantly renewed intrigues retarded its execution. The ratification of it was, however, signed; but precious days had already been lost. Such a desire was felt at Valençay, as at the Tuileries, to make provision for all difficulties, that it was agreed, that if the least opposition to the execution of all the conditions of the treaty was made on the part of the Cortes at Madrid, it should only be looked upon, in case of need, as an engagement destined to become a public treaty when the prince should have resumed his power, and in opportune circumstances.

The Duke of San Carlos had been dispatched to Madrid, three days after the conclusion of the treaty. The king was to follow him without delay.

But through an unpardonable fault of the Duke of

Sueldre, minister of war, the King of Spain could not quit Valençay till the 13th of March.

The king was to be received at the frontier by Marshal Suchet, whose head-quarters had just been established at Figuierès. The Duke of San Carlos informed the marshal of this arrangement on his way to Madrid, and spoke to him at great length of the constitutional fidelity of the king.

The secrecy which it had been wished to maintain concerning the treaty of Valençay, and the promptitude of its execution, were of immense importance.

They would have been the only means of preventing the English cabinet from acting on the spirit of the Spanish government, and thus preparing the reception given by it to King Ferdinand and his envoy.

On the arrival of the Duke of San Carlos at Madrid, the regency listened to him with coldness, and after having heard the object of his mission, asked him what he had been doing at the time when the Spaniards were fighting desperately for their king, and suffering the fatigues, privations, and dangers of war. It reproached him with his pleasures at Paris, with his luxury and dissipation, and even with his love affair with the Princess Talleyrand.

As regarded his mission, it declared that the king should be received as king when he had taken his oaths in the presence of the Cortes; that, till then, he should only receive the honours due to him as Prince of Asturias; that the necessary orders should be given along a certain route, that of Burgos, that he might at each station find an escort of sixty men, and that the authorities might be instructed as to the conduct they were to pursue.

General Elliot and Monsieur de Zagas, nephew of General Ofaril, formerly minister of war under Joseph Bonaparte, were successively dispatched to Madrid by the king, on missions similar to that of the Duke of San Carlos, and were treated in the same manner by the regency—with pride and disdain; it found subjects for criticism in some details of their personal conduct; reproached General Elliot with having allowed himself to be defeated at Valencia; and, in short, its whole conduct announced that when the king should have remounted the throne, the credit of the Duke of San Carlos, Elliot, and de Zagas would not last long, should his majesty be guided by the spirit of the regency.

Ferdinand at last arrived, on the 19th of March, at Perpignan, and on the 22nd, at the head-quarters at Figuierès, where he was to await the return of General Elliot from Madrid; his whole conversation showed that he felt a deep sense of what he owed to the regency, to the Cortes, and to the nation.

" He only desired to reign," he said, " by the laws which his victorious people had made for themselves."

He communicated to Marshal Suchet the proclamation which he was about to publish, declaring his sentiments, and he asked his advice, believing that what he was going to do would be in perfect accordance with what he ought to do. Marshal Suchet, who was well acquainted with the state of Spain, entirely

approved of the proclamation, which contained the most
explicit and candid declarations; he only requested,
with a delicate feeling of propriety, that the king
should insist still more strongly on the praise merited
by the Spanish army. The Marshal breakfasted and
dined every day with the king, who, until the return
of Messrs. Elliot and Zagas, still testified the same
disposition.

But it was soon changed. On the arrival of these
gentlemen, they both advised him to throw off at once
the yoke which the regency wished to impose on him,
and to travel to Madrid by a different route from
that pointed out by the regency. They persuaded
him to pass through Saragossa, in order to see, in the
ruins of this great and illustrious city, the sad proofs
of the courage of his subjects. They sent emissaries
into the country around to excite the people to assemble
in masses along the route to be taken by the king.
They intoxicated him with the enthusiasm of which
he was the object, and which burst forth with especial
strength at Saragossa.

From that moment, Ferdinand's wise resolutions
were banished. The regency, informed of these proceedings, uttered threats; General Elliot began to
collect armed forces, and finding himself at the head
of about 10,000 men, marched towards the capital.
The regency sent a few battalions to oppose him; he
soon put them to rout; Ferdinand entered Madrid as
a conqueror, and the counter-revolution was made.

Marshal Suchet wrote to the Emperor, that on the

first news of the treaty of Valençay, the regency, happy at, and proud of, a deliverance which it regarded as its work, had manifested the intention of proceeding to the frontier, to be the first to salute with its acclamations the return of the constitutional king to Spain ; but that inexplicable delays had excited distrust, and changed these dispositions. " Had the treaty been executed two months earlier," said he, " Spain would have warded off the catastrophes which await her, and France would have been saved."

CHAPTER XV.

AFFAIRS OF ROME AND CONCORDAT OF FONTAINEBLEAU.

DURING these occurrences, letters from Las Cases gave us hopes of seeing him again. He had obtained permission to return to England, and was to pass by St. Helena. Without doubt, our reason, our knowledge of the character of Sir Hudson Lowe, had already convinced us that we should not be permitted to take a last farewell of this so devoted friend of the Emperor; but hope is the support of the suffering soul, and we hoped in spite of ourselves.

The health of the Emperor continued to get worse and worse. I saw him more frequently than any one, and consequently I was better able than any one else to trace the causes of the malady which was manifested so often, and under such different forms. His chest could not endure the effect of the moist atmosphere of

Longwood, and still less the sudden changes of temperature to which it was subject. In fact, the thermometer at St. Helena varies 10° per day, according as the sun is above or below the horizon.

I have remarked that great heat produces no effect on the Emperor; he had already been accustomed to it in Egypt; but moisture of climate exercises a terrible influence on his health. I have frequently seen him, after coming in from a ride at night, suffer from attacks of cough so violent as not to cease till vomiting ensued.

It was in the midst of these new apprehensions for the health of the Emperor, that Sir Hudson Lowe presented himself before me, to complain that we consumed too much fire-wood; and that it was unreasonable for the Emperor, under the tropics, to have a fire every day in his bedroom. He even asserted that this could only arise from a wish, on his part, to cause more expense to England.

I recalled to his recollection that it was not long since the boards of the bedroom had sunk, and suddenly a gush of stagnant water sprang from a sort of marsh which extended along two-thirds of the room.

"But," said he, "since I have had the boards repaired, and the water emptied out, it seems to me that there is no further occasion for a fire."

"In that room, certainly," answered I; "but what do you say respecting the others, where the boards are rotten, and the walls covered with moisture?"

And at the same time I pointed out to him with my finger proofs of what I advanced.

However, Sir Hudson was uneasy on account of the Emperor's state of health, and he proposed to the grand marshal to have one of those wooden barracks, which can be set up and taken down at pleasure, erected for him, at the end of the library, "in order," said he, "that General Bonaparte may be able to take exercise without being exposed to the sun and the rain." When this proposal was repeated to the Emperor, he merely shrugged his shoulders, and murmured between his teeth, "Disgusting irony!"

The Emperor at last decided upon addressing to Lord Liverpool a long memorandum, in the form of observations on the bad treatment he had experienced. The grand marshal committed this sealed despatch to the officer on duty.

The bad temper of Sir Hudson Lowe increased continually, and at last became such, that Bertrand and I did not know what means to use, so that the Emperor might not hear of his outrages. Poor O'Meara, on his part, was exposed to all his ill-humour. Sir Hudson Lowe wished him to issue bulletins after his fashion; the Emperor heard of this, and refused O'Meara's assistance, however much he might have need of it. Long and painful discussions followed; Sir Hudson at length yielded, and it was settled that no bulletin should be issued without having been previously shown to Bertrand or myself; and in order to avoid any occasion for an insult, it was settled that the Emperor should merely be designated as *the patient.*

This simple announcement of a fact will say more than any commentary!

The arrival of a vessel from Europe gave an agreeable diversion to all these ignoble plots during some time. We received pamphlets and some books on the subject of the reign of the Emperor. I profited by them to awaken the recollection of a happier time. and he dictated the following note on the affairs of Rome:

AFFAIRS OF ROME.

" Napoleon had given, in the years 1796 and 1797, in Italy, particular attention to affairs of religion. This knowledge was necessary to a conqueror and to the legislator of the Transpadane and Cispadane republics, in the same way as, when in Egypt, he studied the Koran, because it was necessary for him to be acquainted with the principles of Islamism, the government, the opinions of the four sects, and their relations to Constantinople and Malta. His profound knowledge of each religion contributed to captivate the affection both of the Italian clergy and of the Ilémas of Egypt.

" He never repented of having signed the concordat of 1801; the expressions put into his mouth on that subject are false; he never said, *that the concordat was the greatest error of his reign.* The disputes which he had with Rome proceeded from the abuse made by this court of the mixture of spiritual and temporal power.

" This may have occasioned him some moments of impatience: it was the lion stung by flies; but nothing ever altered his feelings, either with regard to the principles of his religion, or the great act which has had such important results.

The concordat of 1801 was necessary to religion, to the republic, to the government; the temples of worship were closed, the priests persecuted; they were divided into three sects—the constitutional priests, the vicars apostolic, and the bishops who had emigrated to England. The concordat put an end to these discussions, and raised the Roman-catholic apostolic church from its ruins; it was facilitated by the favourable disposition of the venerable Pius VII., who, immediately on hearing the proposal of it, hastened to reply: " Assure the First Consul, that I shall willingly enter into a negotiation, the aim of which is so praiseworthy, so suitable to my holy office, and so conformable to the wishes of my heart." The plenipotentiaries of the Holy See were, Cardinal Spina, and a celebrated theologian; Joseph Bonaparte, Cretel, a state councillor, and Bermir, then a rector, formerly a chief of the Vendean army, were invested with powers by France.

" One would be inclined to think, that the immense interest which the Holy See had in seeing the altars of Christ again raised in France, would have overruled all secondary questions; but with Rome the contrary always happens.

"Canonical institutions, the admission of the priests who had taken their oaths in the re-organisation of the French church, the consecration of the goods of the church, gave rise to acrimonious debates, while the subject of divorce presented no difficulty, and the Roman negotiators declared that they would consent to admit the marriage of priests, if the First Consul would consent to yield to the Pope the right of adjourning indefinitely canonical institution, which consent would have been equal to a renunciation of the right possessed by the chief of the state to nominate bishops.

"But it was necessary to bring these discussions to a close; the French negotiators and the ambassador of France at Rome, received instructions to declare, that if the Holy See did not, within the space of three days, accede to the offers of France, and sign the concordat, the negotiations should be looked upon as broken off, and the First Consul, desirous, above every other consideration, of bringing back the French nation to religious sentiments, would consider, in his wisdom, whether or not he would follow the example of Henry VIII.

"The venerable Pius VII. was troubled by this declaration, the sacred college trembled. Cardinal Gonzalvé set out in haste for Paris; all difficulties were smoothed down, the concordat was signed at

Paris on the 15th of July, 1801, and the Holy See ratified it in the course of the same month, as well as the decree issued by the First Consul, which, under the title of " *Regulations for the execution of the Concordat,*" settled the *organic articles.*

" The question of divorce and that of the marriage of priests, are the two great social questions which have escaped the shipwreck of the supreme jurisdiction of the catholic church; this is not the opinion maintained by the ignorant fanatics of the profanations of the holy sacrament. Councils have always admitted the dissolution of marriage. The council of Trent fixed rules for it; it appointed thirteen cases in which a nuptial benediction, given in contempt of the observance of any one of these thirteen conditions of the nullity of a marriage, should be dissolved and declared null. To discuss the rupture or nullity, to cavil, is not a principle; to render the bond of a marriage indissoluble, is to provoke crime, is to place the curate of a village above the power of the law.

" A separation *in mezzo termine* can only be put in practice among the higher classes; the mass of the people can find no protection, they are obliged to groan during their whole lives under the evil consequences of one day, or to rush to crime, in the hope of an impunity which should secure the return of calm to their homes.

" Henry IV. possessed the religious right of divorce, and that during the reign of a religious fanaticism, which had condemned him to choose between an ab-

juration and a throne; and to debar a simple citizen
from any means of breaking the tie which binds him
to a barren woman, to a Messalina, or to a shrew, is to
establish an inequality in the face of the law between
men of the same nation, is to place ourselves again
under the empire of feudal distinctions, is to retrograde to the middle ages, to an order of things which
was destroyed from the very root by the revolution of
1789.   It is true that marriage is both a civil and a
religious contract; and as the law declares that it
can only be legally contracted by being performed in
presence of the municipal officer appointed to execute
the commands of the law, it must also, in order to obtain
validity in the sight of religion, be subjected to the
formalities imposed by it, in order that the priest
may give the nuptial benediction.   The rupture of
marriage ought then necessarily to be doubly pronounced, by the natural judges of all questions of religious belief,—viz., the metropolitan authorities.

" In this state of things, equally suggested by reason
to the legislator, and by faith to the pious man, perfect equality before the law for all men, entire liberty
to have a marriage dissolved, whatever may be the
religion of the person requiring it, catholics and protestants would be under the dominion of the same
law, while on the contrary, since the abolition of
divorce by the effects of a senseless reaction, the inequality between the catholic and the protestant is
flagrant.   The former cannot dissolve his marriage,
while to the latter it is easy, for a protestant has

only to acquire the right of citizenship in a protestant village on the frontiers of France, to be able legally to divorce his wife.

" The celibacy of priests is only a perfection of holiness, the councils declared this; and this truth cannot be disputed, for these same councils delegated to the Pope the power of releasing a priest from his vows, and permitting him to marry.

" M. de Talleyrand, minister of foreign affairs during the negotiations for the concordat, had been Bishop of Autun before the French revolution; but considering himself free, like every French citizen, through the effects of the laws of the republic, to contract a marriage, he wished to marry a Dutch woman. The Pope released him from his vows, and Madame Gramt became Princess Talleyrand, and not even the most ardent defender of the canons ventured to raise his voice against this marriage.

" Napoleon rebuilt the altars, put an end to all disorders, desired the faithful to pray for the republic, dissipated all the scruples of the purchasers of national domains, and broke the last thread by which the ancient dynasty still communicated with the country by depriving of their places the bishops who had remained faithful to it, denominating them rebels, who had preferred the affairs of the world and terrestrial interests before the affairs of heaven and the cause of God.

" It has been said, 'Napoleon ought not to have interfered in religious affairs, but to have tolerated religion

in practising its worship;' but what worship? Restore
its temples; but to whom? To the constitutional party,
to the clergy, or to the papist vicars in the pay of
England? It was proposed to Napoleon, in the conferences for the negotiation of the concordat, to assign
a delay in the exercise of the right of instituting
bishops, conferred on the Pope; but he had already
made great concessions; he consented to the suppression of those dioceses whose sees dated from the birth
of Christianity; he deprived a great number of
ancient bishops, by his own authority, of their places,
and sold, without giving any indemnity, four hundred
millions' worth of goods belonging to the clergy.

" It was decided, that, even as regarded the interests
of the republic, new stipulations which would have
favoured the ultra-montanes, ought not to be exacted.
It was in one of these conferences that Napoleon said;
' If the Pope had not existed, he must have been
created for this occasion, as the Roman consuls created
a dictator in difficult circumstances.'

" It is true that the concordat acknowledged the
existence in the state of a foreign power, which was
likely to trouble it one day, but it did not introduce
it—it had always existed.

" Being master of Italy, Napoleon considered himself
master of Rome, and this Italian influence served him
as a means for counteracting the English influence.

" The pieces printed at London, concerning the discussions between the court of the Tuileries and that of
Rome, are apocryphal; they have never been avowed.

The effect hoped for from their publication was that of
exalting the imaginations of the Spaniards and those of
the saints of Christendom: the *Petite Eglise* published them about with furious zeal. Some of these
pieces are false, the others are more or less falsified. It
is to be lamented that they should have found place
in an important work; it would not have been difficult to prove their falsity. 1stly, the court of the
Tuileries never promised, either directly or indirectly,
to allow legations, and the Pope looked upon this condition as the price of his journey to Paris. It is possible that he flattered himself with the hope of obtaining
Romagna, in which lay Casena, his native country,
from the gratitude of the Emperor; it is possible that
during his stay in Paris, he spoke of this desire directly
to the Emperor; but it was very slightly, and without hopes of success. 2ndly. How could it be supposed that the court of Rome had been requested to
establish a patriarch in France? A patriarch would
only have possessed influence in France, while the
Pope, who was the patriarch of the great empire,
possessed an influence over the whole universe.
France would then have lost by the change! 3rdly.
How could the Emperor have demanded the acceptance
of the civil code? Did not the Napoleon code rule in
France and Italy? Did he require the assistance of
the court of Rome to frame laws for his own subjects?
4thly. Why should he have demanded liberty of worship? Was not this a fundamental law of the French
constitution. Had this law more need of the sanction

of the Pope, than of that of Maron the minister, and the consistory of Geneva? 5thly. How could he have demanded the reform of the too numerous bishoprics in Italy? Had not the concordat of Italy provided for this? It is true that some negotiations were carried on respecting the bishoprics of Tuscany and Genoa, but in the form established for these kind of affairs. 6thly. What interest could he have in wishing the pontifical bulls relating to the bishoprics and benefices in Italy to be abolished?—was not all this regulated by the concordat of Italy? 7thly. Why should he have demanded the abolition of religious orders?—were not these orders already abolished in France and Italy? How could it be supposed, that, engaged as he was in discussions with the court of Rome, he would demand freedom of marriage for the priests, which would have been, in all gaiety of heart, to give his enemies an advantage? What did the celibacy of the priests matter to him! Had he any time to lose in theological discussions? 9thly. What interest could he have in wishing Joseph Bonaparte to be consecrated King of Naples by the Pope? Had the Pope wished to do so, Napoleon would have opposed his desire, for fear that he should afterwards put forward a claim to be suzerain of Naples.

" The direct correspondence between the Emperor and the Pope, from 1805 to 1809, remained secret; it solely concerned temporal affairs, regarding which he needed neither the consent nor the advice of his bishops; but in 1809, when the Pope, relying on a

passage in the proceedings of the council of Lyons,
endeavoured, by the brief of Savona, addressed to the
chapter of Florence and to that of Paris, to interfere
with the duties of capitular vicars, during the vacancies
of the sees, the discussions began to refer to spiritual
matters. The Pope then felt the need of the counsel
and intervention of the clergy—he established a
council of theologians. The choice which he made was
fortunate; the Bishop of Nantes, who had for half a
century been one of the oracles of Christendom, was
the soul of the council; from this time, all the discussions became public.

"Fox, conversing with Napoleon after the treaty of
Amiens, reproached him with not having obtained
freedom for the priests to marry: Napoleon replied:
"I had and have need of using pacifying measures;
*it is with water, and not with oil, that theological
volcanoes must be calmed; it would have given me
less trouble to have established the confession of
Augsburg throughout my empire.*"

"Ever since the coronation, discussions had been
carried on concerning the cardinals' hats, some
expressions which the Pope had allowed himself to
use in his harangues on the organic laws, and the
briefs relating to the penitentiary tribunal; as
also concerning some circumscriptions of the bishoprics of Tuscany and Genoa, and some secret affairs
relative to the kingdom of Italy; but none of
these discussions directly occupied the two sovereigns;
they were constantly abandoned to the care of the

chanceries, which treated all these affairs with moderation and wisdom.

" The carrying off the Pope was neither foreseen nor ordered by the Emperor: it was a personal act of General Miollis, an old republican who was at the head of the troops stationed in the states of the church.

" The disputes between the cabinet of the Tuileries and that of the Holy See were never caused by any religious question; they were entirely political, and date from the year 1805—a period at which the squadrons of the coalition threatened the shores of Italy with an Anglo-Prussian debarkation.

" The arming of Ancona was included in the general plan for the defence of Italy. The Emperor commissioned his ambassador at Rome to demand it from the Holy See. He made offers of an offensive and defensive alliance between the king of Italy and the court of Rome. The Pope refused, and answered: ' that as father of the faithful, he could enter into no league against his children, and neither could nor would make war against any one.' The Emperor replied: ' The history of the Popes is full of accounts of their leagues with the emperors, the kings of Spain, and the kings of France. Julius II. commanded armies: in 1797, I, General Bonaparte, defeated the army of Pius VI., which was fighting among the ranks of the Austrians against the French republic, and since, in our days, the banners of St. Peter could float, without any derogation to their sanctity, beside

the eagles of Austria; they may well float over the
walls of Ancona, as allies of the eagle of France. Nevertheless, out of respect to the scruples of the holy
father, I consent that the treaty of alliance shall be
confined to the case of an attack from the infidels or
heretics.'

" Events succeeded each other rapidly in this time of
deadly struggle between England and France. Ancona
must be occupied at any price; the safety of the
kingdom of Italy depended upon this being done;
General Miollis received orders to garrison it, and
was charged with the defence of the marches and
legations.   The nuncio quitted Paris immediately on
hearing of this arrangement, and, though minister of
the smallest existing temporal power, unhesitatingly
declared war against the colossal French Empire.
The cabinet of the Tuileries affected not to consider
itself at variance with Rome, and instructed its ambassador to make no change in his diplomatic relations
with the Holy See.

" The battle of Esling for a moment revived the
hopes of the coalition.

" The exasperated feelings of the people manifested
themselves very strongly in several districts of the
states of the church, and General Miollis with alarm
saw himself exposed to the fanaticism of a people
roused by the holy name of religion.   His troops,
extended along a line of sixty leagues in extent,
amounted to scarcely 6000 men, and in Rome itself
he had less than 1500 to keep that great city under

authority. His position was very critical. He recollected the sinister examples of the massacres of
Verona, in 1797, and of Rome, in 1798, when General
Duphot fell under the daggers of the dregs of the
populace, who had been exasperated by the priests;
and he saw no prospect of safety but in one of those
extraordinary and unforeseen measures which are
sometimes taken. General Miollis did not recoil from
the fearful responsibility of violating the supreme
majesty of the Pope; yet he was still hesitating, when
he received a letter, signed by the queen of Naples,
advising and even authorising him to adopt this
measure; from this moment his hesitation vanished—
he carried off the Pope in the middle of the night,
and sent him to Florence. The effect of this measure
was sudden as a thunderbolt—a most profound stupor
reigned throughout the town and in the mountains,
instead of the threatening effervescence of the previous
evening.

" The Grand Duchess of Tuscany was not a little
astonished that a general should dare to act thus
without the Emperor's orders, and became naturally
alarmed at the part of the responsibility which would
rest on her, if the Pope remained in Tuscany; she
sent courier after courier to the imperial head-
quarters, requiring General Miollis to send the cortège
along the sea-shore into the states of Genoa. The Pope
was conducted to Savona.

"Nothing could equal the displeasure of the Emperor;
he immediately understood all the difficulties which

would arise, and his first act was to order the Pope to be taken back to the Vatican. But all the dreams of General Bonaparte, all the projects of the Emperor concerning Italy received from this carrying off of the Pope the possibility of being realized. Of the three obstacles which had always been opposed to the *unity of Italy*, two had disappeared, by the will of the Emperor; the third, the only one which his thoughts had but timidly approached, the residence of the vicars of Jesus Christ at Rome, was now removed by one of those inexplicable combinations of destiny which sometimes occur, and which now transported the chair of St. Peter from the banks of the Tiber to those of the Seine. Paris would be the capital of the great empire, and the residence of the sovereign pontiff of 80,000,000 catholics. The spiritual power of the Popes would naturally be strengthened by the support of the great temporal power of the Emperor; the golden days of the church would be revived. The removal of the Popes was a fact gained to the fortune of the empire; Napoleon accepted it; it was on this occasion that he wrote to the Abbé Duvoisin, Bishop of Nantes, whose great merit he held in high estimation, and with whom he corresponded, in the following words:

" ' Let your mind be perfectly easy; the policy of my state is intimately connected with the maintenance of the Pope's power: I must make him more powerful than ever: he will never have as much power as my policy would lead me to give him.' "

The Bishop of Nantes preached the catholic religion by the wisdom of his reasonings and the excellence of the morality which he professed. In his discussions, he abandoned everything which it was difficult for reason to admit, and thus placed himself on an excellent ground on which to argue with his adversaries. He was a contemporary of Diderot, of D'Alembert, and of the philosophers of this period, and had endeavoured, and with success, to combat their opinions; he had gained the esteem and confidence of the Emperor, who consulted him in all questions relating to the church. The carrying off of the Pope was not an act of the Emperor's will, but one of those accidents which often happen in politics as well as in the course of life. The whole of the Imperial Palace at Turin was put at the disposal of the Pope. At Savona he was lodged in the archbishop's palace, which afforded him every convenience; the intendant of the civil list and the Count Salmatori provided abundantly for everything necessary.

He remained there for several months, during which time proposals were made to him to return to Rome, if he would agree not to disturb public tranquillity, to recognise the government established in that capital, and only to occupy himself with spiritual affairs; but, perceiving that they wished to weary him out, and that the world went on without him, he addressed briefs to the metropolitan chapters of Florence and Paris, to disturb the administration of the dioceses during the vacancies of the sees, at the same time

that Cardinal Pietro sent vicars apostolic into the
vacant dioceses.   Then, first, did the discussions,
which had been carried on for five years, lose their temporal character, and begin to take concern in spiritual
matters; and this gave rise to the first and second
assemblies of bishops, to the council of Paris, to the
bull of 1811, and finally, to the concordat of Fontainebleau, in 1813.   Nothing was yet settled concerning
the temporal affairs of Rome; this uncertainty encouraged the resistance of the Pope; the Emperor, who
had been harassed for five years by the most pitiful
arguments, arising from the mixture of temporal and
spiritual power, decided at length to separate them
for ever, and no longer to allow the Pope to be a
temporal sovereign.   Jesus Christ had said: " *My
kingdom is not of this world;*" though heir to the
throne of David, he had wished to be pontiff and not
king.

In the beginning of the year 1810, Napoleon passed
a decree uniting Rome to the empire.   He made
arrangements on the most liberal scale for everything
relating to the temporal concerns of the Pope and
cardinals, and caused the senate to issue the following
decree:

" CLAUSE I.—*Concerning the Annexation of the States of
Rome to the Empire.*

" 1stly. The state of Rome is annexed to the empire,
and forms an integral part of it. 2ndly. It will
form two departments, that of Rome, and that of

Trasimene. 3rdly. The department of Rome will send seven deputies to the legislative body, that of Trasimene four. 4thly. The department of Rome will be classed in the first series, that of Trasimene in the second. 5thly. A senatorship will be established in the departments of Rome and Trasimene. 6thly. The city of Rome is the second city in the empire. The mayor of Rome will, on his appointment, take the oath of allegiance to the Emperor; he will thus, as well as the deputies of the city of Rome, rank on all occasions next after the mayors and deputies of Paris. 7thly. The heir-apparent of the Imperial Crown will bear the title of King of Rome, and receive the honours due to this rank. 8thly. There will be at Rome a prince of the blood. or a high dignitary of the empire, who will hold the court of the Emperor. 9thly. The estates which will form the dotation of the Imperial Crown, conformably to the decree of the 30th of January last, will be regulated by a special decree. 10thly. The emperors, after having been crowned in the church of Nôtre Dame, in Paris, will be crowned in the church of St. Peter, in Rome, before the tenth year of their reigns. 11thly. The city of Rome will enjoy such particular privileges and immunities as shall be determined by the Emperor Napoleon.

" CLAUSE II.—*Concerning the Independence of the Imperial Throne of all other Authority.*

" 12thly. Any temporal sovereignty is incompatible

with the exercise of spiritual authority in the interior of the empire. 13thly. Immediately on their elevation to the chair of St Peter, the popes will take an oath never to oppose in any way the four propositions of the Gallican church, decreed in the assembly of the clergy, in 1682. 14thly. The four propositions of the Gallican church are declared common to all the Catholic churches of the empire.

" CLAUSE III.— *Concerning the Temporal Affairs of the Pope.*

" 15thly. Palaces will be prepared for the Pope in the various places of the empire where he may wish to reside; he will necessarily have one at Paris, and one at Rome. 16thly. A revenue of two millions of francs, arising from rural possessions, and free of all impost, and six millions in various other parts of the empire, will be assigned to the Pope. 17thly. The expenses of the sacred college, and of the propaganda, are declared imperial. 18thly. The present organic decree will be transmitted to His Majesty the Emperor and King."

During all this time, the deputations of bishops had always instructions to make proposals to the Pope for his return to Rome, provided he would acknowledge the temporal government which had been established there, and would occupy himself solely with spiritual affairs; but he constantly refused.

Napoleon understood the interests of the church;

they were constantly united in his thoughts with those of the crown; and to him the catholic church owes the power which, during the last forty years, it has regained in France. The concordat of 1801 excited violent passions against the First Consul; celebrated generals raised their voices, and accused him of betraying the republic; one of them, the general who commanded the Grenadiers of the guard, dared to carry his reproaches even into the palace; but his excitement soon vanished, as by magic, before the paternal mildness with which Napoleon listened to him; and that very evening he set out on some diplomatic mission for Lisbon. Madame de Staël had placed herself at the head of the *saloon* malcontents, and said at the same time to the republicans: " You have but a moment; to-morrow, the tyrant will have 40,000 priests for his *Seides*."

Napoleon showed, in his disputes with the Holy See, more patience than accorded with his situation and character, and if he sometimes employed sarcasm in his correspondence with the Pope, he was always provoked to it by the bitter style of the Roman chancery, which expressed itself in the same manner as might have been used in the time of Louis le Debonnaire, or of the emperors of the house of Swabia; a style so much the more out of place as it was addressed to a man eminently well-informed concerning the wars and affairs of Italy, and who knew all the temporal intrigues of the popes by heart. The court of Rome might have avoided all these disputes,

by frankly annexing itself to the great system of
France, closing its ports against the English, sum-
moning some French battalions to the defence of
Ancona, and, in short, maintaining tranquillity in
Italy.

As regards spiritual questions, no others were discussed between the Emperor and the Pope, except
those laid down in the two verbal processes—that of
the two ecclesiastical commissions, and that of the
council of Paris; the only important question was
that concerning the bishops.

The Pope rendered him justice; and when he heard
of the disembarkation at Cannes, he said to Prince
Lucien, with a manner that marked his confidence—
" The Emperor having disembarked and arrived,
you will go to Paris. This is well; make my peace
with him; I am at Rome; he shall never have any
annoyance from me."

Man, launched into life, asks himself—" Whence do
I come? What am I? Whither do I go?" Mysterious questions, which draw him towards religion; we
all hasten towards it—our natural inclination urges
us so to do. We believe in the existence of God, because everything around us proclaims it; the greatest
minds have believed in it—Bossuet, Newton, Leibnitz.

We have need of believing, and without doubt
believe most frequently without exercising our reason;
faith becomes wavering, as soon as we begin to reason;
but even then we say in our hearts—" Perhaps I shall
again believe blindly; God grant it!" For we feel

that this must be a great happiness, an immense consolation in adversity and in great trials, and even in accidental suggestions of immorality.

The virtuous man never doubts of the existence of God; for, if his reason does not suffice to comprehend it, the instinct of his soul adopts the belief. Every intimate feeling of the soul is in sympathy with the sentiments of religion.

When Napoleon received the supreme power, his mind became occupied with the great elements of the social body; he recognised all the importance of religion—he resolved to re-establish it; but it would be difficult to believe all the resistance he had to overcome in order to attain his object, and to re-erect the altars of Catholicism. The council of state was not favourable to the concordat. The greater part of its members, those who held the highest places in public esteem, only gave way after taking a resolution to become Protestants, in order to remain independent of Rome, if the church again took up the sceptre which the revolution had broken.

The disposition of the public mind was then tending strongly towards reform. But besides that the First Consul himself firmly maintained his natal religion, the highest political motives for re-establishing it existed. What advantage would he have gained by proclaiming Protestantism? He would have awakened religious fanaticism and created new parties, when the first aim of his ambition was to abolish them in France, and rally the French people beneath the banner of national interest. Parties, under whatever denomination they may rank, weaken the social system, and give favourable opportunities to the intrigues of foreigners. None of these dangers were to be feared from the re-establishment of catholicism. Catholicism had, besides, the great advantage of gaining the favour of the Holy See; and from that time what an influence would it have!—what a lever of opinion on eighty millions of catholics! During his disputes with the vatican, Napoleon had never, either as First Consul or as Emperor, touched upon points of dogma. The Pope had dispensed the Emperor from public communion, and by this determination showed him the value of the sincerity of his religious faith. A council of cardinals had been held on this subject; the most of them had strongly insisted on his receiving the communion in public, and said, that his example would be of great importance to the church, and that he ought to give it. The Pope answered, that if he only performed this action as he would a part of a ceremonial, it would be a sacrilege: " I cannot desire that he should do this—my conscience opposes it. Napoleon is not, perhaps, favourably disposed to it. A time will doubtless come, when faith will urge him to perform this act of devotion. In the meantime, let us not load either his conscience or our own."

Pius VII. was personally attached to the Emperor; their private intimacy was never interrupted by their disputes as sovereigns; and to this esteem and this mutual affection must be attributed the concluding of the concordat of Fontainebleau, by which the Pope renounced all temporal sovereignty.

The Pope left Paris after the coronation, without having obtained the reward which he thought he had merited. He demanded the execution of the famous donation of Countess Matilda, and showed the Emperor some letters, written by Louis XIV., who, in the last years of his reign, had thus compromised the honour of the crown of France. The Emperor, after having read the letters, threw them into the fire, instead of giving them back to the Pope, who stood in amazement at this act of power.

To have executed the donation would have been to sacrifice the interests of the empire in order to pay a debt of personal gratitude; and *that* nothing in the world could have persuaded Napoleon to do. The sacred college became hostile to him, and Rome was thenceforth the centre of all the plots woven against him.

Fanatic priests proclaimed in the senate bulls and letters of the Pope; they represented the Emperor as excommunicated by the vicar of Jesus Christ. A Monsieur Franchet, director of the posts in a department on the frontiers of Savoy, was the intermediate link of all these clandestine webs; and the son of a former minister of religious affairs, who was himself a councillor of state, charged, *per interim*, with their administration, knew all, without informing the Emperor of it. The prefect of Lyons was the first who gave him any intimation of these proceedings. It was necessary to give some example which should stop these madmen; the Emperor wished to give it paternally; he could not resolve to punish as he deserved, the son of a virtuous man, whom he had numbered among his friends.

But when, at the next sitting of the Council of State, he saw Monsieur Portalis enter and take his seat as if he had nothing to reproach himself with, Napoleon could not restrain his indignation. "Monsieur Portalis," said he, "is it your religious principles which have induced you to betray your duty to your sovereign? But should this be so, why come and seat yourself in my council of state? I do violence to the conscience of no one; did I force you to become one of my councillors of state? Was it not rather a signal favour which you solicited from me? You are the youngest here, and perhaps the only one without personal claims; I only saw in you the heir to your father's services. You swore allegiance to me. How can your religion accord with the flagrant violation of an oath? Speak, however; you are here as in a family circle; your colleagues will judge you. Your fault is great—very great! A murderous conspiracy is rendered abortive as soon as we seize the poniard in the hand of the assassin; but a moral conspiracy is a train of powder.

"I have surrounded myself with men of all parties; I have even placed near my person *emigrés*, men from the army of Condé; and I have done this because

I have confidence in French honour. and in serving me
they swore allegiance to me. Since I have been at
the head of affairs you are the first person who has
betrayed me." Monsieur Portalis had nothing to say,
but stammered out some unmeaning excuses.

The Emperor said—"Leave the room, sir; you are
no longer a councillor of state."

Pius VII. had been for six months at Fontainebleau;
his court was composed of the Cardinal of Bayonne. Cardinals Buffo, Rovende, Doria, and Agnani; the Bishop
of Edessa; several almoners. and a staff of physicians;
some French prelates, and some from the kingdom of
Italy, such as Monsieur de Basal. Archbishop of Tours,
Cardinal Mancey, called Archbishop of Paris, the
Bishops of Nantes, Trèves. Evreux, Plaiseur, Ideltre,
and Faenza.

Independently of the great question of the temporal
sovereignty of the Popes, questions of comparatively
secondary importance, but grave in themselves, were
in discussion, and appeared insoluble in the state of
exasperation in which the sacred college had for three
years been. It was impossible to obtain bulls of
consecration for the bishops who had been appointed
to vacant sees; and what was still more important,
the Pope obstinately refused to sanction the establishment of the bishoprics created by the Emperor at
Hamburg, Amsterdam, and Düsseldorf, for the propagation and glory of catholicism.

The Emperor demanded, for the interest of religion,
that the Holy See should be obliged to publish the

bulls, as well as the concordat of 1801, within a given
time, and that the sovereign should have a right,
during a limited period, of nominating to the
bishoprics.

The Pope's resistance to such just demands at
length appeared to be weakened; the ill-will on the
part of the cardinals had sensibly diminished, as
letters from the Bishop of Nantes announced. The
Emperor resolved upon taking a personal step in
order to accomplish a complete reconciliation, which
was rendered so desirable by the interests of his policy
and by his religious sentiments; he relied, and with
reason, on the friendship and esteem which the Pope
had never ceased to exhibit towards him, notwithstanding their disputes as sovereigns.

He demanded of the Prince of Neufchatel to hold a
coursing chase on his estate of Gros Bois, near Melun.
While the chase was yet being actively carried on,
he set out for Fontainebleau, arrived there quite
unexpectedly, and presented himself to the Pope, who,
moved by this unhoped-for homage, received him with
great kindness, and testified a lively and friendly
pleasure at his visit. Their interview lasted for
several hours; and from this moment the Pope's
resistance was vanquished. The conversation was
carried on in Italian, and bore the kindly stamp of
the names by which they addressed each other—
"father," and "son." The Pope agreed provisionally
to the residence at Avignon, and without totally
renouncing his temporal sovereignty over Rome, he

consented to come to arrangements respecting compensation, and agreed to the fixing of a limited time for the expediting of the bulls. These bases being agreed upon, the Emperor immediately dictated the new concordat to which they gave rise. The Pope was present; he expressed his approbation, either by words or signs, of every one of the stipulations. The cardinals were commissioned finally to draw up the document; they were occupied four days in fulfilling this charge. On the 25th of January, 1813, the concordat was signed, in presence of the whole court of France, which had united itself to that of the holy father, in order to give the greatest possible solemnity to this ceremony. The Empress was present. All the actions and words of the Pope were so many testimonies of the joy and serenity of his mind; he seemed happy, in short, to see a good understanding re-established between himself and the Emperor.

The Cardinals of the household received magnificent presents. The Emperor loaded them with benefits; he pardoned the fourteen cardinals who were either prisoners or exiles, and the reconciliation appeared complete; on his side it was so.

The concordat of Fontainebleau being signed, the Pope had a prospect of finding, in riches, homage, and royal pomp, more than a compensation for the loss of his temporal power. The Emperor desired to make an idol of him. Paris was to become the capital of the Christian universe, the centre of action and direction of the religious as of the political world.

This would be a great means of drawing closer the ties of the federative parties of the empire.

"CONCORDAT OF FONTAINEBLEAU.

" His Majesty the Emperor and King, and his Holiness the Pope, wishing to put a term to the differences which have arisen between them, and to provide for difficulties which have arisen concerning several affairs of the church, have agreed to the following articles, which are to serve as a basis for a definite arrangement:

" Art. 1. His holiness will exercise the office of pontiff in France, and in the kingdom of Italy, in the same manner, and with the same forms as his predecessors.

" Art. 2. The ambassadors and ministers of foreign powers at the court of the Pope, and the ambassadors, ministers, or *chargés d'affaires* of the Pope, who may be at foreign courts, will enjoy the same immunities and privileges as were enjoyed by the diplomatic body.

" Art. 3. The domains of the holy father which have not been alienated, will be exempt from all kinds of imposts; they will be administered by his agents or *chargés d'affaires*. Those which have been alienated will be replaced by a revenue of two millions of francs.

"Art. 4. During the six months following the usual notification of the nomination by the Emperor to archbishoprics and bishoprics of the empire, and of the kingdom of Italy, the Pope will give the canonical institution, conformably to the concordats and in virtue of this present. The previous inquiry will be made by the metropolitan bishop. Should the six months elapse without the Pope's having granted the institution, the metropolitan, or, in default of him, the oldest bishop of the province, will proceed to consecrate the nominated bishop, so that by this means a see may never be vacant longer than a year.

"Art. 5. The Pope will have the right of nomination to ten bishoprics, either in France or in the kingdom of Italy; these ten will be afterwards agreed upon.

"Art. 6. The six suburban bishoprics will be re-established. The Pope will have the right of nomination to them. Their existing possessions will be restored, and measures will be taken with regard to such as have been sold. On the decease of the bishops of Agnani and Rieté, their dioceses will be annexed to the said six bishoprics, conformably to an arrangement which will be made between his majesty and the holy father.

"Art. 7. With regard to those bishops of the Roman states, who may from circumstances be absent from their bishoprics, the holy father may exercise in their favour his right of giving bishoprics *in partibus*. A pension equal to the revenue which they enjoyed will be given them, and their vacant sees, either in France or the kingdom of Italy, may be filled.

"Art. 8. His majesty and his holiness will come to an agreement at an opportune time, concerning the re duction to be made, if necessary, in the bishoprics o

Tuscany and Genoa, as well as concerning the bishoprics to be established in Holland, and the Hanseatic departments.

" Art. 9. The propaganda, the penitentiary's court, and the archives, will be established in the place of residence of the holy father.

" Art. 10. His majesty restores to his favour those cardinals, bishops, priests, and laymen, who have incurred his displeasure during the present events.

" Art. 11. The holy father gives his approbation to the above articles through consideration of the present state of the church, and confidently relies on his majesty's powerful aid in administering to the many necessities of religion in the times in which we live.

(Signed)   " NAPOLEON.
" POPE PIUS VII.

" Fontainebleau, January 25th, 1813."

" DECREE OF THE 25TH OF MARCH, 1813.

" Napoleon, Emperor of the French, King of Italy, Protector of the Confederation of the Rhine, Mediator of the Swiss Confederation, &c., &c.

" We have decreed, and decree, as follows:

" Art. 1. The concordat signed at Fontainebleau, which regulates the affairs of the church, and which was published as a law of the state, on the 13th of February, 1813, is obligatory upon the archbishops, bishops, and chapters of France, who will be bound to conform to it.

" Art. 2. As soon as we shall have nominated any ecclesiastic to a vacant bishopric, and shall have made known our nomination to the holy father, in the form laid down by the concordat, our minister of religious affairs will send an announcement of the nomination to the metropolitan, or, in default of him, to the oldest bishop of the ecclesiastical province.

" Art. 3. The person whom we shall have nominated will address himself to the metropolitan, who will make the necessary inquiries, and will inform the holy father of the result.

" Art. 4. Should the person nominated come under the head of some ecclesiastical exclusion, the metropolitan will immediately send us information of the fact; but in case no such motive of exclusion exists, if the institution has not been accorded by the Pope within six months after the notification of our nomination, the metropolitan, conformably with the terms of Art. 4 of the concordat, will be bound to institute the said person in his bishopric, with the assistance of the bishops of the province.

" Art. 5. Our imperial courts of justice will take cognisance of all affairs known under the name of 'appeals against abuses,' as well as of all such as result from the non-execution of the laws of the concordats.

" Art. 6. Our chief judge will present, to be discussed in our council, a plan for a law which shall determine the legal procedures and punishments applicable to these matters.

" Art. 7. Our kingdoms of France and Italy are

charged to execute this present decree, which will be
inserted in the archives of the laws.

                    (Signed)   " NAPOLEON."

The Emperor wished to give great importance to
the curates; he wished to render them useful in forwarding the development of social intelligence.   The
more enlightened and well-informed they are, the
less do they seek to abuse their ministry.   To their
course of theology, the Emperor would have added
elementary courses of agriculture, of the useful arts,
and of a practical knowledge of medicine and law.
They would then truly have been a providence to
their flocks; and as he would have made them entirely
independent with respect to fortune, they would have
formed a very respectable and worthy class of society,
and would have enjoyed great consideration; they
would not have possessed the power of the feudal
seignorial clergy, but they *would* have possessed, and
that without danger, all its influence.   A curate
would have been the natural mediator of peace, the
true moral head, who would have directed the lives of
his parishioners.

If we remember that in addition to the instruction
thus acquired at the seminaries, the priests would
have to pass through their probation and noviciate,
which, in some measure, guarantee the vocation,
and suppose good dispositions of heart and mind, we
are inclined to declare that such a class of pastors
distributed among the people, would have brought

about a moral revolution entirely to the advantage of civilisation. The Emperor had already several times expressed, in the council of state, an opinion that it would be well to abolish the council of the ministers of religious affairs, and had exposed, in order to strengthen his argument, the impropriety of placing the priests in a position in which they were obliged to bargain about the sacred and yet indispensable acts of their office. He wished to replace their casual income by a great increase of salary. A curate would have had at least 6000 francs income. To make up for this, however, the number would have been reduced, and the small parishes, which are for the most part only so in name, would only have had chapels of ease.

To have rendered the offices of religion gratuitous, would have been to increase its dignity and its charitable nature, and to do much for the mass of the people. All are born, many marry, all die. Why, then, should not the expense of religious assistance in these various phases of life be looked upon as a charge of the state, and be included in the list of general taxes?

In principle, convents are useless, and are examples of debasing indolence. There are, however, certain things to be said in their favour; therefore, to tolerate them, to restrict them to a useful number, and only to permit annual vows, is the best policy for France in this respect; for an empire like that of France can and ought to have Trappists. No law could, without revolting tyranny, enforce the practices which they observe, but these very practices sometimes form the delight of him who voluntarily imposes them on himself. The monastery on Mount Cenis was re-established by the First Consul, because the monks were found useful, and heroic in their efforts for the safety of travellers. The monks would perhaps be by far the best of the instructing bodies, if they could be properly kept in check.

But there is a religious society, the tendency of which is highly dangerous, and which should never have been admitted into the territories of the empire— viz., the Society of Jesus. Its doctrines are subversive of all monarchical principles. The General of the Jesuits desires to be sovereign master, the sovereign of sovereigns. Everywhere that the Jesuits are tolerated, they strive for power, at any price. Their society is by nature fond of ruling, and nourishes, therefore, an irreconcilable hatred of all existing power. Any action, any crime, however atrocious it may be, is meritorious, if committed for the interest of the society, or by the orders of its General. The Jesuits are all men of talent and learning. They are the best existing missionaries, and would be, were it not for their ambition of ruling, the best instructing body, for the propagation of civilisation and the development of its progress. They may be of service in Russia for some years longer, because the first need of that empire is civilisation.

Another religious interest had attracted the attention of the Emperor, because it might have been brought to have an influence on the increase of national riches. Millions of Jews were scattered over the earth—their riches were incalculable; France might hope to attract them to her dominions by giving them equal rights in the empire with the catholics and protestants, and by rendering them good citizens; the reasoning on this subject was simple. Their Rabbins taught them that they should not practise usury in transactions with their own people, and that it was only permitted to exercise it towards the Christians; the moment they were placed on an equality of rights with the other subjects of the Emperor, they would regard him as they would have done Solomon or Herod, as the chief of their nation, and consider the rest of his subjects as brethren, of tribes similar to theirs; they would enjoy all the rights of the country, and would think it but just that they should share the charge of paying the imposts, and submit to conscription. The Emperor realised his projects on this point.

The French army gained many good soldiers, great riches poured into France, and much more would have been brought to it, had it not been for the events of 1814, because the Jews would all have successively come and established themselves in a country where equality of rights was secured to them, and where the door to honours was open to their ambition. The Emperor wished to tolerate all religions; he wished every one to think and believe in his own way, and

that all his subjects—protestants, catholics, Mahometans, and even deists—should enjoy equal privileges, so
that a man's religion might in no way influence his
public fortune.

The Emperor proposed to hold religious sessions in
the same manner as he held legislative ones.   The
councils of Paris would be the representatives of the
whole of Christendom; the Pope would preside over
them, but the Emperor would open them—their
sessions would be convoked and closed by his decrees,
and their decisions would be approved and published
by him as they would have been by the Emperor
Constantine or by Charlemagne.   Rome had thrown
off the yoke of imperial supremacy solely through the
fault of the emperors, who had allowed the popes to
reside at a distance from the seat of the empire.

CHAPTER XVI.

CORSICA.

THE Emperor was in the mood for work; I availed myself of it to remind him of his history of Corsica, written under the impressions of a young man of twenty, and proposed to him to re-write it, under those of his experience of things and of men; he laughed at this courtierlike criticism, and answered: "Very well; go and find it, and we will set to work." I give it here as he dictated it to me.

———

"The history of Charlemagne is full of absurdities, which even the most learned critics have not been able to clear up. It would, then, be superfluous to attempt to discover the events which took place in Corsica during the time of that prince. Philippi, the author of the most ancient chronicle of the island,

lived in the 15th century; he was archdeacon of
Aleria. Lampridi wrote at Rome, towards the end
of the last century, a very voluminous history of the
revolutions of this country; he was a man of talent,
and distinguished for literary acquirements. At the
same period, several histories were published in Tuscany and other parts of Italy. We have, in France,
a great number of writings on Corsica, under the
titles of journeys, memoirs, revolutions, histories, &c.,
&c. Public curiosity was excited by the continued
struggles of this people to free themselves from oppression, and to declare and maintain their independence.

" The African Arabs ruled for a long time in
Corsica. The arms of this kingdom are still a death's
head, with a band over the eyes, on a white ground.
The Corsicans distinguished themselves at the battle
of Estié, where the Saracens were defeated, and
obliged to renounce their designs upon Rome. There
are some who think that this shield was given them
by Pope Leo II., as a testimony of their valour.

" Corsica is said to have formed a part of the
dotation of Constantine, and of that of Charlemagne;
but what is more certain, is, that it formed a part of
the Countess Matilda's inheritance. The Colonnas
of Rome affirm, that in the 9th century, one of their
ancestors wrested Corsica from the hands of the
Saracens, and became its king. The Colonnas of
Istria and Cuierca have been acknowledged by the
Colonnas of Rome and by the genealogists of Versailles;
but the historical fact of the sovereignty of a branch

of the Colonna family in Corsica, is not the less a problem. This much, however, is certain, that Corsica formed the twelfth kingdom recognised in Europe, a title of which these islanders were extremely proud, and which they never would renounce. It was in virtue of this title that the Doge of Genoa wore the royal crown; and at the moment when they were the most zealous for their liberty, they reconciled these opposite ideas by proclaiming the Holy Virgin their queen.

" We find traces of this in the deliberations of several councils, among the rest, in that which was held at the Convent de la Vinsalosea.

" Like the rest of Italy, Corsica was under the rule of the feudal system; every village had its superior lord: but the enfranchisement of the commonalties in this island preceded the general movement, which took place in Italy in the 11th century, by fifty years.

" There are still to be seen, on steep rocks, ruins of castles which tradition points out as the places of refuge of the superior lords during the war of the commonalties, in the 12th, 13th, 14th, and 15th centuries. The district called that of the Liamone, and especially the province of La Rocca, exercised the principal influence in the affairs of the island.

" But during the 16th, 17th and 18th centuries, the parishes called the districts of the commonalties, or otherwise of the Castagnichia, in their turn preponderated in the councils or assemblies of the nation.

" Pisa was the nearest town of the mainland to

Corsica; it was the first which carried on commerce with this island, established settlements there, insensibly extended its influence, and finally brought the whole island under its government. Its administration was mild, and suited the wishes and opinions of the islanders, who served it with zeal in its wars with Florence. The enormous power of Pisa was destroyed by the battle of Malaria. On its ruins arose the power of Genoa, which inherited the commerce of Pisa. The Genoese established themselves in Corsica ; this was the commencement of the misfortunes of the country, which constantly increased.

" The senate of Genoa not having found the way of engaging the affection of the inhabitants, sought to weaken and divide them, and to keep them in ignorance and poverty.

" The picture drawn by the Corsican historians of the crimes of the administration of the oligarchs of Genoa, is one of the most hideous presented by the history of mankind; and there are, therefore, but few examples to be found of a hatred and antipathy equal to that nourished by the islanders against the Genoese.

" France, though so close a neighbour to Corsica, never made any claims to it. It has been said, that Charles Martel sent one of his lieutenants thither to fight the Saracens; but this is very apocryphal. It was Henry II. who first sent an army there, under the command of Marshal Cherusco, of the celebrated San Pietro Ornano, and of one of the Unsins, but they only remained a few years in the island.

" Andreas Doria, although very aged, having passed his 85th year, recovered the island for his country.

" Spain, divided into several kingdoms, and solely occupied with its war against the Moors, had no designs upon Corsica till very lately; and was, even then, diverted from them by its wars in Sicily.

" The parishes of the districts of the commonalties, Rostino, Campagnani, Orezza, and La Peuta, were the first to revolt against the government of Genoa; the other parishes of La Castagnichia, and insensibly all the other provinces of the island followed their example. This war, which commenced in 1729, was terminated in 1769, by the annexation of Corsica to the French monarchy; the struggle lasted forty years. The Genoese levied Swiss armies, and had several times recourse to the great European powers, by taking auxiliary troops into their pay. It was thus that the Emperor of Germany first sent Baron Wachtendorf into Corsica, and afterwards the Prince of Würtemberg; and that Louis XV. sent Count Boissieux, and afterwards Marshal Maillebois, thither. The Genoese and Swiss armies suffered defeats. Wachtendorf and Boissieux were also defeated; the Prince of Würtemberg and Maillebois obtained some victories, and subdued the country; but they left the spark among the ashes; and immediately on their departure, the war broke out with fresh fury. The old Giafferi, the Canon Orticone, a cunning and eloquent man, Hyacinthe Paoli, Cianaldi, Gaforio, were successively at the head of affairs, which they conducted with more or

less success, but always with fidelity, and under the
inspiration of the most noble sentiments. The sovereign power was in the hands of a council composed
of deputies from the parishes. This council determined war and peace, and decreed the taxes and
levies of militia; no paid troops were maintained;
but all citizens capable of bearing arms were inscribed
in three lists in every commonalty; they marched
against the enemy at the summons of their chief.
Each individual supported the expenses of his own
arms, ammunition, and provisions.

" It is difficult to understand the policy of Genoa at
this period. Why such obstinacy in a struggle which
was so burdensome to her? she ought either to have
renounced Corsica or have contented its inhabitants.

" If she had inscribed the principal families of the
island in the Golden Book, and had adopted a system
entirely opposed to that in which she succeeded so ill,
and which she was not sufficiently powerful to maintain, she would have conciliated the Corsicans and
attached them to her government. This opinion was
often expressed in the senate: ' The Corsicans are
more in a condition to take possession of Genoa, than
you are to take possession of their mountains. Attach
these islanders to you by a just government; flatter
their ambition and their vanity; you will by this
means have a seminary for good soldiers, who will be
useful in guarding your capital, and you will preserve
settlements so advantageous to your commerce.'

" The proud oligarchy replied: ' We cannot treat the
Corsicans more favourably than the two nations of the

two rivers; the Golden Book would become principally filled with the names of provincial families. This would be a total subversion of our constitution; in proposing it, you propose to us to abandon the heritage of our fathers. The Corsicans are not formidable; it is to our errors that they owe all their success; with more wisdom, it will be an easy matter for us to subdue this handful of rebels, who have neither artillery, discipline nor order.'

" In all the councils, (there were some years in which several were held,) the Corsicans published manifestoes, in which they detailed their causes of complaint, both old and new, against their oppressors; their object was to interest Europe in their cause, and at the same time to excite the patriotism of the people.

" Several of these manifestoes, drawn up by Orticone, are full of energy, good reasoning, and the most noble and elevated sentiments.

" False ideas are entertained respecting King Theodore. Baron Neuchoff was a Westphalian; he landed on the coast of Aleria, bringing four transport vessels laden with guns, powder, and shoes. The expenses of this store were borne by Dutch private persons and speculators. This unexpected aid, arriving at a moment when the Corsicans were discouraged, seemed to descend from heaven. The chiefs proclaimed the German baron king, and represented him to the people as a prince of Europe, who was a guarantee to them of the powerful aid which they would receive. This proceeding had the desired effect, it influenced the multitude for eighteen months; its influence was then spent, and Baron Neuchoff returned to the Continent. He re-appeared several times on the coast, bringing important aid, which he owed to the court of Sardinia and the Bey of Tunis.

" This is a curious episode of this memorable war, and shows what various resources were at the command of the leaders of the Corsicans.

" In the year 1775, Pascal Paoli was declared first magistrate and general of Corsica. He was the son of Hyacinthe Paoli, had been educated in Naples, and was now a captain in the service of the King Don Carlos.

" The parish of Rostino named him its deputy to the council of Alesani. His family was very popular. He was tall, young, well-made, well-informed, and eloquent. The council was divided into two parties; the one proclaimed Paoli chief and general; this party was composed of the warmest patriots, and those who were the most disinclined to any accommodation. The more moderate party supported, in opposition to him, Matras, deputy of Fiumarbo. The two deputies quarrelled on the subject and fought; Paoli was defeated, and obliged to shut himself up in the convent of Alesani. His cause seemed to be lost; he was surrounded by the partisans of his rival. But as soon as the news of Paoli's situation arrived in the parishes of the commonalties, all the mountain-tops were immediately lighted up with alarm-fires; the caverns and forests resounded with the terrible blasts of the trumpet; this was the signal of war. Matras attempted to get the start of these formidable troops; he assaulted the convent; being himself of an impetuous character, he advanced in the foremost rank, and fell, mortally wounded. From this moment, all parties united in acknowledging Paoli; a few months afterwards the council of Alesani was acknowledged by all the parishes. Paoli displayed talent; he conciliated the minds of the people; he governed by fixed principles, established schools and a university, and gained the friendship of Algiers and of the people of Barbary; he formed a navy of light vessels; had correspondents in the maritime towns; and took possession of the island of Capraja, from which he expelled the Genoese, who were not without some fears that the Corsicans would land on the banks of their river. He did all that it was possible to do under existing circumstances, and among the nation which he ruled. He was about to take possession of the five ports of the island, when the senate of Genoa, in alarm, had again recourse to France. In 1764, six French battalions were sent to guard the maritime cities, and under their ægis, these places continued to recognise the authority of the senate.

" The French garrisons remained neuter, and took no part in the war, which continued to be waged between the Corsicans and the Genoese. The French officers loudly expressed opinions greatly favourable to the islanders and opposed to the oligarchs, and this circumstance completed the alienation of the inhabitants of the cities from the Genoese. In the year 1768, the

French troops were to return to France; this moment
was awaited with impatience; no trace of the authority
of Genoa remained in the island; when at this
juncture the Duke of Choiseul conceived the idea of
annexing Corsica to France. This acquisition appeared
to him important, as being a natural dependence of
Provence, and as being fitted to protect the commerce
of the Levant, and to favour the future operations of
the French in Italy.

" After long deliberation, the senate consented to this
measure, and Spinola, the Genoese ambassador at
Paris, signed a treaty, by which it was agreed that
the King of France should subdue and disarm the
Corsicans, and govern them until such time as the
republic should be able to repay him the advances
which this war would have cost him. Now, more
than 30,000 men would be required in order to
subdue and disarm the island, and it would be necessary to maintain numerous garrisons there for several
years; and the expense of all this would necessarily
amount to a sum which the republic of Genoa would
neither be able nor willing to repay.

" Both the contracting parties were well aware of
this fact; but the oligarchs thought by this stipula-
tion to save their honour, and to ward off the odium
which, in the eyes of all Italy, was thrown upon
them by their so lightly yielding a part of their territory to a foreign power. Choiseul saw, in this turn of
the affair, a means of deluding England, and of
retracing his steps, if necessary, without compromis-

ing the honour of France. Louis XV. wished to avoid a war with England.

" The French minister opened a negotiation with Paoli; he demanded of him that he should persuade his countrymen to acknowledge themselves subjects of the French king, and that he should, conformably to a wish which had been sometimes expressed by former councils, freely acknowledge Corsica to be a province of the kingdom. In return for this condescension, he offered Paoli fortune and honours; and the noble and generous character of the French minister could leave the Corsican no cause of uneasiness on this point. Paoli rejected these offers with disdain; he convoked the council, and exposed to its members the critical state of affairs; he did not conceal from them that it would be impossible to resist the arms of France, and that but a vague hope existed of the interference of England. There was but one cry in the assembly — *Liberty or death!* Paoli exhorted them not to engage rashly in this affair, demonstrating that such a struggle should not be undertaken without reflection and in a fit of enthusiasm. A young man of twenty, a deputy in the council, made a speech full of energy, which completed the already enthusiastic tendency of the assembly. He had just come from Rome and Pisa, and was filled with the enthusiasm which is aroused by reading the ancient classical authors, and which reigned in these schools: ' If, to be free, it were sufficient to desire it, all the nations of the earth

would be so.   And yet but few of them have attained
to the blessings of liberty, because but few have possessed the necessary energy, courage, and virtue.'
Others added, that, brought up as they had been for
forty years among arms, they had seen their parents
and their children perish in the struggle for the
independence of their country, a blessing bestowed on
them by nature, which had isolated them from all
other nations.

" They all seemed indignant that France, which had
so often acted the part of a mediator in their quarrels
with Genoa, and had always professed the most dis-
interested motives, should now come forward as a
party in the affair, and pretend to believe that the
government of Genoa could sell the Corsicans like a herd
of cattle, and against the tenour of the *facta conventa*.

" Maillebois had, in the year 1738, levied the royal
Corsican regiment, formed of two battalions, and consisting entirely of Corsicans.   The French carried on a
communication, through the officers, with the principal
chiefs of this regiment.   Many of them showed themselves above corruption; but some yielded, and made
a merit of advancing to meet a domination which was
henceforth inevitable.

" In order to justify themselves and to make proselytes, they   said—' Our ancestors struggled against
the tyranny of the oligarchs of Genoa; but we are
now at length delivered from it for ever.   If Giafferi,
Hyacinthe Paoli, Gaforio, Ortecone, and all the great
men who died in the defence of our rights, could

now see their native country become an integral part of the most splendid monarchy of Europe, they would rejoice, and would not regret the blood which they shed in its cause! Open your records; you have always been the sport of the Pisans or the Genoese— nations, in reality, much less powerful than your own. All the ports of Provence and Languedoc will now be opened to you; you will be respected by the inhabitants of Barbary; you will be an object of jealousy to Tuscany, Sardinia, and even to Genoa itself; calling yourselves Frenchmen, you may show yourselves with pride in any part of Europe. You say, that by following this plan we should acknowledge that Genoa had the right to sell us—this is not so. The treaties concluded between the two powers, in the secrecy of the cabinet, do not · concern us. Let us fulfil the wish of the council of Calca-Sana, and spontaneously request the King of France to include us in the number of his children; he will acknowledge us by this name. Beware of the delusion of your passions; you cannot, without betraying the interests of your countrymen, engage in such an unequal contest. If you wish that the King of France should question you, he will do so; but it will then be too late to stipulate for your privileges, or to claim your rights. You will be slaves, by the incontestable right which governs the world, that of force and conquest. France is a collection of small states; Provence is not governed like Languedoc, nor Bretagne like Lorraine. You may, then, unite all the advantages of liberty and independ-

ence with those attached to a union with the most
enlightened nation of Europe, and to the protection of
the most powerful monarch.'

" The patriots and the mass of the people neither
read the writings nor listened to · the speeches of the
advocates of this course of proceeding: ' We are
invincible in our mountains; we have defended them
against the auxiliary troops of Genoa, against the
imperial army, and against the forces of France itself;
let us sustain the first shock, and England will interfere. You speak of the advantages we should gain by
declaring ourselves subjects of the King of France; we
wish for none of them; we will be poor, but masters
in our own land, governed by ourselves, and not the
sport of a commissary from Versailles. You speak of
stipulating for our privileges: but the French monarchy is absolute; it is founded on the principle—
as the king wills, so the law wills; we should, then,
find no safe-guard in it against the tyranny of a subaltern. *Liberty or death !*'

" The priests and monks were the most enthusiastic.
The mass of the people, and above all the mountaineers,
had no idea of the power of France. Accustomed
frequently to fight and repulse the feeble troops of
Counts Boissieux and Maillebois, nothing that they
had yet seen had alarmed them. They mistook these
weak detachments for French armies. The council
was almost unanimous in favour of war; the people
shared the same feelings.

" The treaty by which Genoa was to cede Corsica to

the king, excited a general feeling of reprobation in France. When it became known, from the resolutions of the council, that France was to make war, and to put part of its forces in motion against this small nation: the *injustice* and *ungenerous character* of this war moved all minds.

" The guilt of all the blood which was about to be shed was attributed entirely to Choiseul: ' What need have we of Corsica? None. Has it only now come into existence? And why is it only now that France turns her thoughts to it? We have but one interest in the matter—viz., that England should not establish its power in Corsica; everything else is indifferent to us. But if this war is not prescribed by necessity, it is still less so by justice. Genoa herself has no right to the island; and if she had, she could not transfer this right to a foreign power. When Francis I., by the treaty of Madrid, ceded Burgundy to Charles V., the whole province revolted, and declared that the King of France had no right to alienate; and yet this was as early as the sixteenth century. What! can men, then, be sold like herds of cattle! Grant to the oppressed party, in this struggle between Genoa and Corsica, a protection worthy of the exalted greatness of the king; this will attach this people to you by the bonds of gratitude; it will spare you an act of injustice, a costly war, and the trouble of, for years, keeping under subjection a country discontented and ill-disposed towards your government, and which would writhe under the hand that oppressed it. Are our finances in too good a condition; or are the imposts which now weigh upon the people too light?'

" This reasoning was, however, in vain; it did not arrest the proceedings of the cabinet. Lieutenant-General Chauvelin landed at Bastia, with 12,000 men under his command. He published proclamations, intimated his orders to the commonalties, and commenced hostilities. But his troops, defeated at the battle of Borgo, and repulsed in all their attacks, were compelled, at the end of the campaign of 1768, to shut themselves up in the fortresses, and only communicated with each other by the help of a few cruising frigates. The Corsicans thought themselves saved; they did not doubt that England would interfere. Paoli shared this illusion; but the English ministry, uneasy at the agitation which was beginning to show itself in the American colonies, had no desire to declare war with France. It transmitted a feeble note to Versailles, and contented itself with the yet more feeble explanations which were given. Some London clubs sent arms and money to the Corsicans; the court of Sardinia and some Italian societies secretly sent them aid; but these were but feeble resources against the formidable armament which was being prepared on the shores of Provence. The check experienced by Chauvelin had been seen with satisfaction throughout the whole of Europe, and especially in France. The French people had the good sense to see that their national glory was not at all compromised in this struggle with a handful of moun-

taineers. Even Louis XV. himself expressed sentiments favourable to the Corsicans; he was by no
means desirous of having this new crown placed on his
head; and the promoters of the scheme were obliged,
in order to determine him to order preparations for a
second campaign to be made, to speak to him of the
joy which would be felt by the philosophers, at seeing
their great king defeated by a free people, and compelled to retreat before them. The influence of this on
the king's authority, said they, would be great; there
were fanatics in the cause of liberty, who would see
miracles in the success of so unequal a struggle.
The monarch no longer deliberated. Marshal Vaux
set out for Corsica; he had 30,000 men under his
command, and the ports of the island were inundated
with troops. The islanders defended themselves, however, during a part of the campaign, but without
hopes of success. The population of Corsica then
amounted, at the most, to 150,000 inhabitants;
30,000 were taken up by the forts and the French
garrisons; there remained 20,000 men fit to carry
arms, but from these must be taken all those who
served under such chiefs as had treated with the
agents of the French ministry.

" The Corsicans fought obstinately at the passage
of the river Golo. Not having had time to destroy
the bridge, which was of stone, they made use of the
bodies of those who had been killed to form an in-
trenchment. Paoli, driven to the south of the island,
embarked in an English vessel at Porto-Vecchio,

landed at Livorno, traversed the Continent, and
arrived in London. He was everywhere received, by
sovereigns and people, with the greatest marks of
admiration.

" It was not possible, without doubt, to resist the
army of Marshal Vaux. And yet there was a moment
when he had scattered all his troops; when he had
deceived himself, believing that the country was
subdued and disarmed; but the fact was that none but
old men, women, and children had remained in the
villages, and that only old guns had been given up to
him on his landing. All the strong and brave men of
the island, inured to civil wars which had lasted
for forty years, were wandering among the woods
and caverns, and on the tops of the mountains.
Corsica is a country so extraordinary, and so difficult
of access, that a San Pietro, in these circumstances,
would have fallen separately on all the divisions of
the French army, hindered them from rallying, and
compelled them to shut themselves up in the fortresses;
which event must assuredly have obliged the court of
Versailles to change its system. But Paoli had
neither the quick sight, the promptitude, nor the
military vigour required for the execution of such a
plan. His brother, Clement, had he had more talent,
would have been suited to the duty by his warlike
virtues. Four or five hundred patriots followed Paoli,
and emigrated; a great number of others abandoned
their villages and houses, and continued for many years
to carry on a desultory kind of war, intercepting the

passage of the convoys, and of all isolated soldiers. The Corsicans called them 'patriots,' the French named them 'bandits.' They merited the latter appellation by the cruelties which they committed, though never upon their countrymen.

" In the year 1774, five years after the subjection of the island, some refugees returned thither, and raised the standard of revolt in the district of Nivlo, a parish lying on the highest mountain. The Count of Narbonne-Fritzlar, lieutenant-general and commandant of the island, marched against the mountaineers with the greatest part of the garrisons. He dishonoured his character by the cruelties which he committed. Major-general Sionville rendered himself odious to the Corsicans; he burnt the houses, cut down the olive and chesnut trees, and tore up the vines; and committed all these ravages not only on the property of the bandits, but on that of their relations to the third degree. The country was a prey to terror; yet the inhabitants still secretly nourished a silent discontent.

" Notwithstanding all this ravage and destruction, the intentions of the cabinet of Versailles were beneficent: it granted to the Corsicans freedom to have provincial assemblies or states, composed of three orders—the clergy, the nobility, and the *tiers état*. It re-established the magistracy of twelve nobles, which the Corsicans had always claimed; this was a Pisan institution, a kind of intermediary commission of the states, which regulated the taxes, and the in-

terior government of the province. At the time of each
sitting of the states, a bishop, a deputy of the nobility,
and a person selected from the *tiers état*, were received at the French court, bringing directly to the
king a summary of the complaints of the country.
Encouragement was given to agriculture. The African
company of Marseilles was compelled to recognise
some ancient customs favourable to the Corsican
fishermen, with regard to the fishing for coral. Fine
roads were cut through the country, and marshes
drained. An attempt was even made to form colonies,
consisting of inhabitants of Lorraine and Alsace, in
order to give the Corsicans models of agriculture.

" The taxes were not heavy, the schools were encouraged; the children of the principal families were
invited to France to be educated there. It was in
Corsica that the political economists made the trial of
the taxation paid in the produce of the land instead
of in money.

" During the twenty years which passed between
1769 and 1789, the island gained a great deal. But
all these beneficent measures did not touch the hearts
of the Corsicans, who, at the time of the revolution,
were as far as possible from being Frenchmen.

" A lieutenant-general of infantry, crossing the
mountains, was once talking to a peasant of the ingratitude of his countrymen; he recounted to him all
the good measures of the French administration: ' In
your Paoli's time,' added he, ' you paid double what
you do now.' ' Very true, sir, but then *we gave,*

now *you take.*' The natural wit of these islanders exhibited itself in all circumstances. A thousand of their repartees might be cited; we take one at random. Some titled officers, travelling in the Nivlo, said one evening to their host, one of the poorest inhabitants of the district: ' Look at the difference between us Frenchmen and you Corsicans; see how we are supported and clothed!' The peasant rose, looked at them attentively, and asked each one his name. One was a marquis, another a baron, the third a chevalier. ' Bah!' replied he; ' it is true, I should like to be clothed like you; but is every one in France, a marquis, a baron, or a chevalier?'

" The revolution changed the disposition of the Corsicans; they became Frenchmen in 1790; Paoli quitted England where he had been living on a pension, granted him by the parliament, but which he now resigned. He was received by the *Constituante*, by the national guard of Paris, and even by Louis XVI. His arrival in Corsica caused a general rejoicing. The whole population hastened to Bastia to see him. His memory was extraordinary; he knew the names of all the families, *though it was with the previous generation that he had to do.* In a few days his influence was as powerful as ever. The executive council appointed him general of a division, and commander of the troops of the line in the island.

" The corps of national guards conferred the command on him; the electoral assembly made him president. He thus united, in his own person, all the offices of power. This proceeding of the executive council was by no means politic; but it must be attributed to the spirit which then reigned. However this may be, Paoli faithfully served the revolution till the 10th of August. The execution of Louis XVI. completed his rising disgust for the revolutionary government. He was denounced by the popular societies of Provence, and the convention, whose proceedings no consideration could arrest, summoned him to appear at the bar; he was approaching his eightieth year; this was desiring him to lay his own head on the scaffold; he had no resource but to appeal to his countrymen; the whole island, excited by him, rose in insurrection against the convention.

" The commissaries, representatives of the people, who were charged with the execution of the decree, arrived at this moment: all they were able to do was to retain, by the help of a few battalions, the fortresses of Bastia and Calvi. Had the decision of the course to be taken by Corsica depended on an assembly of the principal families, Paoli would not have succeeded. The excesses committed in France were generally blamed by these persons, but they thought that they were transient, that it was easy to defend themselves from them in Corsica, and that it would not be well, in order to obviate the evils of the moment, to endanger the happiness and tranquillity of the country. Paoli was astonished at the little influence he had in private conferences. Several even of those who had

accompanied him to England, and who had passed the
last twenty years in cursing France, were now the most
averse to his designs, among others General Gentili;
among the mass of the population, however, at the
appeal of their old chief, there was but one cry.   In a
moment the flag with the death's head was hoisted on
every tower, and Corsica ceased to be French.   A
few months afterwards, the English seized Toulon;
when they were expelled from it, Admiral Hood cast
anchor at San Fiorenza; he landed 12,000 men there,
and placed them under the command of Nelson;
Paoli added a reinforcement of 6000 men.   They invested Bastia; Lacombe, St. Michel, and Gentili defended the town with the greatest intrepidity; it only
capitulated at the end of a four months' siege.   Calvi
resisted forty days of open trenches.   General Dundas,
who commanded an English corps of 4000 men, and
who was encamped at St. Fiorenza, refused to take
part in the siege of Bastia, not wishing to compromise his troops without a special order from his
government.

" And now was to be seen a strange spectacle; the
King of England placing on his head the crown of
Corsica, which was no doubt much surprised at find-
ing itself side by side with the crown of Fingal.

" In the month of June, 1794, the council of Corsica, at which Paoli presided, declared that the
political ties of that country with France were broken,
and that the crown should be offered to the King of
England.   A deputation composed of the following

persons—viz., the president Galeazzi; Filippo, a native
of Vescovato; Negroni, of Bastia; and Cesare Rocea,
of the district of Rocea, proceeded to London, and the
king accepted the crown. He named Lord Gilbert
Elliot viceroy. The council, at the same time that it
had determined on offering the crown to the King of
England, had desired a constitution, which secured
the liberties and privileges of the island; it was
modelled after that of England.

" Lord Elliot was a man of merit; he had been
viceroy in India; but he very soon quarrelled with
Paoli. The old man had retired into the mountains;
he now testified his disapprobation of the conduct of
the viceroy, who was influenced by two young men,
Pozzo di Borgo, and Colonna; the one was in his
service as a secretary, the other as an aide-de-camp.
Paoli was reproached with being of a restless character,
with not being able to resolve to live as a private
person, and with always endeavouring to take the state
of master of the island upon himself. Yet, the influence which he had in Corsica, and which was never
contested, the services which he had rendered to
England in the late affair, and all the honourable and
worthy points of his career and of his character, led
the English minister to act towards him with circum-
spection and respect. Paoli had several conferences
with the viceroy and the secretary of state. It was
at one of these that, piqued by some observations, he
said to them: " Here I am in my kingdom; I made
war for two years against the King of France; I

expelled the republicans; and if you violate the
privileges and rights of the country, I can still more
easily expel your troops." A few months after this,
the King of England wrote him a letter, suitable to
the circumstances, in which, expressing the interest
he felt in his tranquillity and happiness, he advised
him to come and finish his days in a country where
he was respected, and where he had been happy. The
secretary of state took this letter to Paoli, then at
Porto Vecchio. Paoli felt that this was a command;
he hesitated; but nothing then announced that the
Reign of Terror in France was about to come to an end.
The army of Italy was still in the province of Nice. By
declaring war against the English, Paoli would have
exposed himself to the attacks of both the belligerent
parties. He submitted to his fate, and went to London,
where he died in the year 1807. We must do him
the justice to say, that in all his letters from England,
during the last eight years of his life, he advised his
countrymen never to separate themselves from France,
but to associate themselves with the good and evil
fortunes of that great nation. He left a considerable
sum, by will, to be appropriated to the foundation of
a university at Corte.

" If the English wished to preserve their influence
in Corsica, they should have acknowledged its independence, consolidated the power of Paoli, and granted
some slight subsidies, for the purpose of retaining a
kind of supremacy, as well as the privilege of anchoring
their squadrons in the principal roads, especially that

of S. Fiorenza. They would then have had a point
of rest in the Mediterranean, would have been able,
in case of need, to levy an auxiliary body of from
5000 to 6000 brave troops, which might be employed
in that sea; the ports of Corsica would have been at
their service. The numerous refugees who were in
France would insensibly have rallied round a national
government; and France itself would easily have been
brought, at the peace, to recognise a state of things
which opinion had recommended to Choiseul. The
Corsicans were extremely dissatisfied with the English
governors; they did not understand their language,
their habitual gravity, or their way of living. Men
continually at table, almost always somewhat intoxicated, and not at all communicative, formed a
strong contrast with the Corsican manners. The
difference of religion was also a cause of repugnance.
This was the first time, since the birth of Christianity,
that Corsica had been profaned by a heretical worship;
everything they saw confirmed them in their prejudices against the Protestant religion. This worship,
devoid of ceremony, these bare and melancholy temples
could not accord with southern imaginations, excited
as they were by the pomp of the catholic worship, its
beautiful churches, adorned with paintings and
images, and its imposing ceremonies.

" The English scattered their gold lavishly around;
the Corsicans received it, but it inspired them with
no feelings of gratitude.

"At this period, Napoleon entered Milan, took possession of Livorno, and collected all the Corsican refugees there, under the orders of Gentili. The excitement of the mountaineers became extreme. At a grand fête, at Ajaccio, the young Colonna, the viceroy's aide-de-camp, was accused of having insulted a bust of Paoli; he was incapable of such an action. The insurrection broke out; the inhabitants of Bogognano intercepted the communications between Bastia and Ajaccio, and surrounded the viceroy, who had marched against them with a body of troops; he was obliged to abandon his two favourites, and send them from his camp. Disguised, and escorted by their relations, they went to Bastia, by cross roads, and arrived there before the viceroy. Elliot saw that it was impossible to maintain his position in Corsica; he sought a refuge, and took possession of Porto-Ferrajo. Gentili and all the officers landed, in October 1796, in spite of the English cruisers. They organised a general rising of the population. All the crests of the mountains were covered at night with alarm fires; the harsh sound of the mountain-horn, the signal of insurrection, was heard in all the valleys. They took possession of Bastia and of all the fortresses. The English hastily embarked, and left many of their prisoners behind. The king of England wore the crown of Corsica but two years; and the affair only served to unveil the ambition of his cabinet and throw ridicule on himself. This fancy cost the treasury five millions sterling. The treasures of John Bull could not have been worse employed.

"Corsica formed the third military division of the republic. General Vaubois was appointed to the command of it. In the beginning of the year 1797, some ill disposed persons, under pretext of religion, raised an insurrection in a part of Fiumarbo; and wishing to give the weight of a great name to their enterprise, placed General Giafferi at their head. General Vaubois marched against them, and took Giafferi prisoner; he was ninety years old, and entirely ruled by his confessor. He had been educated at Naples, where he had served, and had attained the rank of major-general; he had for eight years previous to this affair enjoyed a pension and had lived peaceably in retirement; Vaubois had him taken before a military committee, which condemned him to death: he was shot. This catastrophe drew tears from every Corsican; he was the son of the celebrated Giafferi who had led them during thirty years in the struggle for their independence; his name was eminently national. The old man should have been considered as in his second childhood, and the punishment should have been made to fall on the hypocritical monk who guided him.

"Corsica lies at a distance of twenty leagues from the coast of Tuscany, forty from that of Provence, and sixty from that of Spain. Geographically regarded, it belongs to Italy; but as this peninsula does not form a power, Corsica is very naturally an integral part of France. Its extent is about 500 leagues square; it has four maritime towns, Bastia, Ajaccio, Calvi, and Bonifaccio, 60 *dales* or valleys, 450 villages or hamlets, and three large roads, capable of containing the largest fleets —San Fiorenza, Ajaccio, and Porto-Vecchio. The island is mountainous; it is traversed from the northwest to the south-east by a high range of granite mountains, which divides the island into two; the highest peaks are always covered with snow. The three largest rivers are, the Golo, the Liamone and the Tavignano. From the high mountains there flow rivers, or torrents, which empty themselves into the sea in all directions; at their mouths there are small plains of one or two leagues in circumference. The coast on the side next Italy from Bastia to Aleria is a plain, twenty leagues long, and three or four broad. The island is wooded; the plains and hills are, or may be, covered with olive-trees, mulberry-trees, fruit-trees, orange and pomegranate trees. The backs of the mountains are covered with woods of chestnut-trees, in the midst of which lie villages which are naturally fortified by their position. On the tops of the mountains are forests of pines, fir-trees, and green oaks. The olive-trees are as large as those in the Levant; the chestnut trees are of enormous size, and the fruit is of the largest kind; the pines and fir-trees are not inferior to those of Russia in height and size; but when used as masts, they are only serviceable for three or four years; at the end of this time they have become dry and brittle, whereas the pines of Russia always retain their elasticity and suppleness; oil, wine, silk, and wood for building are four great branches of exportation which contribute to enrich this island. The population amounts at the least to 180,000; the country produces corn, chestnuts, and cattle, sufficient for their wants. Before the invasion of the Saracens, the sea-shore was all peopled: Aleria and Mariana, two Roman colonies, were two great towns, containing each a population of 60,000 souls; but the incursions of the Mussulmen, in the seventh and eighth centuries, and afterwards that of the people of Barbary, drove the Corsicans to the mountains; the plains became uninhabited, and consequently unhealthy.

" Corsica is a fine country in the months of January and February, but in the dog-days the drought is felt; a scarcity of water occurs, especially in the plains; and the Corsicans are fond of residing on a declivity, from whence they descend, in winter, to the marshes, to pasture their cattle or to cultivate their plains.

" San Fiorenza is designed by nature for the capital of the island, the bulwark of its defence, and the centre of all the government magazines, because its roads are the largest in the island and the nearest to Toulon. This point ought to be regularly fortified; in all the other towns, only side-batteries ought to be maintained.

" The air of San Fiorenza is in the present day insalubrious—not in the roads, but at the place where the little town is situated; yet it would not be difficult to drain the marshes. A part of the population of Bastia,

which is but a few leagues distant, would naturally
go to this new town. In default of San Fiorenza,
Ajaccio should be the capital, the centre of administration and of defence, because it is the second road
on the side towards Toulon, and the nearest to it after
S. Fiorenza. An Italian interest predominated in the
choice of Bastia as a capital, because it is the town
which lies the nearest to Italy; the direct communication from thence with France is difficult; the inhabitants are obliged to double Cape Corso; this town,
besides, has no roads, and its port can only receive
merchant vessels.

" To fortify any other town except S. Fiorenza or
Ajaccio would be useless, since it could not be
defended against an enemy who was master of the sea,
and since the national guard would suffice for the defence of the interior of the island. In case of an
attack, the troops of the line should collect in one
maritime town, in order to prolong their defence and
await succour.

" The most urgent wants of Corsica are the following :
1stly, a good rural code which should protect agriculture against the incursions of cattle, and ordain the
destruction of goats; 2ndly, the draining of the
marshes, in order gradually to bring back the population to the sea shore; 3rdly, premiums for the purpose of encouraging the plantation and grafting of
olive and mulberry trees; they should be double for
the plantations made on the sea-shore; 4thly, a just
but severe police; a general and absolute privation of

all arms, large and small, such as stilettoes, poniards, &c.; 5thly, 200 places reserved exclusively for young Corsicans, in the lyceums, military schools, seminaries, veterinary schools, schools of agriculture, the arts and trades in France; 6thly, a regular exportation for the royal navy of building timber; and advantage should also be taken of this circumstance to found hamlets on the sea-shore, and on the skirts of the forests; for all the endeavours of the government should tend towards drawing the population down into the plains."

CHAPTER XVII.

MEMOIRS OF BONAPARTE WHEN YOUNG—CROWNED AT
THE ACADEMY OF LYONS.

THE 1st of January, 1817, arrived, yet more
melancholy than the 1st of the January preceding
had been. The departure of Count Las Cases had
left painful impressions on us all.

There are some anniversaries more dreary than all
others, because they naturally bring back a series of
recollections which force one to compare the past with
the present. The 1st of January—this family festival,
at which the Emperor at the Tuileries was first
saluted by a wife whom he adored—by a son, who
was his hope—by a people whose happiness was his
principal occupation—by four beings who were his
brothers by blood—and, finally, by ten or twelve
more who called themselves his brothers in affection—
presented itself this time as a dreary gateway to a
year still more dreary than that which had just passed.

Instead of the Tuileries, our miserable habitation; instead of our France, so often regretted, St. Helena, so often lamented; instead of the caresses of a family, the congratulations of courtiers, the shouts of a nation, and the homage of Europe—the good wishes, though without hope, of some companions in captivity, whose numbers might at any moment be diminished by the caprice of an odious gaoler. The Emperor received with kindness our good wishes and our homage. " I believe you," said he to us; " but I only expect from fate that death, which will terminate my misfortunes. You yourselves see that every day is marked by some new outrage; I pity you, for the more proofs you give me of your devotion, the more you must feel my sufferings. Let us hope, at least, that Mr. Lowe will allow me to pass this day without condemning me to remain shut up in my room to avoid meeting him in the garden.

" Your children shall dine with me. I wish their joy to be complete. Come, Hortense, you shall have the first present."

The hopes of the Emperor were not, however, to be realised; and the insult would forcibly have brought back his thoughts to his cruel position, had not General Gourgaud kept, till the next day, the secret of the pretended mistake, which caused him to remain for an hour the prisoner of a sentry.

One of the sentries of Hut's-gate interpreted his orders wrong, and arrested General Gourgaud, who was only set free at the expiration of this sentry's guard by the corporal who relieved him. The grand marshal hastened to Sir Hudson Lowe to complain, but obtained no other answer than the general one, that it was an error which should not be repeated; and yet a week afterwards the same error occurred. How, indeed, could it be otherwise, when a sentry, who interpreted his orders in our favour, received a hundred lashes, whilst the interpreting them against us was merely considered as an excess of zeal, a proof of fidelity, a mark of bad intentions towards us. We learned on this occasion that Sir Hudson very frequently gave orders to the sentries during his rides, without the commanders of the detachment knowing anything of them, except by the report of the corporal who had relieved the sentinel to whom such extraordinary orders had been given, in direct opposition to the rules of military service.

We heard also, that the soldier who had arrested General Gourgaud, had received from Sir Hudson positive orders to arrest any Frenchman who should present himself at Hut's-gate to pass, except he were accompanied by an English officer, even if it should be *General Bonaparte himself.* But Hut's-gate was within our limits, which extended for more than a mile beyond this in two directions; in the third direction alone, Hut's-gate formed the boundary.

The dinner was really a family dinner; all the expenses were borne by our children, and their childish happiness awakened in the Emperor the remembrance of his youth; his first love and his first meditations on happiness returned to his recollection.

He took pleasure in repeating to us his long conversations with the Abbé Raynal, in speaking to us of his correspondence with this celebrated man, and of what he had written under his inspiration. The correspondence of the Emperor with the Abbé Raynal, and the manuscript of his first literary work, had been confided by him to an inhabitant of Lyons, whose name he had forgotten. He related this to M. de Talleyrand, in one of his after-dinner chats with him under the shade of that beautiful allée of horse-chestnut trees, which began at St. Cloud, just opposite to his cabinet, and he witnessed some regret at not being able to see again these first impressions of his youth. M. de Talleyrand was too good a courtier to let such a good opportunity of doing something agreeable to his master escape him. He said nothing, but his first care on returning to Paris was to send for M. Dérenade, one of his most intimate friends, and the most suitable man in France, by reason of his acuteness, his general information, and his literary connexions, to discover the person with whom the manuscript had been deposited. A fortnight had not elapsed when M. de Talleyrand presented himself at St. Cloud, having carefully placed in his portfolio, as minister of foreign affairs, the packet, which he had received from Lyons the evening before. The Empetor eagerly looked through it, and found there to his great surprise, some fragments of letters to M. Butafoco, and a republican profession of faith, under the title of ' Souper de Beaucaire.'

These writings bore the impression of the excitement produced in the head of a young man by the events of the revolution. He committed them to the flames; but he preserved, notwithstanding their quite as republican tendency, a history (partial) of Corsica, and a memorial of the sentiments which it was most necessary to impress upon men for their happiness. The Academy of Lyons had rewarded this treatise with a gold medal, and this homage from a learned body was a precious *souvenir* of his youth.

The manuscript concerning Corsica served him as a basis for his history of Corsica, which I shall mention further on. I give here the treatise crowned by the Academy of Lyons:

" Literary societies ought never to have been animated by any other feeling than the love of truth and honour; but there is no truth without prejudice. There are no men where kings are despotic; there is only the slave *oppressor*, still more vile than the slave *oppressed.* This explains why literary societies, since the beginning of time, have offered the melancholy spectacle of flattery and the most disgraceful adulation.

" This explains why the really useful sciences, those of morals and of politics, have been suffered to languish in oblivion, or have been lost in a labyrinth of obscurity. They have, however, made rapid progress in latter times. This has been owing to some men of spirit who, urged forwards by their genius, have feared neither the thunder of a despot,

nor the dungeons of a bastile. These rays of
light illumined the atmosphere; threw a new light
upon public opinion, which, proud of its rights,
destroyed the enchantment which had bound the
world, as by a spell, for so many centuries. Thus
was Rinaldo restored to virtue and to himself, as soon
as a courageous and friendly hand held up to him the
buckler, in which were traced, at the same time, his
duties and his apathy.

" To what can we with more propriety compare the
immortal works of these great men, than to the divine
buckler of Tasso?

" The liberty thus acquired after an energetic
struggle of twenty months, and the most violent
exertions, will be for ever a glory to France, to phi-
losophy, and to literature. Under these circumstances,
the academy proposes *to determine those truths and
feelings which it is most necessary to inculcate upon
man for his happiness.* This question, really worthy
of the consideration of the free man, is in itself an
eulogy on the sages who have proposed it. None is
more likely to answer the purpose of the founder.

" Illustrious Raynal! if, in the course of a life
harassed by prejudice, and the great whom thou hast
unmasked, thou hast ever been constant and im-
movable in thy zeal for suffering and oppressed
humanity, deign this day, in the midst of the applause
of an immense nation, which, called by thee to liberty,
renders to thee its first homage, deign to smile upon
the efforts of a zealous disciple, whose feeble attempts

thou hast been kind enough sometimes to encourage. The question which I am about to consider is worthy of thy pencil; but without aiming at possessing its power, I have exclaimed to myself with courage, ' *I too am a painter.*'

" It is indispensably necessary, in the first place, to fix clearly our ideas of happiness.

" Man is born to be happy. Nature, a beneficent mother, has endowed him with all the organs necessary to this first design of his creation. Happiness, then, is nothing more than that enjoyment of his life, which is most conformable to his organisation. Men of all climates, of all sects, of all religions—are there any among you, the prejudices of whose dogmas should prevent them from acknowledging the truth of this principle? Let such, if any there be, place their right hands on their hearts, their left on their eyes, let them enter into themselves, let them consider truly and honestly—and then let them say whether they do not believe with me in this.

" We must live, then, in a manner conformable to our organisation, or we can enjoy no happiness.

" Our animal organisation feels certain indispensable cravings; those of eating, drinking, of procreation; nourishment, therefore, a lodging, a covering, a wife, are indispensably necessary to our happiness.

" Our intellectual organisation gives rise to demands no less imperious, and the satisfaction of which is much more precious. It is in their full development that happiness is really to be sought. Perception and the reasoning powers form the essence of man. These are his titles to the supremacy which he has acquired, which he retains, and will retain for ever.

" Our feelings revolt against restraint, render dear to us the beautiful and the just, and disagreeable to us the oppressor and the wicked. Woe to him who does not acknowledge these truths! He knows nothing of life but the shade; he knows no pleasures but the enjoyments of sense.

" Our reasoning powers lead us to make comparisons. From reasoning arises perfection, as fruit from the tree. Reason, the inexorable judge of our actions, ought also to be their invariable guide. The eyes of reason preserve man from the precipice of his passions, in the same way as its decrees modify even the feeling of his rights. Feeling gives rise to society; reason maintains it entire.

" It is necessary for us, therefore, to eat, to drink, to procreate, to feel, and to reason, in order to live like a man; that is, in order to be happy.

" Of all the legislators whom the esteem of their fellow-citizens has raised up to give them laws, none appear to have been more convinced of these truths than Lycurgus and Paoli. It was by very different courses, however, that they have put them in practice in their legislations.

" The Lacedæmonians enjoyed an abundance of food, they had convenient habitations and dress, their wives were robust, they reasoned in their social meetings, and their government was a free one. They enjoyed their strength, their skill, their glory, the esteem of their countrymen, the prosperity of their country. These were all means of gratifying their feelings. Their affections were excited—their families, their emotions roused by the varied views and the beautiful climate of Greece: but it was principally at the sight of strength and of virtue that they felt moved. Virtue consisted in courage and strength. Energy is the life of the soul, as well as the main-spring of reason.

" The actions of a Spartan were those of a strong man; the strong man is good, the weak man wicked. The Spartan lived in a manner conformable to his organisation: he was happy.

" But all this is but a dream. On the banks of the Eurotas, at the present day, resides a pasha of three tails; and the traveller, grieving over this sight, retires affrighted, almost doubting, for a moment, the goodness of the governor of the universe.

" But to conduct men to happiness, must they then be equal in means? To what point must the love of an equality of faculties be inculcated upon them? Since feeling is necessary to a happy life, what are the feelings with which they should be inspired? What are the truths which ought to be explained to them? You say, without reasoning no happiness can exist.

" Man at his birth brings with him into the world a right to that portion of the fruits of the earth necessary for his subsistence.

" After the buoyancy of childhood comes the commencement of passion. He chooses from among the companions of his sports her who is to be the companion of his destiny. His vigorous arms, in connexion with his wants, demand labour; he casts a glance around him; he sees the earth, divided among a few possessors, affording the means of luxury and of superfluity. He asks himself, by what right do these people possess all this? Why is the idler everything, the labourer almost nothing? Why have they left to me nothing of all this—to me who have a wife, an aged father and mother to maintain?

" He runs to the minister, the confidant of his secrets; he explains to him his doubts: ' Man,' answers the priest, ' never reflect upon the existence of society—God conducts all—abandon yourself to Providence—this life is only a passage—all things are disposed by a justice, the decrees of which we should not seek to explain—believe, obey, never reason, and work: these are your duties.'

" A proud soul, a sensitive heart, a natural reason, cannot be satisfied with this answer. He wishes to communicate his doubts and his inquietude, and goes to the wisest man of the country—a notary. ' Man of wisdom,' he says, ' they have divided the goods of the country and have given me nothing.' The wise man laughs at his simplicity, takes him into his study, leads him from act to act, from contract to contract, from testament to testament, and proves to him the legitimacy of the division of which he complains.

" ' What! are these the titles of these gentlemen?' he exclaims, indignantly; ' mine are more sacred, more incontestable, more universal; they are renewed with my breathing, circulate with my blood, are written on my nerves and in my heart; they are the necessity of my existence, and above all, of my happiness.' And with these words he seizes these papers, and casts them into the flames.

" He immediately begins to fear the powerful arm called Justice; he flees to his hut, and throws himself in violent emotion on the cold body of his father. This venerable old man, blind and paralysed by age, seems only still to live by the forgetfulness of the great tyrant Death. ' My father!' he cries, ' you gave me life, and with it a lively desire for happiness; and now, my father, robbers have divided everything among themselves. I have but my arms left; for those they could not take from me. I am condemned, then, to the most ceaseless labour, to the most degrading toil for money. Neither under the sun of August, nor during the frosts of January, will there be any repose for your son. And as the reward of such great labour, others will gather the harvest pro-duced by the sweat of my brow! And if I could even supply all that is necessary ! I must feed, clothe, lodge, and keep warm a whole family. We shall be in want of bread, my heart will be torn at every moment, my sensibility will be blunted, my reason will be obscured. Oh, my father! I shall live stupid and miserable, and perhaps wicked. I shall live unhappy. Was I born for this?'

" ' My son,' answers the venerable old man; ' the sacred characters of nature are traced in your bosom in all their energy; preserve them carefully, in order to live happy and strong; but listen attentively to what the experience of eighty years has taught me. My son, I reared you in my arms, I witnessed your young years; and now, when your heart begins to palpitate, your nerves are doubtless accustomed to labour, but to moderate labour, which refreshes the body, excites the feelings, and calms the impatient imagination. My son, have you ever wanted for anything? your dress is coarse, your habitation rustic, your food simple: but once more I ask, have you ever had a desire unsatisfied? Your sentiments are pure as your sensations, as yourself. You wished for a wife; my son, you have chosen one. I aided you with my experience to direct your youthful heart. Oh! my tender friend, why do you complain? You fear for the future; act always as you have hitherto done, and you need not fear it.

" ' My son, if I had been among the number of those miserable men who possess nothing, I should have trained your body to the animal yoke; I should myself have stifled your feelings and your ideas; I should have made you the first of the animals in your shed.

Bent under the dominion of habit, you would have lived tranquil in your apathy, contented in your ignorance—you would not have been happy, oh my son! but you would have died without knowing that you had lived; for, as you yourself say, in order to live it is necessary to feel and reason; and then, not to be weighed down by physical wants. Yes, good young man, let this information refresh and console you; calm your inquietude; these fields, this hut, these cattle are ours. I have purposely kept you in ignorance of this; it is so happy and so sweet to rise, so hard to descend!

" ' Your father will soon be no more; he has lived long enough, he has known true pleasures, and now feels the greatest of all, since he once more presses you to his bosom. Impress one thing on your heart, my son, if you wish to imitate him; your soul is ardent; but your wife, this sweet gift of love, and your children, what objects are these with which to fill the void in your heart—do not nourish a cupidity of riches. Riches only influence happiness, in as far as they procure or refuse physical necessaries. You have these necessaries, and with them a habit of labour; you are the richest man in the country; bridle, then, your disordered imagination: you require but to call reason to your aid.

" ' Are the rich happy? They have it in their power to be so, but not more than you have; they have it in their power, I say; for they are rarely happy.

Happiness resides especially in your station of
life, because it is that of reason and feeling. The
station of the rich is the empire of a disordered
imagination, of vanity, sensual enjoyments, caprice,
and fantasy—never envy it; and even should all the
riches of the country be offered you, cast them far
from you; except indeed you should receive them
for the purpose of dividing them immediately among
your fellow citizens. But, my son, this struggle of
strength of mind and magnanimity is only fitting for a
god. Be a man, but a true one; live master of yourself. Without strength of mind, there is neither
virtue nor happiness.'

" I have thus demonstrated the two extremities of
the social chain; yes, gentlemen, let the rich man be
the one, I consent to this; but let not the miserable
man be the other; let it be the small proprietor, or
small merchant, or the skilful artisan, who may, by
moderate labour, feed, clothe, and lodge his family.
You will recommend then to the legislator, not to establish the civil law under which a few men might possess
everything. He must resolve his political problem in
such a manner that even the least may have something. He will not by this means establish equality;
for the two extremes are so distant, and the latitude
so great, that inequality may exist in the intervening
ranks; man can be happy in the hut as well as in the
palace, covered with skins as well as clothed in
embroidery from Lyons; at the frugal table of Cincin-
natus, as well as at that of Vitellius; but then, he

must have this hut, these skins, this frugal table. How can the legislator bring this about? How can he resolve his political problem in such a manner that even the lowest may have something? The difficulties are great, and I know of no one who understands better how to overcome them than Monsieur Paoli.

"M. Paoli, whose solicitude for the welfare of humanity and of his fellow-countrymen is his distinguishing characteristic; who for a moment revived in the middle of the Mediterranean the splendid days of Sparta and of Athens; M. Paoli, full of those feelings and of that genius which nature sometimes unites in one man for the consolation of nations, appeared in Corsica, and drew the eyes of Europe upon himself. His fellow-citizens, tossed hither and thither by wars at home and abroad, recognised his ascendant, and proclaimed him nearly in the same manner as the citizens of Athens formerly did Solon, or those of Rome the triumvirs.

"Affairs were in such disorder that a magistrate clothed with great authority, and possessing transcendent genius, alone could save his country.

"Happy the nation in which the social chain is not firmly enough riveted to cause fear of the consequences of such a rash step!—happy, when it produces men who justify this unbounded confidence, who render themselves worthy of it!

"Placed at the helm of affairs, and summoned by his countrymen to give them laws, M. Paoli established a constitution, founded not only on the same principles as the existing one, but even on the same administrative divisions; there were municipalities, districts, procurators, and a syndic of the procurators of the community. He overthrew the clergy, and appropriated the property of the bishops to the nation. In short, the course of his government was almost that of actual revolution. He found, in his unequalled activity, in his warm and persuasive eloquence, and in his penetrating and supple genius, means of protecting his new constitution from the attacks of the malicious and of his enemies, for Corsica was then at war with Genoa.

"But M. Paoli's principal merit in our eyes is that he seemed convinced of the principle, established by civil law, that the legislator should assure to every man such a portion of property as would suffice, with moderate labour, for his support. For this purpose, he separated the territories of each village into two kinds; those of the first order, plains fit for sowing or for pasture land; and those of the second order, mountains, fit for the cultivation of olive trees, chestnut trees, and trees of all kinds. The lands of the first order, called pasture-ground, became public property; but the temporary use of them was enjoyed by individuals. Every three years the pasture-ground of each village was divided among the inhabitants. The lands of the second order, susceptible of peculiar cultivation, remained under the inspection of individual interest.

" By this wise arrangement, every citizen was born a proprietor, without destroying industry, or injuring the progress of agriculture; in short, without having helots.

"But all legislators have not found themselves in the same circumstances; they have not all been able to manage affairs and to conduct them to such a happy issue; but yet, pressed by the principle, they have rendered homage to it by excluding from society all those who possessed nothing, or did not pay a certain tax. Why this second injustice? Because the man whom the laws have not enabled to be happy, cannot be a citizen; because the man who has no interest in the maintenance of the civil law, is its enemy; a portion of property ought to have been secured to him, in order to interest him in, and attach him to this law, but in default of this, it has been necessary to exclude him, as a degraded, dull creature, and as such incapable of exercising a portion of the sovereignty. These are doubtless the political reasons— but what are they in the eyes of morality, of humanity! When I see one of these unfortunate creatures transgress the law of the state, and suffer for it, I say to myself: 'It is the strong making the weak their victim.' I imagine I see the American perishing for having violated the law of the Spaniard.

"After having persuaded the legislator that he should care equally for the fate of all ranks of citizens in the reaction of his civil law, you will say to the rich man: 'Your riches constitute your misfortune: remain within the limits of your senses; you will then no longer be uneasy or fantastical. How many young

housekeepers run to ruin, because they are in want of
the very thing which makes you so uneasy; you have
too much, and they have not enough. Your lot is the
same, with this difference, that you being wiser might
remedy it, whilst they can only groan. . . Man of ice,
does your heart, then, never beat? I pity you, I ab-
hor you; you are unhappy, and the cause of unhappi-
ness in others!'

" Without marriage, we have said there is neither
health nor happiness; you will, therefore, teach the
numerous class of advocates of celibacy that their
pleasures are not true ones; except you find that,
convinced that they cannot live without wives, they
seek in those of other men the gratification of their
appetites; you will then publicly denounce them.
You will denounce the extravagant presumption of
the minister of Brahma; you will teach him that
the happy man alone is worthy of his Creator; that
the Fakir who mutilates himself is a monster of de-
pravity and folly.

" You will laugh with indignant disdain, when they
endeavour to persuade you that perfection consists
in celibacy. You have opened the great book of
reason and feeling, and will, therefore, disdain to
answer the sophisms of prejudice and hypocrisy.

" Let the civil law secure to every one physical
necessaries; let the inextinguishable thirst for riches
be replaced by the consoling feeling of happiness.
At your voice let the old man be the father of all his

children; let him divide his property equally among them; and let the pleasant sight of eight happy households cause the barbarous law of primogeniture to be for ever abhorred. Let man, in short, learn that his true glory is to live as a man; and at this voice let the enemies of nature be silent, and bite their serpent tongues with rage. Let the minister of the most sublime of religions, who should bring peace and consolation to the wounded souls of the unfortunate, learn to know the sweet emotions of love; let the nectar of pleasure make him sincerely sensible of the greatness of the Author of his being; then, truly worthy of public confidence, he will be a man of nature, and an interpreter of her decrees; let him choose a companion; that day will be the triumph of morality, and the true friends of nature will celebrate it heartily. The minister, awakened to a feeling of those new joys, will bless the age of reason as he tastes its first benefits.

" These, gentlemen, are the truths, as far as regards animal necessities, which must be taught to men for their happiness.

" SECOND PART.

" What is sentiment? It is the bond of life, of society, of love, of friendship! It is that which unites the son to the mother, the citizen to his country; it is especially powerful in the child of nature; dissipation and the pleasures of sense destroy its delicacy and refinement, but in misfortune man always finds it again; it is that spirit of consolation which never abandons us but with our lives.

" Are you not satisfied? climb to one of the peaks of Mont Blanc; watch the sun emerging by degrees, bringing consolation and warmth to the hut of the labourer. Let the first beam which he sheds, dwell and be remembered in your heart. Bear in mind the pleasure you enjoy.

" Descend to the coast of the sea; observe the god of day sinking majestically into the bosom of infinity; melancholy will overpower you—you will abandon yourself to its impression; no one can resist the melancholy of nature.

" Stand under the monument of St. Remi—contemplate its majesty; the finger of these proud Romans traced in past ages, transports you into the society of Emilius, Scipio, and Fabius; you return to yourself to gaze on the mountains at a distance covered with a dark veil, crowning the immense plain of Tarascon, where a hundred thousand Cimbrians lay buried. The Rhone flows at its extremity more rapid than an arrow; a road lies upon the left, a small town in the distance, a flock in the meadows; you dream, without doubt—it is the dream of sentiment.

" Wander abroad into the country; take shelter in the miserable cabin of a shepherd; pass the night stretched upon sheepskins, with your feet to the fire. What a situation!—midnight strikes; all the cattle of the neighbourhood go forth to pasture, their lowings commingle with the voices of their conductors. It is midnight—forget it not; this is the moment to hold deep communion with yourself; to meditate on the origin of nature, and to taste its most exquisite delights.

" On your return from a long walk, you are overtaken by the night; you arrive by the light of the silvery rays in the perfect silence of the universe; you have been oppressed by the burning heat of the dog-star; you taste the delights of the evening freshness, and the salutary balm of meditation.

" Your family is gone to bed, your lights are extinguished, but not your fire; the cold and frosts of January obstruct vegetation in your garden. What do you do there for several hours? I do not suppose that you wander forth possessed with the passion or ambition for wealth; in what are you engaged? You commune with yourself.

" You know that the metropolitan church of St. Peter's in Rome is as large as a town; a single lamp burns before the great altar. You enter there at ten o'clock in the evening, and grope your way; the feeble light does not enable you to see anything but itself; you believe you are only entering, when the morning has already arrived; Aurora sheds her light through the windows, and the paleness of the morning succeeds to the darkness of the night; you at length begin to think of retiring, but you have been there six hours! Could I have written down your thoughts, how interesting to morality would they have been!

" Curiosity, the mother of life, has led you to embark for Greece; you are driven by the currents on the isle of Monte-Christo,—at night you seek for shelter; you traverse the little rock, and you find one upon a height, in the midst of the ruins of an old monastery, behind a crumbling wall covered with ivy and rosemary; you arrange your tent; you are surrounded on all sides by the mighty sea, and the hoarse roaring of its waves as they dash against the rocks, suggests to you the idea of this element so terrible to the feeble voyager. A light covering and a wall fifteen centuries old form your shelter ; you are agitated by the agitation of sentiment.

Are you, at seven o'clock in the morning, in the midst of flowery thickets, or in a vast forest, during the season of fruit? Are you asleep in a grotto surrounded by the waters of the Dryads, during the raging heat of the dog star? You will pass whole hours alone, unable to tear yourself away from the scene, or to bear the intrusion of those who come to interrupt your enjoyment.

" He is not human who has not experienced the sweetness, the melancholy, the thrill which most of these situations impart. How deeply do I pity him who cannot comprehend, or has never been affected by the electricity of nature! If sentiment made us experience these delightful emotions only, it would even then have done much for us, it would have afforded us a succession of enjoyments without regret, without fatigue, without any kind of violent excitement; these would have been its precious gifts, had not patriotism, conjugal affection, and divine friendship been also amongst the number of its bounties.

" You return to your country after many years of absence; you traverse the scenes of your youth, which were witnesses to the agitation which the first knowledge of men, and the morning of passion produced in your senses. In a moment you live through the life of your youth, and participate in its pleasures. You say you have a father, an affectionate mother, sisters still innocent, brothers, at the same time friends; oh, happy man! run, fly, lose not a moment! Should death stop you on the way, you will not have known the delights of life, those of sweet gratitude, of tender respect, and of sincere friendship. But you say, I have a wife and children. A wife and children! It is too much, my dear friend; it is too much; never leave them more, pleasure would overwhelm you on your return, grief oppress you at your departure—a wife and children, father and mother, brothers and sisters, a friend! And yet we complain of nature, and say why were we born? we submit with impatience to the transitory evils of life, and run with wild impetuosity after emptiness of vanity and riches. What then, oh! unfortunate mortals, is the depraving draught, which has thus altered the inclinations inscribed in your blood, your nerves, and your eyes? Had you a soul as ardent as the fires of Etna, if you had a father, a mother, a wife and children, you have no reason to dread the anxieties and wearisomeness of life.

" Yes, these are the only, the real pleasures of life, from which nothing can distract you, of which nothing can deprive you. It is vain for man to surround himself with all the blessings of fortune—as soon as these sentiments fly from his heart, tedium seizes upon him; sadness, gloomy melancholy, and despair succeed; and if this condition continues, he relieves himself by death.

" Pontaveri was torn away from Tahiti, conducted to Europe, watched with care, and loaded with attentions; no means of distraction were forgotten or neglected. One single object attracted his attention, and snatched him from the arms of grief. It was the mulberry tree; he embraced it with transport, exclaiming: ' Tree of my country! tree of my country!' All that the court of Copenhagen could offer was lavished in vain on five Greenlanders; anxiety for their country and their family brought on melancholy, and melancholy was the precursor of death. Instead of this, how many English, Dutch, and French are there who live among savages! These unhappy men were degraded in Europe, the sport of the passions, and the melancholy refuse of the great, whilst the man of nature lives happily in the bosom of sentiment and natural reason.

" We have now seen how sentiment enables us to enjoy ourselves, nature, our country, and those who surround us. It remains to observe how it makes us thrill at the contemplation of the different vicissitudes of life. Here we become convinced that if it makes us friends of what is lovely and just, it fills us with repugnance towards the oppressor and the wicked.

" A young beauty has just entered her sixteenth year; the roses on her cheek are changed for the lily, the fire of her eyes is extinguished; the vivacity of her graces degenerate into the languor of melancholy : she loves. Does she inspire you with respect, with confidence? it is the respect, the confidence of sentiment. Does she inspire you with contempt for her weakness? Be it so, but never utter it, if you value my esteem.

" Nina loved; her well-beloved died; she would have died with him—she survived him long, but only to remain faithful to him. Nina knew well that the object of her affections was dead, but sentiment could not conceive his annihilation. She waited for it always, she would wait for it still. You complain contemptuously of her folly—harsh man! Instead of that, feel esteem for her constancy and the tenderness of her heart. This is the esteem and tenderness of sentiment.

" An adored wife has died—she was the wife of your enemy. The unfortunate husband is overwhelmed with his loss. He flees from the society of men; the drapery of mourning replaces the garments of rejoicing. Two torches are upon the table—despair in his·heart. Thus he passes the languishing remnant of his life. With a good soul you feel your hatred appeased—you run to her tomb, and lavish upon it marks of the reconciliation of sentiment.

"You have read Tacitus; which of you has not cried out with Cato the younger, ' Let some one give me a sword, that I may kill this monster.' Now, at the expiration of two thousand years, the recital of the deeds of Marius, Sylla, Nero, Caligula, and Domitian, excite feelings of apathy and repugnance. Their memory is that of hatred and execration."

———

It was thus, that those days which were a kind of living ephemeris, led the Emperor by the subtle and capricious thread of memory, sometimes to the days of his youth; obscure, indeed, but always laborious— sometimes to the years of his triumphal consulate, and sometimes to the more gloomy and stormy period of his imperial power.

CHAPTER XVIII.

RECOLLECTIONS OF RUSSIA—RECOLLECTIONS OF EGYPT.
PAUL I.—KLEBER.

IN the meanwhile, the Spey arrived with despatches and news from England. She brought accounts of the bombardment of Algiers by Lord Exmouth. This event made an impression upon the Emperor: "The destruction of these barbarian powers," he said to us, as soon as he heard the details of the news, "was one of my projects; I have never been able to understand how the maritime powers of Europe could submit to these corsairs. During the peace of Amiens, I proposed to England to put an end to them, and I do not at this moment recollect what prevented us from coming to an understanding on the subject. At a later period, I, at several times, gave orders to the minister of marine to study the question of Algiers; I do not think that England has adopted the best method by

attacking their batteries by force; this was exposing
their ships to almost certain destruction; a rigid
blockade, or the landing of a few thousand men, and
an attack by land, would appear to me likely to have
produced a more certain result than could be obtained
by the other course, and without the useless exposure
of brave men to such a *canaille.* And besides, what
would Lord Exmouth have done, if, on the next day
after the bombardment, the Dey of Algiers had
refused to consent to any one of the conditions which
England imposed upon him? it would have been
impossible for him to renew the combat with his shattered vessels; he would have been obliged to change
his tone, to await the arrival of a new squadron,
or to depart without having accomplished anything,
and to have all the disgrace of failure.

" If the Algerines are really struck with terror, and
if they execute the treaty which Lord Exmouth has
dictated at the cannon's mouth, England will have
rendered a signal service to humanity; I cannot,
however, believe that it will be so; and besides, these
barbarians do not alter their practice with respect to
their prisoners, and will only treat them the more
cruelly, because they have no longer any hope of
obtaining a ransom.

" The order of Malta entertained a noble thought,
and had the English faithfully executed the treaty of
Amiens, the Emperor Paul would certainly have restored this order to its former importance. This prince
attached great importance to the title of Protector of

Malta; his chivalrous spirit was pleased with the design of the flag of the order again becoming the terror of the barbarians, and the protection of commerce in the Mediterranean. When he heard of the refusal of the English minister to deliver Malta into his hands, his anger knew no bounds; he is said to have driven his sword through the despatch which conveyed the intelligence, and to have ordered his minister of foreign affairs to send it back directly to London.

" Paul was a man who had a soul, and was accessible to noble resolutions, but all his moral faults were concentrated by the restless forebodings of that animal instinct which I have so often observed in some of my bravest soldiers: Lasalle, for example, who in the middle of the night wrote to me from bivouac on the battle-field of Wagram, to ask me to sign immediately the decree for the transmission of his title and his *majorat* of Count to his wife's son, because he felt that he was about to fall in the battle on the ensuing day; and the unfortunate man was right. Cervoni, who stood near me at Eckmühl, and now faced cannon for the first time since the war in Italy, said to me, ' Sire, you forced me to quit Marseilles, which I loved, by writing to me that the Cross of the Legion of Honour was only to be won by soldiers in the presence of the enemy. Here I am—but this is my last day.' A quarter of an hour afterwards, a ball carried away his head. Paul I. was constantly dreaming of conspiracies and assassination. He had brought a skilful mechanic from abroad, in order to make him a number of secret passages by which he might escape from the different chambers which he most frequently used in his palace. There was one man alone who had his entire confidence, and that was Count Pahlen, governor of St. Petersburg, and chief director of the police. He was at supper with the general the night before his assassination, when he received a letter revealing to him to the most minute details, the whole scheme of the conspiracy, naming Count Pahlen as the chief, and warning him that the plot was completely ripe for execution. Some fatality prevented him from breaking the seal, and he thought no more of it when he retired to his private apartments. Had he opened the letter, he would have been saved!

" On the evening before, he had received a similar warning, and having immediately commanded the presence of Count Pahlen, the following singular conversation ensued; ' There is,' said the Emperor, ' a plot against my life. The English ambassador is the prime mover; the consultations take place at the house of Madame de Gerbsdorf, and Prince Sabof is one of its most zealous promoters.'

" ' I believe it,' replied Count Pahlen. ' My son Alexander is in league with the conspirators.' 'I believe it,' Pahlen again laconically replied. ' But you yourself are concerned in it.' ' If I had not been,' said Count Pahlen, interrupting him, ' how could I have found it out and saved you?' This *sang-froid* imposed upon the unfortunate Paul the First. Count Pahlen having perceived that the handwriting on the letter delivered during supper was the same as that of the informer of the evening before, no sooner left the supper table, than he ran directly to Prince Sabof, Count Orloff, and General Benigsen to inform them of their impending danger. The whole four went immediately to the house of the grand Duke Alexander, whose hesitation was likely to compromise them all. They said to him, ' It is absolutely necessary to finish the affair this very night; the Emperor, within these twenty-four hours, has received two important revelations; to-morrow your head and ours will fall upon the scaffold, if to-morrow Russia does not salute you as her Emperor.' ' Save the life of my father!' cried Alexander; covering his face with his hands. ' The will of God be done!' replied the conspirators, and they quitted him to proceed to the house of the grand Duke Michael, where the Emperor was then residing.

" Prince Sabof, being commander-in-chief of the guards, all the doors were opened to him, but the Cossack who was on duty at the door of the Emperor's chamber refused him permission to enter. The conspirators could not hesitate; they rushed upon him, and entered by force. Paul, terrified by the clash of arms, lost his presence of mind, and attempted to escape by the secret passage; but whilst he was trying to open the door, the conspirators, conducted by General Benigsen, surrounded him, and one of them,

Prince Sabof, presenting an act of abdication for his signature, said to him—' Sire, I arrest you, in the name of the Emperor Alexander.' On his refusing to sign and attempting to defend himself against his assassins, they fell upon him and strangled him; it is said that the General was the one who inflicted the mortal blow. The name of Benigsen reminds me, that after the battle of Friedland, an exchange of the *cordon* of our orders took place between Alexander and myself, and he asked me to bestow the cross of the Legion of Honour on this same general, which I refused, from the recollection of his crime. I said to him, ' I will bestow it with pleasure on the soldier whom you shall point out to me as the bravest in your army; but I must refuse it to a general who laid the hand of an assassin on his sovereign.'

" There can be no doubt that the Emperor Alexander retained the conviction up till the last moment, that the Emperor Paul would abdicate and save his life; but he ought to have delivered up the assassins of his father into the hands of justice; the bonds of nature imposed this upon him as a sacred duty; and if it be true, unfortunately for him, that the conspiracy imposed upon him a yoke of iron during the first years of his reign, he ought to have recollected that the hand which directed all, did not protect the murderers. It was of little consequence to the cabinet of St. James's what became of the Emperor's murderers—what they desired they purchased at the price of a great crime, and that was, a complete change in the policy of the cabinet of St. Petersburg. Alexander might, without fear, have avenged the death of his father, by the exemplary punishment of the assassins, on the day on which he broke with me, and placed the whole power of Russia at the disposal of England. The Empress-mother was inflexible in the pursuit of vengeance, and never suffered the conspirators to approach her person."

In the meantime, the insult offered to General Gourgaud, by the sentinel at Hut's gate, could not be long concealed from the Emperor. These repeated shocks affected his health, so that he always remained shut up for several days in his miserable apartments, and on each occasion, it was a species of diplomatic victory on our part, to prevail on the Emperor to agree to take the fresh air; and we only succeeded, when the want of exercise produced serious effects, and manifested itself by the swellings of his legs and pains in his head. The Emperor always persuaded himself that a bath of some hours and working by night, were specific remedies against the discomforts arising from want of exercise. It is certain he often found them to produce salutary effects.

The Emperor conceived the hope of obtaining from the Prince Regent, some modification of the despotic power exercised by Sir Hudson Lowe. He could never bring himself to believe that a King of England, had no other power than that of naming his ministers. He dictated to me a long *exposé* of all the useless vexations of which he was daily made the victim, but this labour was laid aside, up till the moment when it served as a basis for the observations of the Emperor Napoleon on the speech of Lord Bathurst.

A visit made by Admiral Malcolm gave new life to the negotiations for a better understanding, which some concessions on the part of Sir Hudson Lowe, seemed at length to render possible. He came personally to the house of the grand marshal to inform him, that henceforward, the free enjoyment of the road from Miss Masson's cottage and Woody Range would be restored to us, as before the restrictions of the 9th of October. On the next morning, however, all was changed. The restless and tormenting humour of Sir Hudson had resumed its empire, and taking his text from the observations made by the grand marshal on the restrictions of the 9th of October, he said to him, that " the person who had dictated to him observations couched in such terms and containing so many falsehoods, could not have been guided by any desire of conciliation, and that he had decided on not doing anything which would be regarded as a concession on his part to such observations; that in consequence, he had returned to his determination of the preceding evening, and that things should remain as they had been prescribed by the restrictions of the 9th of October, — that he thought the person who offered his mediation only did it with a view of previously obtaining an excuse, rather than in any hope of gaining concessions."

" Let General Bonaparte," he added, " send me his proposals by Admiral Malcolm, and I will give him an answer." In the meantime, the admiral came to Longwood, and the Emperor, after having received an assurance from him of his confidence in Sir Hudson Lowe's desire to put an end to those quarrels which closed the doors of the audience room at Longwood against him, authorised him to say to the governor that he would receive with pleasure any explanations transmitted through the mediation of the admiral, and that if he would re-establish all things on the footing on which they stood in the time of Sir George Cockburn, all should be forgotten.

Journals, pamphlets, and letters received from England by way of the Cape, put an end, for some days, to these painful discussions. M. Miot's work on the Campaign in Egypt, as well as the articles in the Quarterly Review, and Pillet's collections upon the same subject, attracted the Emperor's attention. The accusation of having caused 1500 prisoners to be shot, and especially that of having poisoned those who were suffering from the plague, at Jaffa, excited his indignation, and he passed a considerable part of the night in dictating to me the following remarks:

" 1st. El'Arish, the first port in Egypt, is a poor village in the desert which separates Africa from Asia. Five or six springs, furnishing the quantity of water necessary for an army of 30,000 men, are there found in the midst of a wood of palm-trees, and it is to this circumstance that the village and

port of El'Arish are indebted for their existence;
4000 men, under the command of Djezzar Pasha, the
new Seraskier of Egypt, were in possession of this important position, when Napoleon was crossing the
desert to occupy Syria.　Orders were issued to
General Regnier to make himself master of El'Arish;
on the 9th of February, he attacked the village,
drove out the Turks, and took 300 prisoners; 2000
Arnauts succeeded in shutting themselves up in the
fort; these troops were commanded by chiefs independent of one another; their cavalry, 1500 strong,
retired half a league from the fort, and took up a
strong position with a view to protect the road to
Syria.　Regnier had only 900 hussars, and could not
therefore venture to assail the Turkish cavalry, which
were thus able to wait tranquilly for the army of
Abdalla.　On the first news of the presence of the
French at El'Arish, this army commenced its march,
consisting of from five to six thousand men, infantry
as well as cavalry, among whom were the Mamelukes,
with twelve pieces of cannon.　On the evening of
the 12th, this force pitched its camp within 1500
toises of El' Arish, which would have rendered General
Regnier's position very critical, had he not been
joined at break of day on the 13th, by Kleber's division, and 300 cavalry, under the command of Murat.

　" Kleber undertook the blockade of the fort, and
Regnier posted his division on the sides of the ravine,
or hollow way, in order to keep the Turkish army in
check.　He remained in this position during the 13th

and 14th, and on the night between the 14th and
15th, he quitted his camp, ascended the hollow way
a league, and then crossed it.   His division was composed of three regiments of infantry which he drew up
in order of battle, changed his front, his right in advance, and his left resting on the ravine. His order of
battle was formed in three close columns at a sufficient
distance to be able to extend their ranks.   Two
hundred paces in advance of each column, he placed
the grenadiers and light company of each regiment,
forming, in all, about 150 men, and sixty men of the
cavalry.   About two o'clock in the morning, when
he was a little distance from the enemy's camp, he
ordered a halt, arranged his men, marched forward
with the advanced guard of the three columns, and
dashed into the midst of their camp on three different
sides.   This produced the greatest confusion among
the Turks; he marched directly to the tent of the
Pasha, who had only time to escape on foot half
dressed.   The whole army was dispersed, and abandoned their tents, baggage, artillery, and provisions,
with about 150 killed, and more than 1200 prisoners,
1000 saddle and draft horses, and 500 camels.   The
fugitives did not begin to rally till they reached
Kanzouses.   On the next morning at day-break,
Napoleon, who had crossed the desert in all haste
upon a dromedary, arrived and summoned the garrison
of El'Arish, which returned a haughty reply of defi-
ance.   A battery of 4—12 was erected by means of
a quantity of stones, which lay at about a pistol shot

from the fort; a partial breach was soon effected, and then the four chiefs proposed a parley. With this view, they came to the tent of the general·in·chief, asked an armistice of fifteen days, and offered to surrender, if they were not relieved in the mean-time. At the end of two hours' useless discussion, during which these four chiefs, who exactly resembled four leaders of brigands, appeared very resolute, and confident of being relieved, the conference was broken up. The success of an assault was infallible, but it would probably have cost from six to seven hundred men, wherefore the artillery was again directed against the fort, and the fire was kept up with such spirit and precision, that 800 bombs were thrown in the course of the morning, the greatest number of which burst in the fort. As it was very small, they committed fearful destruction, and covered it with dead bodies and streams of blood. The garrison lost courage, new parleys took place, and the four chiefs signed a capitulation. The fort was surrendered at the break of day, the enemy marched out with the honours of war, laid down their colours and arms, and took an oath not to carry arms against the French, but to return to Bagdad, and not to set foot in Syria for a year. Three hundred of them (Maugrabins) volun·teered to join the French army, 500 had been either killed or wounded, and 3200 were escorted by a detachment, two days' march into the desert in the direction of Bagdad.

" ' CAPITULATION OF EL'ARISH.

" ' The Commandant of the Fort of El'Arish, and the other Commanders of the troops to the General-in-chief.

" ' We have received the terms of capitulation, which you have addressed to us; we agree to surrender the fort of El'Arish, and will return to Bagdad by the desert. Herewith we send you the list of Agas in the fort, who promise and swear, for themselves and their soldiers, not to serve in the army of Djezzar, and not to re-enter Syria for a year from this date. We shall receive a passport and colours from you, and will leave in the fort all the ammunition which is there. All the Agas who are in the fort solemnly swear by God, Moses, Abraham, and the Prophet, (to whom may God be gracious!) and by the Koran, to execute faithfully all these articles, and especially not to serve under Djezzar. The Most High and the Prophet are witnesses of our sincerity.

(Signed)

" ' IBRAHIM, Commandant of the fort of El' Arish.

" ' EL HADJY MAHOMMED, Col. of Maugrabins.

" ' EL HADJY, Aga of the Arnauts.

" ' MOHAMMED, Aga, Chief Commissary.'

" There were found in the fort—three pieces of cannon, 200 horses, several hundred camels, and great quantities of provisions.

" On the 22nd of February, two hours before day, Kleber formed the advanced guard of the army, and

marched towards Syria, with orders to advance on
Kanzouses, although the distance was equal to twelve
leagues. Napoleon set out with one hundred dromedaries and one hundred cavalry, to join his advanced
guard; he proceeded at a trot, but as he passed by
Santon Caaba, he remarked, with astonishment, that
the ditches in which the Arabs concealed their straw,
their corn, and occasionally their roots, had not been
plundered by his soldiers. He found no sledges,
which however was not extraordinary, as the fear of
the Arabs prevented them from having any in the
army. Having arrived at the sources of the Rapho,
where the two columns stand which mark the limits
between Asia and Africa, he was surprised to find no
traces of spilled water, as the advanced guard must
have passed the place about two hours previously.
He was only then about two leagues distance from
Kan-zouses, he continued his march, and arrived in
the neighbourhood of the village towards the close
of the day. The Chasseurs of the advanced guard
fired two shots, and immediately afterwards a very
fine camp, belonging to the Turkish army, appeared in
sight, and the Turks instantly flew to arms. What,
then, became of Kleber and the advanced guard? A
hasty retreat was determined on, although the horses
were fatigued, and the French arrived at the sources
of the Lawi, at ten o'clock at night, after having been
pursued by the Turkish cavalry for more than half
a league. The night having become dark, the Pasha
became afraid of an ambuscade, and returned to the

camp. For several hours the detachment was a prey to a thousand gloomy reflections, and seemed to have no resource from despair. However, at two o'clock in the morning, a detachment of dromedaries returned which had been in a direction in which they hoped to méet with a miserable hut occupied by Arabs who possessed some herds of camels; they brought back intelligence that a French army, as numerous as the stars of the firmament, or the sands of the desert, had taken the route of Kanzouses.

"Napoleon, guided by an Arab, mounted his dromedary and set out at day·light. He soon fell in with some dragoons, who appeared worn out with fatigue, and from them he learned that Kleber had mistaken his way, and that the soldiers, surprised at not having arrived at Santon Caaba, where, according to what had been told them, they were to find the ditches filled with roots, began to suspect that they had missed their way; that Kleber had ordered a halt, and that there was no more water than was sufficient to make soup; that in consequence of the original project, according to which the advance·guard was to avail itself of the wells of Rapho, and would arrive at Kan-zouses in a day, they had taken supplies of water merely for a day. Two hours afterwards Napoleon came up with the division, and as soon as the soldiers saw him, they uttered shouts of joy. Worn down with fatigue, and dying of thirst, their spirits were completely broken; and some of the young soldiers, in their despair, had even pro-

ceeded to break their firelocks. Hope, however,
returned at the sight of their General, who collected
them and addressed them in the following terms:—
' There are on the way several camels loaded with
water, which will arrive in less than three hours. I
admit that there is still a great distance to march,
but if it be necessary, learn how to die with honour
and without complaint.' In fact, they did not
arrive at Jassy till midnight, where they met the
detachment and the camels laden with skins of water.
Napoleon now proceeded on the march, with Lasne's
division, and arrived at Kan-zouses on the 24th,
from whence the Turkish army had departed. The
armies did not meet till they were near Gaza. The
Turks did not resist the charge of the French for a
moment; the fort and city of Gaza were taken. On
the 1st of March, the French head-quarters were
established at Azola, and on the 2nd, at Rumsté. An
advanced-guard was pushed forward towards Jerusalem, where multitudes of Christians were in irons
and in momentary dread of the poniards of the Turks.
Napoleon, however, secretly concluded an armistice
with the Pasha, and finding all thus tranquil on his
right flank, on the 4th he marched to Jaffa, which was
regularly invested, and several batteries of 12-pounders
made ready for action. Jaffa was only fortified by
a wall, but it contained a garrison of from 6000
to 7000 men, among whom were a body of artillery
sent from Constantinople, and trained by French
officers. As soon as the batteries were ready to play,

a cartel was sent to summon the place; a quarter of an hour afterwards, the army saw the head of the unfortunate bearer stuck on a pike, and his dead body was thrown over the wall. This was the signal for attack; in three hours, a breach was effected in one of the towers, forty or fifty grenadiers and a dozen of sappers made good a lodgment; the column followed, and the town was carried by assault. Nothing could arrest the fury of the soldiers; every person who came in their way was killed, and the place delivered up to plunder. During the night the disorder was terrible, and order could not possibly be restored even at daylight. All that were saved of that unfortunate garrison were sent prisoners to Egypt, with the exception of 800 men who were shot. These 800 were the remnant of the garrison of El' Arish, who, after having proceeded three days' march in the direction of Bagdad, had changed their route, violated the terms of their capitulation, and thrown themselves into Jaffa. Prudence did not allow them to be sent to Cairo. Accustomed to the desert, they would have found means to escape on the way, and they would have been found again in Acre. About 4000 Turks perished at Jaffa, and nearly 3000 were saved. Of these, 1200 were sent prisoners to Egypt; 1300 soldiers and servants, natives of Egypt, were set at liberty as countrymen, and 500 were sent to carry and diffuse the news of the victories of the French, to Damascus, Jerusalem, Aleppo, &c.

"2nd. The army which had just raised the siege of St. Jean d'Acre was destitute of the means of transport. Its general, nevertheless, succeeded in conducting it, without loss, as far as Jaffa; a thousand sick, and about the same number who had been wounded during the siege. On his arrival at Jaffa, he caused them to be put on board ship for Damietta, as well as all the sick who were in the military hospital, which he had taken care to establish at Jaffa. At this time the plague was making the most frightful ravages in the French hospitals: five or six daily fell as victims to this dreadful scourge. Those of the sick who were the strongest were sent away first, as soon as the vessel was loaded. The next vessel contained those of whose recovery there was but little hope. Napoleon gave orders for the departure of the army on the 27th of May, and on the 26th, according to custom, he sent one of his aides-de-camp (Lavalette) to visit the stores and hospitals, and to see that his orders had been punctually observed and executed. The aide-de-camp reported that the whole had been removed, with the exception of seven men, of whom the officers of health despaired, and who could not be removed, because they would infect with the plague all those whom they approached; that some of these unfortunates, seeing themselves thus about to be abandoned to their unhappy fate, earnestly entreated to be put to death, crying out that the Turks, on their arrival, would inflict upon them unheard-of cruelties. It was, in fact, the custom of these barbarous monsters horribly to mutilate the persons; to slit the noses and pull out the eyes of

those who had the misfortune to fall into their hands.
The surgeons on duty asked permission of the aide-
de-camp to gratify their desires by giving them
opium, at the last moment, for it would have been
horrible and inhuman thus to have abandoned these
unfortunate men in this condition; the maxim—" *Do
unto others, as ye would they should do unto you,*"
ought here to be applied. Napoleon sent for Desguettes,
the physician-in-chief, and Larrey, the surgeon-in-
chief, in order to learn with certainty whether it was
impossible to convey these unfortunate men; he recommended that they should be put on horseback, with
others to lead the horses, and offered, in fact, his own
saddles.   The medical officers assured him, that it
was impossible, and observed that these men could not
survive four-and-twenty hours.   During this consulta-
tion on the possibility of removing them, they added,
that they had consulted on the proposition of allowing
opium to be administered, but that Desguettes said,
that his profession being to cure, he could not give
his authority to such a measure. After this, Napoleon
put off the departure of the army for twenty-four
hours.   There was nothing urgent in the case; he
was master of the country, and Djezzar Pasha had
not set out from Acre.   The rear-guard, consisting
of 800 cavalry, did not leave the town till the
next day at four o'clock in the afternoon, twenty-four
hours after the aide-de-camp's visit to the hospitals,
and only after being informed that the seven patients
were all dead.

" This circumstance, which has been so grossly mis-represented by libellers and enemies, is, in reality, a proof of Napoleon's humanity, and of his solicitude for his soldiers. All of them regarded him as a father, and they were right, for he loved them as if they had been his own children,

" After the battle of Heliopolis and the re-taking of Cairo, in the months of March, April, and May, Kleber imposed a contribution of six millions of francs upon that city. Sheik Suddah, who was descended from a relation of the prophet, and very highly revered in the East, was taxed at a very con-siderable sum, which he refused to pay. Although the evil disposition of this sheik towards the French was very well known, Napoleon was accustomed to manage and flatter him, for which he was often even blamed by many persons in the army. It happened that this Suddah was guilty of some acts of imperti-nence, for which Kleber caused him to be arrested and conducted to the citadel, where, according to the custom of the country, he was punished by the *bastinado*. This caused a great noise in the city, and the Ulemas were extremely indignant at his being exposed to such treatment. Some weeks afterwards, a person named Soliman, a native of Aleppo, was sent from Gaza by the Aga, who was with the grand vizier, to wage a SACRED WAR against Kleber. This man established himself at the Mosque of Semil Azar, and it was confidently said, that the sheiks were informed of his intentions, but that, being offended at the treatment inflicted on the Sheik Suddah, they did not interfere to prevent him.

The assassin, seizing upon a favourable moment, when Kleber was walking in his garden, advanced, and presented a petition; and whilst he was reading the papers, plunged his *kandjar* into his body; he was condemned and executed together with four sheiks, his accomplices. Before this, several persons had been dispatched in 1798 and 1799, by Djezzar Pasha, to wage *sacred war* against Napoleon, but as the latter was a very great favourite with the sheiks, they opposed these designs, *and thus saved his life."*

CHAPTER XIX.

DETAILS OF THE PRIVATE LIFE OF NAPOLEON
AT ST. HELENA.

THINGS had just taken place which cast a fresh portion of acrimony into the disputes between us and the governor of St. Helena, when Sir Hudson Lowe adopted the very inexplicable idea of performing an act of politeness, and sent to General Bonaparte a small case of superior Bourbon coffee for his personal use, expressing his desire that this offer should be accepted as a testimony of his respect, and of the anxiety which he felt to anticipate the smallest wishes of the general. This, I repeat it, was an inexplicable circumstance, considering those feelings of irritation which prevailed in all our relations to one another, and above all, the sinister impressions which his visits and expressions had left upon the Emperor's mind. I hesitated to convey this strange message, so much was I convinced that the answer would be throwing oil upon the fire, but to my great astonishment, the Emperor merely said, " Cause the case to be carried to the pantry—good coffee is a precious thing in this horrible place." Cipriani thought me mad, when I put the case into his charge to be used by Pièrron, the chief cook. I was obliged to repeat the Emperor's order, before he would consent to obey, declaring to me over and over again, that he would first of all submit it to a variety of trials before he allowed any of it to be served up to his master. In short, the coffee was excellent.

The weather had now become fine; the Emperor went out and terminated his walk by a visit to the grand marshal; he had not put his foot out of doors for forty-three days. On the next day, he complained of violent sickness, and remained four hours in the bath.

We have already spoken of the offers made to his brother Joseph by the Spanish Americans. The news of this offer was agreeable to him; he said, however, on hearing of it, "Joseph will certainly refuse; although possessing the mind, talents, and all the qualities necessary to make a nation happy, he loves his liberty and the enjoyments of social life too much to have any wish a second time to launch into the storms of royalty. His acceptance would be useful to these unfortunate people by saving them from the calamities of a long civil war, and would be also very advantageous to England, because she would acquire all the commerce of Spanish America. Joseph neither would nor would have any diplomatic connexion with the kings of France and Spain; and as Spanish America could not do without European productions, it would become necessary that all her markets should be supplied with English merchandise. Moreover, Joseph loves me sincerely, and he would avail himself of this new means to obtain from the English ministers some change in my position."

Some months afterwards, the crown refused by Prince Joseph was offered to the Emperor himself and rejected. The leader of the Spanish Americans, whose message reached Longwood, had foreseen all the obstacles resulting from the Emperor's captivity, and forgotten nothing to ensure the success of their design; but that great mind, which had twice laid down the crown of France rather than be indebted for its preservation to a civil war, could not possibly accept the sceptre offered to him by a people at war among themselves and with the mother country, had not even a regard for his own dignity dictated a refusal.

Sir Hudson thought to make sure of victory in our incessant disputes, by inditing a voluminous memoir, justifying his conduct, and throwing the whole blame upon Las Cases, the grand marshal, and myself. We had misrepresented everything—words, writings, actions; he was the best man in the world, and the most desirous of softening the rigours of the Emperor's captivity, and we were execrable calumniators.

The Emperor indignantly did justice to this mean accusation against us by throwing it in the fire.

This document contained one very remarkable passage.   " Neither in the instructions given to me, nor in those given to Sir George' Cockburn, have his majesty's ministers entered into any details.   They have referred these to my own judgment, and I am at liberty to take such precautions as may seem to me desirable, and to do as I please.   I have received, in general terms, the order to take the necessary precautions to prevent General Bonaparte's escape, as well as not to allow any correspondence to reach him which does not pass through my hands.   The rest depends upon me."   " All that," said the Emperor, " is a mass of absurd and infamous insinuations.   I maintain that the acts of this man are worse than those put in force in Botany Bay; for even there, the convicts are not forbidden to speak.   The man must be a fool to pretend to persuade me, that he has not treated us badly; we are neither fools nor ordinary persons, to suffer ourselves to be imposed on by such gilded phraseology. There is assuredly no free born man living whose hair would not stand on end with indignation, on finding himself made the butt of such disgraceful proceedings as those which restrain us from addressing such persons as we may accidentally meet with in the narrow limits destined for our promenade. It is merely adding wrong to barbarism, to pretend that such measures as these are adopted from any feeling of their necessity. Am I deceived when I see in this man an exe-

cutioner sent to assassinate me, a man wholly without
a heart, and merely capable of discharging the office
and duties of a gaoler?"

I have already mentioned the great lack of water
to which we were exposed. There was no sufficient
supply for the Emperor's bath, and the governor
caused some to be carried to Longwood in casks used
for providing water for ships; but this water exhaled
such an unhealthy smell in the course of being warmed,
as made its use unfortunately impossible; and the works,
commenced with a view of providing an adequate supply for Longwood, were yet far from being finished.
When I complained to Sir Hudson Lowe, he replied,
" that he would accelerate them as much as possible,"
and excused himself by saying, "that he was not,
hitherto, at all aware, that General Bonaparte had any
need of being *boiled* in hot water for several hours
every day." This strange pleasantry gives a complete
picture of the man!

At length a store-ship arrived with the famous iron
grating, so long and so impatiently expected by Sir
Hudson Lowe. One hundred and thirty-five sentinels
were insufficient to calm his nocturnal terrors, and he
must have a grating by which we should be as it were
hermetically sealed, and the key at night under his
pillow.

The sudden variations of temperature always
affected more or less the Emperor's health, but these
effects had hitherto given us no serious uneasiness.
On this occasion, it was different. Symptoms of

dysentery appeared, and we knew too well by daily experience, what were the dangers of this disease in the burning climate of St. Helena. For three days our uneasiness was extreme, although the disease did not increase, but there was danger as long as the calomel did not, as the physicians say, produce its effect. At length, on the 5th, improvement became sensible, and on the 8th, the Emperor felt himself sufficiently recovered to wish to breathe the fresh air in the garden. As soon, however, as he perceived Sir Hudson Lowe, accompanied by two or three officers, at full gallop towards our residence, he precipitately returned into his chamber.

Two vessels, arrived from Europe and the Cape, brought us newspapers, pamphlets and letters. We heard the contents of our letters from the officers of the camp, who being persuaded that we had read them, spoke to us on the subject of their contents; they had been on the preceding evening at a ball given by Lady Lowe.

Among the number of our pamphlets, there was one written by Dr. Warden, surgeon of the Northumberland, which the Emperor read with interest, and to which he dictated in reply, eight or ten letters supposed to be written from the Cape. The notes which he had previously dictated to me on Egypt, were used in these letters. This was an occasion, which he did not wish to allow to pass by without refuting some of those odious calumnies. Count Las Cases, to whom those letters from the Cape were attributed, has denied being their author, and has published notes or observations on this subject during his exile in Germany, which, like all his actions, are a proof of his fidelity and attachment to the Emperor.

Notwithstanding the pains taken by Sir Hudson Lowe to envelope Longwood in an impenetrable veil, the Emperor's attack of dysentery became known in the island. The commissioners were alarmed, called for official communications respecting the Emperor's health, and renewed their importunities to be allowed to see him. The governor did not yield upon the question of free communication with Longwood, but he consented to give a copy of the physician's bulletin, which he received. This circumstance was the commencement of his serious and personal disputes with Dr. O'Meara. He wished the medical attendant to perjure himself; to prepare bulletins according to his convenience—or, to speak more correctly, to write them under his dictation. The bulletin of health would furnish him with an opportunity of making a report of all that he had seen, heard or learnt from the Emperor or concerning the Emperor during the course of the day. He wished to make the physician a spy.

About this time the Emperor received a visit from Admiral and Lady Malcolm, and saw again with great pleasure, Mr. Mackenzie, an officer of the navy, who served on board the Indomitable, when she was at the isle of Elba.

The tragical death of an employé of the governor, and one who possessed his fullest confidence, was for some days the subject of universal conversation on the island. It was wrongfully said that this man had hung himself, because Sir Hudson Lowe had discovered that he had betrayed him, by sending to me some copies of all the despatches from the ministry, as well as bulletins of all the news which he wished to conceal from us.

Several ships arrived from India and the Cape, and almost all the officers of these vessels obtained permission to be presented at Longwood. It was on this occasion that Captain * * * availed himself of the opportunity to place his services at the disposal of the Emperor, and offered to conduct him wherever he pleased. He said that this feeling was inspired by his strong indignation at the conduct pursued by the English government, and above all, at that of Sir Hudson Lowe—an indignation, he added, which was shared by all classes in England, with the exception of a few private friends of the ministers.

The Emperor listened with the kindest interest to this noble and generous offer—but refused to accept it. It was about the same period, that one of the officers of the garrison conceived a plan of escape, the success of which was almost certain. His plan was to reach the shore at a point of the coast opposite to James' Town, which was guarded merely by a post of infantry; small boats alone could approach the shore at this place, but a boat well provided with rowers would have been sufficient to enable the fugitives to reach the vessel appointed to receive them. This point was only an hour's walk distant. But whether the Emperor at this time had relinquished all idea of desiring to escape, or whether he doubted the sincerity of the offers which were made to him, or the possibility of their success, he refused to accept them. In its proper place, I will record another offer of a more serious kind, which I was commissioned to make to him, and the reasons which he assigned for its refusal. Two ships just arrived, the one from India, and the other from China, brought to Longwood new subjects for grave disputes with Sir Hudson Lowe; a master gunner had been commissioned to present the Emperor with a beautiful marble bust of the King of Rome, made at Florence, and which was said to have been made in compliance with the orders of the Empress Maria-Louisa, to be presented to the father and husband as a testimony of her affectionate remembrances.

But what consequences might not such a message produce, according to the imagination of Sir Hudson Lowe! It was perhaps all a conspiracy! The bust might contain a correspondence of the very highest political interest! Not to suffer it to go to Longwood, and to break it in pieces, was in his opinion the advice of sound reason; but what recriminations, and what an echo would these recriminations find in public opinion, should we become acquainted with these facts, and happen to divulge them! *When you are in doubt, abstain*, says the proverb, and Sir Hudson Lowe followed its advice. Six days were allowed to pass without the bust being brought to Longwood, although on the day after the arrival of the Baring, we had been informed of the gunner's commission. At length, on the 11th, Sir Hudson Lowe came to the grand marshal's house, and told him, with an air of extreme embarrassment, that a statuary in Leghorn had made a bad bust of the son of the Archduchess Maria Louisa, and had sent it to St. Helena by the ship Baring, accompanied by a letter in which he states that the bust has been already paid for, but that he hopes the Emperor's generosity will lead him to send an additional 100 Louis-d'ors; a claim which in his, Sir H. Lowe's judgment, appeared exorbitant—so exorbitant, he added, as to be a sufficient reason for not accepting the bust—as it was evidently a shameful speculation of some inferior Tuscan sculptor. The grand marshal did not suffer himself to be imposed upon by the cunning governor, and assured him that the Emperor was all eagerness and joy at the hope of seeing again the features of his son, and he begged him earnestly to send it that evening to Longwood. He did not, however receive it till the next day. So much cunning and malevolence of purpose cruelly wounded the Emperor. He dictated the following letter to the grand marshal, to be sent to the gunner of the Baring.

" Mr. Radwick.

" Sir,—I have received the marble bust of the young Napoleon, and given it to his father. Its reception has given him the most lively satisfaction.

" I regret that it is not in your power to come and

see us, and communicate to us details which would have the greatest interest for a father, and especially for one placed in such circumstances as he is.

"According to the letters forwarded to us, the artist values his work at £100 sterling. The Emperor has commanded me to put into your hands the sum of £300 sterling;* the overplus is intended to indemnify you for the losses to which you have been exposed in the sale of your merchandise, by not having been allowed to send your goods on shore, and for the prejudice which that event may have raised against you, but which will secure you the esteem of every gallant man.

"Have the goodness to transmit to the persons who have paid him this obliging attention, the Emperor's best thanks.   I have the honour to be, &c.,

"COUNT BERTRAND.

"P. S.—I beg you to acknowledge the receipt of the enclosed letter of credit."

This precious article was succeeded by other presents not less unexpected. The honourable Mr. Elphinstone, with a view of discharging a debt of gratitude to the Emperor, sent to St. Helena several small cases, containing a set of chessmen in ivory, of marvellously beautiful workmanship, a box of dice, another of counters, and two magnificent baskets of

---

* In consequence of some unworthy manœuvres the poor gunner did not receive his money till nearly two years afterwards.

large dimensions, all exquisitely carved. Each of these objects was ornamented with the imperial crown —eagles and letter N. We have already said, that this was an act of grateful homage on the part of Mr. Elphinstone, which arose from the following circumstances.

On the evening before the battle of Waterloo, Captain Elphinstone, brother of the gentleman in question, had been grievously wounded, and was lying stretched on the field in a hopeless condition. The Emperor happened to pass near him, observed his situation, and sent the surgeon in attendance on his person, to make the necessary application to staunch his wounds, from which the blood was copiously flowing. His natural goodness towards the wounded, prompted him also to give him some wine from the silver flask which one of the chasseurs of the guard always carried on service near his person, in case of a halt or bivouac. This providential assistance saved Captain Elphinstone's life. These presents, as well as some others, gave rise to very lively discussions between Sir Hudson Lowe and the grand marshal, whilst more than a month elapsed between their arrival at St. Helena and their being delivered to the Emperor. Mr. Manning, who had received the commission to deliver them, yielded to the wish of Sir Hudson Lowe, of leaving us in ignorance of the fact, and left the boxes at James Town, in order to wait for the decision of the government, as to whether they should be delivered to the Emperor or not.

This conduct of Sir Hudson Lowe gave rise to the following correspondence:

" SIR,—I have received the five cases which you have taken the trouble to send me, containing a set of chessmen, a box of counters, and two carved caskets in ivory, sent from Canton by Mr. Elphinstone. The Emperor was surprised to see by your letter that you thought it would have been your duty not to have transmitted these articles to Longwood. ' Did I act,' you say, ' in entire conformity with the established regulations, I ought not to forward them.' In this case, sir, you would have acted politely to keep them.

" But to what does this apply? Did not these articles arrive through the channel of the ministry? It is indeed ordained in the minister's restrictions that all letters must come through this channel; but not articles of dress, busts, furniture, &c. We have frequently received from the Cape articles which have been sent us. And besides, Lord Bathurst, in his speech, and you in your letters, indignantly denied that letters which came here through the post, or other opportunities, had been sent to London, to return to St. Helena. Your instructions therefore could not, nor cannot, authorise you to keep back such articles as busts, furniture, books, or any other effects which have no connexion with the security of the Emperor's detention.

" Is it because there is a crown on each of the counters? But no regulation can exist without our knowledge; now, we are not aware that we may not be permitted to possess any article on which there is a crown; if so, it would also be necessary to make new packs of cards, because there are crowns on those which are now used. The Emperor's linen, and the small quantity of plate still in his possession, are often taken to the town; they are marked with a crown.

" But from whom did this regulation, which you say is in force, emanate? From your government, which alone, by passing a bill, has a right to make regulations? Your minister declared, in open parliament, that no restrictions had been made since those which had been printed and communicated to Europe, which your predecessor had, and which he delivered over to you; he added, that you had no restriction, but had only taken measures of execution. In fact, then, you have no right to make restrictions.

" The Emperor wishes for favour from no one, and will have nothing from the caprice of any person whatever; but he has a right to know the restrictions which are imposed on him. Your government, the parliament, and all nations have the same right; I beg you then, sir, to communicate to us these fresh restrictions; if such as these did exist, they would be in contradiction of Lord Bathurst's assertion, ' that the only aim of the restrictions was to secure the Emperor's safe detention.'

" The Emperor charges me to protest against the

existence of any restriction or regulation which shall not have been legally notified to him before being put into execution.

" I have the honour to be,

" &c., &c., &c.,

" COUNT BERTRAND."

THE GOVERNOR'S ANSWER TO THE FOREGOING LETTER.

" SIR,—I have received your letter, dated the 9th instant. The frequent use which you make in it of the title, of ' Emperor,' and the tone in which you express your feelings to me when you employ it, would sufficiently authorise me to be silent respecting its contents, as having been addressed to me under an inadmissible form, and to refer you to my letter of the 30th of August, 1816, addressed to Count Montholon. I will not, however, avail myself of these motives to refuse to reply to them.

" The only object which I had in writing to you on the 8th of this month was, to prevent a belief from being entertained that I tacitly acknowledged, or approved of, the imperial rank being recognised in the crown placed everywhere above the initial letter of Napoleon, in presents sent to St. Helena, particularly by an English subject, and coming from an English factory.

" If I had forwarded these articles without any remark, it would necessarily have been taken for granted that I saw nothing improper in this; and I know but too well how far this precedent would have been used at any future departure from it, had I not explicitly declared the motives which induced me, on this occasion, to allow these articles to be forwarded to you.

"The person who sent these presents has his personal opinions, but I have the right of exercising my judgment in not permitting him to express them through me; and in forwarding the presents to their destination, without any other remarks than those contained in my letter, I did the utmost which could be required of me by the respect which the wishes or expectations of General Bonaparte demand from me. You ask me, sir, ' whether these articles did not come through the channel of the ministry ?' &c. &c.

" I should have considered myself, according to the general tenour of my instructions, and even without reference to the decorations of these presents, fully justified in retaining them until I received from my government express orders to transmit them— except I made use of my discretionary power in examining them, and convincing myself that they contained no means of communication which might serve for a clandestine correspondence. The letter which I sent you, even before· the articles were disembarked, is a sufficient proof that the latter alternative was that on which I was always ready to act, instead of awaiting the arrival of instructions from England.

" You remark, sir, that I repulsed with indignation the accusation of having sent back to London, to be re-sent to St. Helena, letters which had come through

the post, or by private opportunities. I did without
doubt, sir, indignantly repulse this accusation, as
well as the reflections to which it had given rise,
because they contained neither truth nor justice; because I was disgusted at the feeling which turned
into sources of vexation and reproach, the marks of
attention which I had shown, (for on seeing their
family letters, I had used, in favour of the persons
who applied to me, a discretionary power not
authorised by my instructions;) but I did not admit
that I had not a right, and was not perfectly authorised, to return letters to England, if I thought fit,
when they came through irregular channels. Presents
may be as contrary to the safety of General Bonaparte's detention as a letter, and might be liable
to an examination which would entirely prevent
their serving, in any way, either for ornament or
utility. A letter can be concealed in the square of
a chess-board, or under the binding of a book, as well
as in the lining of a flannel waistcoat; and I am not
obliged to confide in the person who sends them,
whoever this may be. If I have allowed articles to
be forwarded to you, it was because I was persuaded
that they were not of a reprehensible nature; and
you have certainly, sir, no reason to complain of the
manner in which I have used my discretionary power,
by consenting, as a general principle, to the transmission of all articles arriving here, and even by
forwarding several others which arrived under cover
to me, and the transmission of which was left by the

persons sending them, through delicacy, entirely to my choice.

"You observe, sir, 'Is it because there is a crown on each of the counters?' &c. &c., and ask whether there exists any regulation forbidding you to have in your possession any article on which there is a crown?

"Without doubt, sir, there does not exist any special and written regulation, forbidding any article surmounted with a crown, to be forwarded to Longwood, or preventing you from possessing any effects adorned with one; but, in the present case, we find the imperial crown above the initial letter of Napoleon, cut and gilded, or engraved, and placed on every article. His abdication, the treaty of Paris, and the acts of the English parliament, render useless the existence of any regulation on this point. The effects surmounted with an imperial crown now at Longwood, bore this mark before the abdication. I have never disputed the possession, nor the satisfaction they may procure.

"As regards the passage which you quote from the debates of parliament, allow me to observe that it is inexact, according to all the newspapers which I have seen. The papers themselves do not agree; one speaks of regulations, another of instructions, not restrictions, as being the same, at least without any substantial change, as those before prescribed.

"You say, sir, 'You have no right to make restrictions.'

"The act of parliament, the commission, and the

instructions with which I am provided, are, sir, my
surest guides in this respect. I shall, however, be
allowed to add, that the first instructions which you
demand should be my only rule, have received a more
ample interpretation than their - strict and literal
sense would seem to bear, relative to the degree of
exemption from personal constraint which General
Bonaparte now enjoys.

" You add—' The Emperor wishes for no favour,'
&c. &c.

" I have not the presumption to grant a favour to
General Bonaparte, and still less the arrogance to
subject him to any act of my caprice. He is subjected to no restriction with which the government is
not acquainted, and which the whole world may not
know.

" I will take advantage of this opportunity to recall
to your mind, that General Bonaparte, himself, in two
interviews which I had with him, told me that, as a
general officer, I ought to act according to my instructions, and not like an officer on duty; but it seems
that now he wishes me to fulfil it like one. Another
time he declared that he would not recognise any
direct or public *surveillançe*. How do these suggestions agree with the narrow limits within
which you now seek to restrain the exercise of my
duties?

" The views which you have expressed coincide the
most with mine, (seeing that all exercise of my discretionary power, even when I endeavour to act most

favourably, only brings on new discussions); but when none but such opposite sentiments are manifested, you will acknowledge, sir, the difficulty of reconciling them.

"You say, 'The Emperor charges me to protest against the existence of any restriction,' &c. &c.

"It is essentially my duty, whenever circumstances permit, to pay attention to any communication made to me in the name of the person you thus designate. It would, however, be impossible to notify a regulation called for by a sudden occurrence, before the circumstance which gives rise to it has taken place. The measure of which you speak was not of a nature to be communicated beforehand, but I venture to affirm, that it was not put into execution before information had been given of it.

"I have the honour to be, &c. &c. &c.

"H. Lowe, Lieutenant-General."

CHAPTER XX.

LORD AMHERST.

EVERYTHING had been prepared for Lord Amherst's audience, as it had been for that of Sir Hudson Lowe on his arrival in St. Helena. The presentation was to be performed by the grand marshal, one of us was to be in the topographic cabinet, which would serve on this occasion as an ante-room, and the valets-de-chambre, St. Denis and Noverras, were to be stationed at the doors of the ante-room and of the saloon in which the Emperor was. The suite of Lord Amherst were not to be presented till after the audience. Everything was done as had been arranged; and if Lord Amherst and his embassy had been received at the Tuileries, in the most splendid days of the empire, they could not have been more courteous and respectful, in manner as well as speech.

The mission of this ambassador formed the first

subject of the conversation, and politics would not, probably, have been introduced at all, had not Lord Amherst offered to take charge of, and transmit to the Prince Regent, the requests which the Emperor might have to make to him.

This offer aroused in the Emperor's mind the recollection of the perpetual outrages which daily poisoned his life.

" Neither your king nor your nation have any right over me," said he, in a tone of deep suffering. " England sets an example of twenty millions of men oppressing one individual. Sylla and Marius signed their decrees of proscription in the midst of combats, and with the still bloody points of their swords; but the bill of the 11th of April was signed in the midst of peace, with the sceptre of a great nation, and in the sanctuary of the law.

" The right of nations should, at least, have been the law of your ministers; but it would have paralysed the savage hatred of some of them; they wanted the arbitrary right; they lied to the parliament; they pushed the audacity of falsehood so far as to say, that they demanded the right of regulating my captivity, in order to treat me with more liberality than it was usual to grant to prisoners of war; and what use have they made of it? They have delegated this discretionary power to a man chosen *ad hoc* amongst men of a character known by their preceding missions, and have said to him—" *If your prisoner escape, your career and your fortune are lost.*" Is not this telling

him to abuse his power? Does not this interest all
that is dear to man? A gaoler in Europe cannot
impose restrictions according to his own caprice or
panic terrors, on the prisoner entrusted to his charge;
he is obliged to confine himself to the execution of the
regulations established by the laws or magistrates.
There is but one means of taking from a prisoner all
chance of evasion—to enclose him in a coffin. The
parliament which gave Charles I.'s head to the axe—
the convention which condemned Louis XVI. to die
by the hand of the executioner, found excuses for
their crimes in national interest; the bill of the 11th
of April only serves the purposes of personal hatred;
it will, sooner or later, be the shame of England; the
parliament which voted it forgot its sacred character,
and, as a legislative body, committed a crime against
English honour. I am not allowed to leave this unhealthy hut, unless accompanied by a guard; I am
forbidden to receive letters from my wife, my mother,
or my family, except they have been read and com-
mented on by my gaoler.

" But of what use are these odious restrictions here?
What man of sense can admit the possibility of my
escape, when numerous cruising vessels hover round
the island; when posts are established at all points;
when there are signals always ready to correspond
with each other; when no vessel can approach or leave St.
Helena without having been visited by the Governor's
agents; and, finally, when hundreds of sentinels are
posted round the limits of this place, from six in the
evening till six in the morning?

" But they do still more, if possible; they want me to deny a glorious fact—to acknowledge the shame of my country. They will have it that France had no right to place the imperial crown on my head; and pretend to wash away, by a decree of Sir Hudson Lowe's, the holy oil with which the vicar of Jesus Christ anointed my forehead. The name of General Bonaparte was the one which I bore at Campo-Formio and at Lunéville, when I dictated terms of peace to the Emperor of Austria; I bore it at Amiens, when I signed the peace with England; I should be proud to bear it still, but the honour of France forbids me to acknowledge the King of England's right to annul the acts of the French people. My intention was to take the name of Duroc; your ministers, and their hired assassin, Sir Hudson Lowe, oblige me, by their ignoble intrigues on this subject, to retain the title of the Emperor Napoleon.

" If your government denies my right to this title, it acknowledges implicitly that Louis XVIII. reigned in France at the time when I signed the peace of Amiens, and when the Lords Lauderdale and Castlereagh negotiated with my plenipotentiaries. It does more: it acknowledges that the Cardinal of York reigned in England when George III. signed the peace of 1783, at Versailles; and denies the royalty of Charles XIII. of Sweden. To assert this opinion would be to give instability to all thrones, and to propagate the germ of revolution in every monarchy.

" Your ministers were not contented with giving

parliament false information respecting my position;
one of them said, in a numerous assembly in Ireland,
that I had only made peace with England for the
purpose of deceiving, surprising, and destroying.
Such calumnies against a man suffering under their
oppression, and held by the throat to prevent his
raising his voice, must be disapproved by all men of
truth and honour.

"I always desired peace, and sincere peace, with
England; and I know of no rivalries which should
prevent two great nations from coming to an understanding with each other, and from advancing conjointly towards the end aimed at by my government.
I wished to fill up the abyss of revolutions, and to
re-construct, without shaking, the European edifice,
to the advantage of all, by employing kings to bestow
on continental Europe the blessing of constitutions,
a blessing which your country, as well as mine, only
acquired at the price of a fearful social commotion.
England had nothing more to fear from me, as soon
as she would listen to me. If Fox had lived, the face
of Europe would have been changed—his genius and
his patriotism understood me—every great and national idea vibrated in his soul. He died, unfortunately
for England, unfortunately for the world. Not a
cannon-shot would have been fired on the Continent
after the battle of Austerlitz, if Lord Lauderdale's
negotiations had been continued. I repeat, that I
always desired peace; I only fought to obtain it. The
congress of Vienna thinks it will secure this blessing

to Europe; it is deceived.   War, and a terrible war,
is being hatched under the ashes of the empire.
Sooner or later, nations will cruelly avenge me of the
ingratitude of the kings whom I crowned or pardoned.
Tell the Prince Regent—tell the parliament of which
you are a principal member, that I await, as a favour,
the axe of the executioner, to put an end to the outrages of my gaoler."

Lord Amherst had heard with emotion these complaints of a great and deeply wounded soul; he did
not seek to conceal the interest which he felt in them.
He promised to tell all to the Prince Regent; and re-
spectfully offered his services to intervene with Sir
Hudson Lowe.

" It would be useless," said the Emperor, interrupting him; " crime, and hatred towards me are equally
in this man's nature.   It is necessary to his enjoyment to torture me; like the tiger, who tears with
his claws the prey whose agonies he takes pleasure in
prolonging."

The evening after this audience, the Emperor said
to us : " Lord Amherst has failed in his mission, but
he is nevertheless a diplomatist of talent and skill.
The precedent of Lord Macartney's embassy was an
insurmountable obstacle at the moment when Lord
Amherst determined not to submit to the Ko-ton.   It
appears that the ministers had foreseen this exaction
of the Court of Pekin, but that bad counsels had

determined Lord Amherst to use, in refusing to submit to it, all the latitude left him by his instructions.
An ambassador is not the sovereign, whatever the old
diplomacy may say. No king ever regarded the ambassador of another king as his equal. The last
prince of the royal blood takes precedence of the ambassador of the first king in Europe. The erroneous
idea that an ambassador stands in the place of his
sovereign, is a feudal tradition; because, when the
feudal system was in operation, if a great vassal found
himself unable to render oath and homage in person
to his suzerain, he sent an ambassador as his representative, and to him all the honours due to his
master were paid. The character of an ambassador
is, in relation to that of a plenipotentiary minister,
what the character of this latter is to that of an
envoy—it is a hierarchy of rank; the ambassador
in the first rank, the minister in the second, the
envoy in the third; as negotiators, they all three
have the same rights, their signatures are equally
good, and must equally acquire their definitive value
by the ratification of the sovereign. The difference
between these three diplomatic degrees of rank, only
exists as far as regards the honours to which they give
a right. An ambassador, for example, has a right to
be treated with all the honours, and to be granted all
the privileges, allowed to men of the highest rank in
the state; the ministers have a right to be treated as
the chief nobility of the court would be; and the envoy
has a right of precedence over the social masses.

The *chargés-d'affaires* are merely accredited agents sent to the minister of foreign affairs.

" Lord Amherst recognised the truth of this diplomatic position; but he affirmed, that from this situation evidently resulted his right to exact that a deputy, of a rank equal to his own, should perform before the portrait of the King of England the ceremony of the Ko-tou, which he would then himself perform before the Emperor of China, unless the Emperor signed a declaration that if he sent an ambassador to England, this ambassador should perform the Ko-tou before the King of England. This demand was refused, and with justice; the same things could not be exacted from a Chinese ambassador in London, as were exacted from other ambassadors.

" Lord Amherst demanded that the Emperor of China would at least accept, as a compromise, the etiquette of presentation at the English court, which requires the ambassador to put one knee to the ground at the foot of the throne, and present his letters of appointment.

" The court of Pekin persisted in its rejection of any modification of the Ko-tou.

" Lord Amherst did not comprehend all the force of the only reasonable objection against the Ko-tou, which was, the representing it as a religious act, a ceremony of paganism, which his religion forbade him to perform; he combated but feebly the demands of the mandarins, who displayed in this discussion much cunning and spirit of chicanery. And in short, this embassy will have cost a great deal of money, and have only served to increase the unpleasantness of the relations between the two countries.

" Mr. Ellis, secretary to the embassy," added the Emperor, " interested me deeply by the details which he gave me of the intrigues at the court of Persia, at the time when I sent General Gardanna thither; Mr. Ellis was then the chargé-d'affaires at this court on the part of England."

General Gourgaud meanwhile was melancholy; some letters which he had received from his mother had deeply affected him; the Emperor had perceived his sadness, but tried in vain to learn the cause of it. Two or three days passed thus. A vessel was about to sail for Europe. The Emperor sent for Gourgaud, and put into his hands an open letter, commissioning him to forward it to Paris, and giving him permission to read its contents. It was a bill for a pension of 12,000 francs, to be paid to M. Gourgaud, and transferred, at his death, to his son; this manner of proving to his officers the interest which he took in them was a custom of the Emperor's; I have often experienced it.

The affair of the bust was not yet terminated, and was fated to give rise to more vexations to the Emperor. Sir Hudson Lowe sent him information, that General Bertrand's letter was the most impertinent he had ever received in his life; that General Bonaparte must keep in mind in future, that General Bertrand only remained on the ·island through the favour of Sir Hudson Lowe; and that if he again committed such a fault, he should immediately be sent to the Cape; and begged General Bonaparte to inform him˙ who was the author of the infamous calumny which accused him of having intended to break the bust, and of having hindered the gunner of the Baring in the sale of his venture.

The Emperor replied: " The gunner himself said this to the grand marshal. The governor complains of the letters which I caused to be written to him; let him fully understand that I wish to be under no obligations to him; if he is not authorised by his instructions to let me purchase the bust of my son, and to allow me to receive the presents offered me by Mr. Elphinstone, in gratitude for my having saved his brother's life on the eve of the battle of Waterloo, why did he forward these articles to Longwood? But where are these pretended restrictions, and why has he never communicated them to us? The fact is, that they do not exist; and I protest against any restraints on my liberty of action, which shall not have been communicated to me before being put into execution. Lord Bathurst declared in parliament that Sir Hudson Lowe had no right to add, in any way, to the established restrictions, which have been communicated to me. If by chance he took a fancy to protest against the crowns on the chess-men, why did he not do it? I should have laughed heartily at it; but no; what he wanted to do was simply to torment me by quoting the tenour of imaginary regulations, in order to have an opportunity of insinuating, that it is to his extreme goodness that I owe the bust of my son, and some articles of Chinese workmanship. A man becomes accustomed to the dungeon of a prison, even if he has irons on his feet and hands, but never to the caprice of his gaoler. I wish for no favour from him; the only thing now wanting to his pretensions is that he should exact that I should write to him every day, to thank him for the air I breathe. Sir Hudson Lowe fatigues me with his insinuations; he is killing me by pin-wounds, morally as well as physically; an executioner would kill me with one blow; the governor's conduct is in everything crooked and mysterious; it is the way the petty tyrants of Italy act: crime alone walks in darkness; sooner or later, his king and his nation will be informed of his unworthy conduct, and if he escapes the chastisement of the laws which he is violating, he will not escape the decree of infamy and reprobation which will be pronounced on him by all enlightened and humane men; he is an unfaithful deputy; he deceives his government;— the twenty falsehoods contained in Lord Bathurst's speech, are an incontestable proof of this. His conduct with regard to the bust of my son, is odious, and worthy of all his acts since his arrival here."

END OF VOL. II.

T. C. Savill, Printer, 4, Chandos Street, Covent Garden.

Lightning Source UK Ltd.
Milton Keynes UK
11 July 2010

156838UK00001B/3/P